PRACTICAL SOCI

Practical Social Work Ethics
Complex Dilemmas Within Applied Social Care

Edited by

MALCOLM CAREY AND LORRAINE GREEN
University of Manchester, UK

ASHGATE

Published by
Ashgate Publishing Limited
Wey Court East
Union Road
Farnham
Surrey GU9 7PT
England

Ashgate Publishing Company
110 Cherry Street
Suite 3-1
Burlington, VT 05401-3818
USA

www.ashgate.com

British Library Cataloguing in Publication Data
A catalogue record for this book is available from the British Library

The Library of Congress has cataloged the printed edition as follows:
Practical social work ethics : complex dilemmas within applied social care / [edited] by Malcolm Carey and Lorraine Green.
    pages cm
 Includes bibliographical references and index.
 ISBN 978-1-4094-3825-0 -- ISBN 978-1-4094-3826-7 (ebook) -- ISBN 978-1-4724-0101-4 (epub) 1. Social service--Moral and ethical aspects. 2. Social workers--Professional ethics. I. Carey, Malcolm.
 HV10.5.P693 2013
 174'.93613--dc23

2013020837

ISBN 9781409438250 (pbk)
ISBN 9781409438267 (ebk – PDF)
ISBN 9781472401014 (ebk – ePUB)

Printed in the United Kingdom by Henry Ling Limited, at the Dorset Press, Dorchester, DT1 1HD

Contents

List of Tables

Notes on Contributors

About the Editors

Malcolm Carey teaches social work at the University of Manchester. His past experience relates to social work with older adults and people with a disability before moving into higher education. His research interests embrace applied ethics, qualitative research and identity within adult social work: this has included care management and agency employment as labour process, and the ethical implications of service user and carer participation, fragmentation, deviance and cynicism within statutory social work. His books include the best-selling *The Social Work Dissertation*, the second edition of which was published by Open University Press/McGraw Hill Education in 2013.

Lorraine Green lectures in social work at the University of Manchester. She is interested in developing eclectic cross-social science underpinning knowledge for social work and her last book integrated sociological and psychological approaches to the life course. She focuses predominantly on topics concerned with marginalisation, abuse and social justice and their relevance for social work, having previously published on childhood and child abuse in their various manifestations, gender and sexuality, disenfranchised grief, resilience and social work education.

About the Contributors

Kylie Agllias (PhD) is a lecturer in social work in the School of Humanities and Social Science at the University of Newcastle, New South Wales, Australia. She has published in the area of women and families (including family estrangement, mentoring and refugees), and social work education.

Donna Baines is a Professor in Labour Studies and Social Work at McMaster University, Canada. She has taught in universities since 1995. Prior to this she worked in a variety of social work settings in Canada and the USA including: medical, mental health, child welfare and community development. Her PhD explored the experiences of class, race and gender in everyday social work practice (University of Toronto, 1999). Her research and activism continues to focus on questions of social justice, equity and fairness in the workplace and larger society.

Sarah Campbell is a researcher within the Dementia and Ageing Research team in the School of Nursing, Midwifery and Social Work at the University of Manchester. She is currently working on the Hair and Care Study with Richard Ward. She is also a part-time doctoral student investigating gender, embodiment and emplacement in dementia care. Prior to this she has worked as a freelance researcher, a trainer and support worker for a community-based mental health charity, and for a number of years as a research support worker.

Sean Cordell is currently a visiting researcher at the University of Sheffield, having previously lectured in philosophy there and having held a research fellowship at the University of Birmingham. His interests are in moral and political philosophy and particularly in the ethics of social roles, i.e. how the nature of political and social institutions helps define, or should help define, the ethical demands of those roles.

Stephen Cowden is a senior lecturer in social work at Coventry University where he has been teaching for over 10 years. Previous to this he worked as a Social Worker in the field of community mental health and learning disability. Originally from Melbourne, Australia, Stephen has lived in the UK for over 20 years. His PhD, which he gained from the University of Kent, was concerned with Australian nationalism and the construction of discourses of 'white' identity. His approach to social work is concerned with issues of social justice, inequality, the construction of social problems and ethics. Stephen is co-author of *The Ethical Foundations of Social Work*, published by Pearson in 2012.

Ros Day is a lecturer in social work at the University of Leeds. Ros has taught social work at Leeds University for over ten years but prior to that taught on both pure and applied social science degrees at the Open University and Huddersfield University. Ros has a sociological and social policy background and is particularly interested in the application of sociological ideas to the study of social work and the relationship between social policy and social work.

Paul Michael Garrett works at the National University of Ireland, Galway in the Republic of Ireland. He is the author of *Remaking Social Work with Children and Families* (Routledge, 2003), *Social Work with Irish Children and Families in Britain* (Policy Press, 2004), *Transforming' Children's Services:*

Neoliberalism and the 'Modern' World (Open University/McGraw Hill, 2009) and *Social Work and Social Theory* (Policy Press, 2013). For a number of years he has been a member of the editorial collective of *Critical Social Policy* (where he is the Editor of the Reviews Section). He is also a member of the editorial board of the *European Journal of Social Work*.

Mel Gray is a Professor of Social Work in the School of Humanities and Social Science at the University of Newcastle, New South Wales, Australia. She has published extensively on social work ethics. Her recent books include *Ethics and Value Perspectives in Social Work* (with Webb, Palgrave, 2010). Mel is Associate Editor of *The International Journal of Social Welfare*.

John Hopton has a professional background in mental health nursing, nurse education and social work education dating back to 1975 and currently teaches social work and nursing students at the University of Manchester in the School of Nursing, Midwifery and Social Work. He has written about mental health issues in a range of publications, including a long-running series of articles for *Openmind* magazine co-written with Peter Beresford in which they debated controversial issues in mental health.

Kenneth McLaughlin is a senior lecturer in social work at Manchester Metropolitan University where he contributes to modules on sociology, social policy and mental health. He has over 20 years' experience in social work and social care, taking up his present position in social work academia in 2001 and prior to this working as an administrator in a social service training department, a support worker for homeless families, and an Approved Social Worker/Acting Team Manager within a social services mental health team.

Gurnam Singh is a principal lecturer in social work at Coventry University where he has worked since 1993. Prior to this he worked as a social worker and training officer for Bradford Social Services. Gurnam's scholarship and activism is built around linking social justice to emancipatory research and critical pedagogy. He was awarded a PhD from the University of Warwick in 2004 for a thesis on anti-racist social work, and in 2009 he was awarded a National Teaching Fellowship by the Higher Education Academy for his work on critical pedagogy and higher education.

Richard Ward is a lecturer in Dementia Studies in the School of Applied Social Science at the University of Stirling. A registered social worker, Richard has worked with older adults and people with dementia for nearly 20 years. He is currently leading the Hair and Care study, an ESRC funded investigation of appearance and the work invested in maintaining it in dementia care settings. He is co-editor of *Lesbian, Gay, Bisexual and Transgender Ageing* (2012) published by Jessica Kingsley.

Lynne Wrennall teaches criminology at Liverpool John Moores University. She was awarded her PhD in Child Welfare gained by the University of Liverpool and has presented some of her research findings around child care social work at the Houses of Parliament. Lynne's interests include critiques of exclusion or violations of human rights within child protection services. Lynne previously coordinated the Service Users' Joint Statement on Child Protection which influenced policy development by the British Government and addressed the parliamentary conference held by the All Party Group on Abuse Investigations.

Introduction: Practical Social Work Ethics, Professionalism and Ethical Space

Malcolm Carey and Lorraine Green

It appears as if ethics are now an integral part of almost everything we do, as if they are everywhere. We are now encouraged to carefully consider the implications of the choices we make as consumers, including their impact upon other people or the environment. What are the moral ramifications of eating meat or buying battery farmed eggs, purchasing low-cost clothing or television sets made in the Majority World? Is it unethical to avoid public transport and drive alone and are our personal beliefs or attitudes towards disability or 'race', among many other constructs, continually open to question? Many more examples persist, but in general the ethical and moral implications of our day-to-day activities, relationships or personal beliefs now remain a central part of Western (late) modern life.

At heart, practical (or applied) ethics attempts to draw from 'moral principles' to clarify, and perhaps help to resolve in some way 'the practical issues of life'. As Kasachkoff (1992: 5) suggests, practical ethics in many respects returns us to the origins of philosophy (especially the early work of Plato, Aristotle, John Stuart Mill, Thomas Hobbes and John Locke), whilst also often striving to keep more of a distance from the sometimes introspective and abstract moral debates stimulated by academics, at times generated for fellow academics:

> In many respects, what we now call "applied philosophy" is a return to philosophy having as its primary subject not problems generated from within academic philosophy itself, but those which arise naturally, sometimes with urgency, out of the practical exigencies of the lives we lead, personal and professional.

In general, practical ethics look to interrogate the implicit nuances, *meaning* and *consequences* of our day-to-day actions, work and leisure, relationships,

1

values and beliefs, typically following a 'philosophical examination' of sorts. From such understanding or analysis we then attempt to draw conclusions – and possibly find and offer solutions – such as the right course of action to take in particular circumstances (Singer, 1979; 1986). Again, an underlying component of such a response remains the *consequences* of what we do and believe, including their impact upon other people or settings and systems. There is also often an implicit drive to explore 'real world' issues and concerns that may move away from traditional, scientific or analytic philosophy and its related preoccupation with objectivity, logic and theory. Within one of his many inspired books, *Beyond Good and Evil*, Friedrich Nietzsche famously caricatured the pretensions and arrogance of many philosophers that preceded him; noting, for example, that more than just a few articulated 'a desire of the heart that has been filtered and made abstract'. Warburton (2004: 38) reiterates this point when he notes that such thinkers may 'give complicated analyses which *appear* to involve impersonal logical reasoning but which always end up by demonstrating that their pre-existing prejudices were correct'. Peter Singer (1986: 1) has added that the revival of applied ethics since the 1960s also reflects civil discontent with traditional authority figures such as politicians, priests or members of the traditional professions such as medicine and law, alongside a more general interest taken by the empowered and less passive consumer in the invariably political nature of modern life. We might argue that doubt within a more fluid social work discourse felt towards professionals by Users and/or Carers – or the questioning of senior managers and policy makers by front-line practitioners – provides further evidence of this principled scepticism.

Most people involved in applied ethics seek to discover practical *conclusions* drawn from relevant *facts* or detailed *cases*, which have erstwhile been examined carefully with moral *principles* (rules, standards, values, beliefs, and so on). However this general, often informal process still leaves us with one significant problem: that of the different possible interpretations or explanations attached to any ethical problem(s) or dilemma(s). As any social worker knows there are typically different explanations and interpretations (or indeed 'assessments' or 'evaluations') of any social problem, issue or casework within the all too often uncertain or precarious fields of practice: consequentially, there inevitably emerge different possible understandings, responses and interventions. This uncertainty is what is generally termed 'moral relativism' (as opposed to certainty) in philosophy, and in our opinion this ambivalence remains a crucial – perhaps inevitable – component of not merely practical social work ethics but also most forms of social work more generally. Most of the chapters in this book therefore do not seek to serve up a one-size fits all, universal, pre-packaged or 'superior' moral outlook or law (sometimes termed 'McDonaldised Ethics') – more readily associated with traditional normative ethics (discussed further below) – but instead they offer one of a series of *possible* standpoints and explanations; thus allowing the reader to decide for themselves, or to look further, before drawing firm conclusions about the issues or problems explored. This relativism is more in keeping with the spirit of critical and libertarian social work from which most of the authors draw influence.

Social work as an *applied* 'ensemble of functions' (Pierson, 2011) has tended to be dominated by more grounded Kantian and Utilitarian ethics (or normative ethics), which in general look to *prescribe* how people ought to reflect or behave in given situations. Such models may have positive outcomes, especially if they are tied to other care-centred theories that promote justice or fairness (e.g. feminist or ethics of care). Despite this they still however often tend to promote adherence *in principle* to more dominant cultural or organisational traditions and rules; and such an interpretation has strongly influenced many professional codes of ethics, policy and practices within social work and welfare. In contrast, there is a more implicit tradition within applied ethics of interrogating and questioning established beliefs, traditions and practices, as well as sometimes offering alternatives that may counter more conventional norms or beliefs. Indeed Aristotle famously considered ethics a synonym for politics and clearly each entwine now as much as in the past. Many of the chapters in this book attempt to build upon this critical tradition.

Practical Ethics for Social Work

Practical ethics for social work focuses more specifically on the meaning and moral implications of our practices and beliefs within the different fields of social work and social care: whether at a policy-led, legal, organisational, group or personal level. In essence, practical ethics reflect what we do each day and the choices that we make within the narrow or wider contexts in which we practice. Practical ethics might be concerned with the support and care we may provide, the restrictions that we may face or impose on others or the impact of the power we may maintain over families or other service users and carers as we interpret and bring policy, law, or organisational rules and norms *to life*. As a specific domain of knowledge, practices and beliefs, practical social work ethics also aim to interrogate and query our taken for granted or unconscious assumptions and activities. These might include the ethical *implications* of higher eligibility criterion set by a local authority for a service user with late stage dementia, the many delicate decisions made by a practitioner regarding the adoption of a child with a learning disability, or the likely 'life chances' of a child recently placed into a residential children's home.

Practical ethics may also be deeply personal or help us to create a bridge, from practitioner as subject within the knowledge based, legal and quasi-market domain of social care, to a raft of contingent day-to-day decisions and related activities. We might, for example, ask how does the practitioner relate with users or understand and more importantly interpret and apply policy and law at ground level? We may have limited resources within an organisational context, but does this justify the non-provision of essential support? Might there be more we can do (or not) to make our work more ethical and meaningful?

We believe that as a profession social work has unique qualities for many different reasons. For example, social work deals with multiple contingent and unpredictable factors in peoples' lives, more often than not within capricious *community* settings. Unlike nursing or teaching, many of its often 'invisible' tasks are applied outside of confined spaces or institutions where control, treatments or less risky and ambivalent techniques or methods may prosper. Social workers also disproportionately accommodate or process potent emotional themes such as poverty, abuse or neglect as their *core* day-to-day business. In tandem, they overwhelmingly work with stigmatised, disempowered, marginalised, vulnerable and sometimes challenging individuals who often exist at the peripheries of society. Nearly all other welfare professionals tend to accommodate a wider socio-economic or class-based demographic and this will affect their role and relations with their clients as well as their professional identity. The issues that social workers address – such as those relating to poverty or neglect or the impact of emphatic market policies and/or human intolerance – are also not easily 'treated' by clear procedures, techniques or 'evidenced-based' treatments or services. This is not simply due to limited resources or time but also because problems such as exclusion, poverty or neglect, among many more examples, tend to be powerful, complex, nuanced and multifaceted. As a consequence, ethical anxieties or uncertainties are regularly embedded, if not all pervasive, within social work practice, perhaps much more so than in most other welfare related activities. Should a child be removed from a family living in abject poverty or is it fair to encourage a woman with later stage dementia to enter residential care? In an age of welfare austerity exactly who should be privileged with our seemingly ever-shrinking services and dwindling budgets: the man living alone with dementia or the lone parent struggling to raise her son with Autism? Adding further to such difficult questions, in Chapter 4 Gurnam Singh and Stephen Cowden ask us to reconsider common assumptions now often made that cultural sensitivity necessarily remains 'a good thing', whilst John Hopton in Chapter 6 again challenges many practitioners almost taken for granted assumption that psychiatry and the bio-medical model remain deeply unethical, if not almost sinister, in relation to attempts to meet patient needs.

Practical ethics therefore affect everyone within social work, and although we are unlikely to be allowed the time or resources to carefully consider them all, we believe that social workers have a professional and moral duty to reflect , identify and consider the consequences of their actions and beliefs. This book seeks to discuss just a few important ethical topics and dilemmas spanning diverse settings, different contexts or policy and a variety of service user groups.

Social Work on the Brink and 'Ethical Space'

These remain extremely difficult times for social work as a professional or state-sponsored activity. Considerable pressures continue to be placed on social work which means it is very much under threat by factors such as: governments who repeatedly demand greater accountability and evidence of the purpose or efficacy of social care related interventions and services; a sometimes hostile media and sceptical public; the greater involvement of other welfare professionals or unqualified staff in core roles or activities once dominated by social work such as mental health and safeguarding assessments, counselling, care management and person-centred or therapeutic welfare; and on-going processes of outsourcing, fragmentation and the implementation of intense austerity programmes that significantly reduce social care budgets for many vulnerable groups such as older people in most Western political economies. This has led in many quarters to a further retreat of positive social work and the intensification of social control or equally reductive risk-orientated activities. As Pollack, (2010: 1276) has recently noted in her discussion of 'risk thinking' in work with female offenders, modern social work stands ever more on 'the front lines of governing marginalized populations'; which seriously brings into question the profession's repeatedly bold claim that it is able to promote human rights and extend social justice for disadvantaged or socially excluded people. There are, however, some more positive outcomes that have emerged, such as the sometimes non-tokenistic and creative involvement of service users or informal carers in sectors of social work education, greater independence for some users and carers who transfer to personal budgets or calls for greater professional discretion as opposed to adherence to government targets or organisational bureaucracy as an organisational and policy-led norm (e.g. Munro, 2011). There is evidence also that there are social workers who against the odds may use their ethical intelligence more creatively to achieve positive outcomes for users and carers (see for example; White, Hall and Peckover, 2007; Carey and Foster, 2011) and also that newer independent or voluntary sector services can improve support to users or carers.

It seems inevitable that social work will continue to encounter ongoing reforms and change. Sarah Banks (2012: 1), for example, opens the latest edition of her now classic *Ethics and Values in Social Work* textbook by noting that social work 'is always in a state of change, as it is linked so closely to social welfare systems that shift with global economic trends and in response to government social and economic policies'. Others, however, such as Linda Davies and Peter Leonard (2004) or Beth Humphries (2004) believe that social work is still far too uncritical and 'state' compliant; and indeed too readily abandons humanitarian ethics in favour of authoritarian policies aimed at asylum seekers or other vulnerable groups in order to survive or extend its legitimacy or relatively limited power base. As Keith Brown notes, market driven policies have also generated pernicious outcomes in the 'support' of many core members of social work's traditional client groups, such as older or disabled people:

> There is a strange pressure which says "please do not be effective in finding new clients who want help as we cannot afford to meet their needs". In other words in financial terms, it is better to employ social workers whose skills and abilities are in preventing new clients from wanting, seeking or finding help. (2006: 1)

This alludes to another trend within social work, which is that although change regularly occurs as Sarah Banks suggests, there also remains continuity in some themes and practices. For example, tensions between social work practitioners and service users or their family members due to poverty, deprivation and class anxieties were prevalent in Victorian times and this continues today (Ferguson, 2010; Pierson, 2011). Practitioners assessing people for their eligibility to receive support or more recent government attempts to encourage 'self-help' among vulnerable populations were again just as central to social work over a century ago as they are now amidst many policy makers (Jones, 1983; Cruickshank, 1999; Davies and Leonard, 2004). Again as in the past, welfare professions are now being disproportionately encouraged to monitor and control seemingly 'deviant' or disenfranchised populations: from the surveillance or regulation of the apparently 'mad' and the 'bad' to the expansion of cheap and predominately short-term (cognitive-behavioural) 'therapies' which seemingly encourage the stressed or alienated to integrate more and be more 'happy' (Davies and Leonard, 2004; King, 2008); despite other causal and structural factors such as poverty which may be the key contributors to their relative unhappiness. In Chapter 5 Kenneth McLaughlin and Sean Cordell bring into question government policies that seek to extend 'happiness' in subject populations – such as in their example of the use of Controlled Treatment Orders with patients with mental health needs. Happiness as they note is a widely contested concept within philosophy, and one that stands on fragile grounds if seeking to use it to extend forced treatment orders on objectified client populations.

We have also witnessed the further promotion of related normalising paradigms such as behavioural, systemic, task-centred or attachment approaches within social work which may again decontextualise complex human relations or needs and ultimately squeeze them into simple rational processes, standardised routines or cost effective 'technologies of care' (Webb, 2006). In some instances at least social work would appear to be following aspects of Althusser's (2003) claim of helping to fulfil (along with the Church, family, workplace, school, etc.) an ideological 'new reality' that surreptitiously supports and disseminates the established moral rules, practices and traditions of a dynamic, almost fluid, free-market Capitalist enterprise. Ethics (deontological, humanist and others) can aid this process by offering another convenient 'mask' behind which the professional as one of a number of 'high priests' of the ruling ideology may hide their implicit or forthright normalizing and 'interpellating' objectives. However, although these traits may be prevalent, it appears increasingly the case that social work now spends so much of its time and resources responding to and managing human crisis and risk, that practitioners perhaps now only possess limited time to also transmit dominant norms or values!

Despite considerable external pressures, we still assert that most social workers do have at least some choices or options in their respective roles and responsibilities. For example, social workers are not legally enshrined to view service users or carers with deep suspicion or even contempt, and they may also decide that extra time and effort spent on an eligibility 'panel' application to support the carer of an older person with dementia will make a difference. For example, Sue White and her colleagues (2007) recently discovered that social work practitioners were able to generate their own subjective autonomy in their work despite regularly being restricted within a bureaucratic child and family 'safeguarding' system. Such employees were at times able to creatively draw upon their tangible life experiences and moral intelligence to make initial decisions about the practical safety and possible risks that children or parents may face.

There are more examples but overall practitioners can if they choose carve out 'ethical spaces' in their work; including in their attitudes towards or relationships with users and carers. Positive emotions or virtues such as empathy and altruism are obvious examples, but so also are creative attempts to advocate on behalf of clients, access support and provide advice, make referrals to agencies that will offer help, and so forth. It is these types of relatively small-scale practical support which are likely to have the greatest impact upon users and carers. Creating ethical space and perhaps engaging in 'creative resistance' is clearly difficult in the often harsh or even dystopian environments of resource-limited or bureaucratic social work, yet wherever possible such altruistic or even recalcitrant approaches are likely to make our work more meaningful, fulfilling and less oppressive to ourselves as well as disadvantaged families and other groups. Again this point is embedded within some of the chapters within this book: such as Lorraine Green and Ros Day's chapter on the use of physical touch within social care settings and Donna Baines exploration of the ethical practices of resistance within voluntary sectors.

Ethical Theory and Practice

Ethics fosters a broad understanding and many different interpretations. There is no one all-encompassing definition of ethics – instead there are several interpretations. For example, ethics is regularly tied to our understanding of what is 'right' or 'wrong', or even 'good' or 'evil' (Singer, 1993). Ethical actions may also be interpreted as our capacity to follow organisational rules and procedures or how to behave correctly in specific environments and settings. For many people, however, ethics is not simply concerned with making a clear distinction between what is right and wrong, a moral binary that is not always easy to draw. In some cases the choice may be between two less than desirable outcomes rather than between an uncontested right and wrong or an unalienable good or bad outcome. In other cases we may have limited choice, for example if being pushed economically into undertaking paid employment for an organisation whose policies and practices we strongly disagree with. As stated earlier, in social work however, despite the prevalence of often unhelpful opposites or binaries (for example, professional/client; good/bad parent; dependent/ independent user; care/control; normal/abnormal personality; and many more examples), we regularly enter grey areas of uncertainty within practice. For example, which of several 'vulnerable' people should receive support from limited resources and where does our loyalty lie as a social worker or care manager: with the state and its laws, the wishes of a supervisor or our employing organisation or with a relative or the service user? Is it really possible to serve all four?

Social work has tended to be influenced by different and competing or associated ethical theories. Stan Houston (2011) proposes four key theories of ethics which have influenced social work. Very briefly these include:

- *Utilitarianism*: considers the best options, consequences or utility for the greatest numbers of people, especially of our actions. In privileging the pleasures or happiness of a majority this approach may exclude or discriminate against the many diverse minority groups that social workers work with. Utilitarianism, because it is more concerned with consequences rather than the moral applicability of individual acts, may also legitimate an immoral act if it yields a positive outcome for the greatest number. On the plus side, Utilitarianism can sometimes be applied with a more focused light to justify preventative and community-orientated social work with families in need.

- *Deontology*: historically the most influential paradigm that impacts upon social work theory and practice, deontology stresses reason, autonomy, duty and respect for others. It also privileges the importance of respecting service users, encouraging their autonomy and the following of universal moral rules. This approach is also closely tied to adhering to professional codes of ethics or laws. There are however times when following legal, professional or organisation rules may not be in best interest of service users or informal carers. This duty-centred approach may also yield more questions and uncertainties than answers, particularly if different ethical dictates and codes conflict with each other.

- *Virtue ethics*: concentrates more upon personal character, substance, and conviction from which it is assumed ethical practices can grow and flourish. It stresses individual choices and *positive* virtues such as integrity, honesty, loyalty, wisdom and kindness, and hopes to shape character which will then influence our actions. Yet virtue again throws up multiple uncertainties and questions, particularly if virtues conflict in different situations, are culturally relative and a choice needs to be made as to which virtues to prioritise. Can the hard-pressed social worker with competing demands realistically be virtuous to everyone in different situations?

- *Ethics of care*: influenced by feminism and attacks individualism whilst recognising wider social factors such as sexism or class-based discrimination that may disadvantage a service user or carer. Stresses inter-dependence, the mutuality of the caring relationship and emotional intelligence, empathy or informal care for users, including recognition of their potential suffering. Again the validity of this approach has been questioned by some within the perhaps paradoxical care/control realm of state sponsored social work.

From the four key schools we can also note implicit ties. For example, Utilitarianism and deontology both stress being impartial and unbiased as a 'good professional'. Both these theories, despite their considerable influence within policy and practice, may also struggle to accommodate ongoing change or different beliefs, cultures or traditions. Virtue ethics shares with the ethics of care a strong humanistic and less formal slant, yet striving to be empathetic or kind may not always be in the best interests of a service user. Indeed Meagher and Parton (2004) note that the ethics of care (and the virtuous social worker) may quickly wither within the bureaucratic and resource-starved domain of risk-orientated social work. Others, however, insist that the ethics of care have a role to play in social work. This is because they emphasise not only the importance of character (as in Virtue Ethics), but also 'the *relationships* in which the ethical issues take place and the centrality of such concepts as responsibility and caring in the definition of the morally right action' (Pullen-Sansfacon and Cowden, 2012: 175–6).

Bauman (1993), however, has challenged our claims to create clear ethical rules which it seems may bind with equally suspect social/political constructs such as reason, progress or supposed regimes or games of one dimensional 'truth'. He argues any such systematic or grand constructs may be highly subjective and ultimately promote conformity, compliance and, yet again, the elevation of dominant interests. Foucault (1984: 4; 1986) argues that ethics links the citizen to not only other people and their environment but also themselves and their soul. That is, in addition to promoting dominant sciences or discourses and established relations of power that regulate such discourses, there is also a third micro-level at which citizens are 'able, are obliged' to 'focus their attention on themselves, to decipher, recognize, and acknowledge themselves as [ethical] subjects'. Within this complex process, an ethical identity encourages citizens to reflect and monitor or regulate themselves, to control and contain their urges or motivate and direct their personal autonomy. In relation, alongside other welfare professionals, but more particularly through casework or group work, social work has long claimed a role in regulating such practices of the self, as Dean (2010: 20) asserts:

> The criminal might be regarded as a victim of circumstance and environment who requires reformation; the unemployed person as someone at risk of welfare dependency who requires group counselling to provide self-help and increase self-esteem; and the national population as lacking the capacities of enterprise and entrepreneurship required to be internationally competitive ... ethics can be reconceived in these terms as the arena of the government of the self, as a form of action of the "self on self".

We might ask nevertheless whether such forms of normative cajoling, reflexivity and self-control are obligatory or uncontested in social care fields, it seems that practitioner responses are likely to be more uncertain, contested and diverse.

Estes, Biggs and Phillipson (2003: 92–4) nevertheless warn of the increasing influence of bio-medical ethics within welfare domains, for example with regard to the formal care of older people. Here within medical science, *autonomy* (the decision making capacity of the patient) takes increasing precedence alongside the equally durable impact of other universal themes such as clinical priority being given to the *choices* made available to consumers (within a market economy). As part of this seemingly pervasive professional discourse special attention is drawn to clinical examinations of need which are translated through 'technical gatekeeping within the symbolic space of a special, one to one bond'. However, such a hegemonic culture is much less able to 'digest issues of institutionalised ageism or imbalances of power between patients and health care professionals'. Indeed choice it seems is more likely to translate into arguments in favour of increased privatisation and freer markets, whilst autonomy will not uncommonly digress into priority being given to 'quality' processes such as monitoring and audit which again obfuscate the impact of structural and personal inequalities upon patients:

> In so far as ethicists deal in universals, they are likely to ignore the social and historical specificity of their own conclusions. There is therefore little attention to issues outside the ethical bubble and, most particularly, the power environment that shapes ethical discourse itself. Ultimately decisions come down either to the ethical judgement of the clinician in so far as this, paradoxically, allows the patient autonomy, or is left to the universal yet hidden hand of market forces ... wider circumferences of policy and power relations are not addressed as it is assumed that the application of general moral principles rather than the interactive dialogue and legitimizing discourses that shape relationships are sufficient to aid professional judgement.

Promoting 'freedom' as opposed to autonomy, choice, control, conformity and self-regulation should instead be the business of a more radical ethics according to Foucault (1984; 1986). In support, Richard Rorty (1989) vociferously eschews reductive or essentialist standpoints embedded within traditional morality. He instead promotes a more pragmatic and personal 'ethics of taste' that is embedded with irony, humour, satire and explicit scepticism for established, rational and objectifying beliefs, values, identities and practices. This perhaps entertaining and deviant stance that – draws more from the cultural traditions set within literature rather than philosophy – has, however, been criticised for being individualistic and prioritising aesthetic rather than moral concerns (Hall, 1994).

The tentative and contingent solution, it would seem, from relatively different quarters, is to be less dogmatic, fixed and static in our viewpoints and practices; and more questioning, inventive, fluid and creative, drawing eclectically from different perspectives and theories (including Kantian and Radical, among others) to challenge and change, depending upon the circumstances (for example, Gray, 2010; Houston, 2011; Banks, 2012). We could, however, question whether such creativity and eclecticism is again practically realistic, alongside dissent, within the high pressured arenas or cauldrons of 'risk-averse' social work in which the capacity to make quick decisions may be one of the most important skills we can possess. Yet again might organisational rules and limited resources or time restrict our options or choices? As Singer (1993) and others note, the availability or otherwise of choice remains central to making any practical interpretations of ethics come to life.

Some possible solutions have been suggested in attempts to accommodate any such obstacles facing social workers who try to practice more ethically. Pullen-Sansfacon and Cowden (2012: 31), for example, have argued for more 'practical reasoning' as a key part of a more ethical social work. This includes an implicit assumption made by each of us that 'just because a norm is formally accepted by a given society, it is not necessarily ethical'. Such an approach asks us to critically question the taken-for-granted, as well as challenge with reason and 'critical judgement' organisational rules if they do not appear to support or assist the disadvantaged or excluded. We may also query professional or moral codes if our 'ethical deliberations' suggest that they again contradict or undermine the altruistic maxims which may (ideally) permeate our endeavours. Gray and Macdonald (2006) also propose that 'ethical reasoning' which draws from different theories, beliefs and experiences, can offer a more viable alternative for practitioners regarding direction and insight than the more conceptually narrow and theoretically reductive paradigms and processes fashioned within evidence-based practices. We can also see from these perspectives that ethics clearly provides us with a type of moral identity – as indicated by Foucault and others – which offer not merely a means of normative self-governance; but also a potential platform from which to question or challenge *unethical* organisational objectives, policy mandates, provider standards, professional claims, and much else. How we manage our moral identity within a role as precarious, unstable and reliant upon contingencies (relationships, accommodation, resources, services, etc.) as social work clearly remains a relentless task in itself.

Professional Ethics and Modernisation

As part of ongoing change within social work since the 1970s we have witnessed a rapid growth in professional codes of ethics. According to the

National Association of Social Work (2011) professional social work ethics (PSWEs) fulfil core objectives which, among others, include: identifying the core values on which social work's mission is based; summarizing broad ethical principles used to guide social work values and practice; providing standards and public accountability; assessing whether social workers have engaged in unethical conduct or are culturally competent, and so forth. In practice PSWEs are grounded in Kantian or deontological duty-based principles yet they also draw in part from other sources (Utilitarian, ethics of care, feminist, and so on). At face value such codes offer a practical and moral foundation upon which practitioner norms, behaviour and values can be based and judged against. Such codes may help to make us more accountable to the public yet the National Association of Social Work (2011) also argues that codes of ethics are rarely intended to determine the moral acts or beliefs of practitioners, but instead seek to *guide* and *inform*.

Codified social work ethics have, furthermore, faced criticism. For example, Downie and Calman (1994) highlight the widening gap between *personal* practitioner ethics 'on the front-line' and formal codes. This may relate to the increasingly fragmented and market-led nature of health or social care service provision. Bowles et al. (2006: 77–8) also note that codes may be out of touch with modern life, such as within more 'flexible' organisations; for example due to the 'multiple realities, or discourses that colour how people see the world, rather than a single "truth"'. Indeed Steph Petrie (2009) offers a damning critique of the British Association of Social Work's *Codes of Ethics* (2002). In particular, the reformed and ever changing nature of modern social work means that such a code fails to offer appropriate guidance to front-line practitioners:

> The BASW code is too grandiose in some areas and too detailed in others. In common with many welfare policies of the UK government in recent years, it could be described as an amalgam of a "blue skies" wish list and tick-box template and in attempting to cover everything achieves little. (ibid.: 3)

Ian Butler (2002), however, in discussing a code for social work research, proposes that codes do not necessarily provide a moral template as such but instead help to carve out a distinct professional culture and identity.

Nevertheless one of the more significant obstacles to ethical practice is the implementation of a now long running modernisation agenda in the UK, propagated by successive New Labour governments (Harris and White, 2009). These have built upon neo-liberal ideological reforms and principles set by the Conservatives during the 1980s, key aspects of which have impacted in many other countries. Modernisation has had many consequences for front-line practice but the most apparent include the continued demise of public sector service provision; the extension of independent (private and voluntary sector) social and health care practices; the increased regulation and accountability of social work practice (such as through performance targets and added or best value) and education; greater coordination between different service provider agencies (especially between health and social care and public and private sectors) and the growth of service user and carer participation. The many ramifications of modernisation are detailed implicitly or explicitly in a number of the chapters running throughout this book. This is most prominently within Part III, yet elsewhere. Among other examples, Paul Michael Garrett in Chapter 1 identifies links between the past abuses of children within the industrial schools of Ireland and more recent relations of implicit fear within modern organisations.

Although some reforms within modernisation have benefited user or carer groups by providing more effective and coordinated services, there are nevertheless also many recognised drawbacks. As well as splintering many previously consistent social work provisions, modernisation has also intensified further already bureaucratic systems which, among other consequences, erect and fortress increasingly higher walls between practitioners and users or their carers. As Galpin (2009: 88–9) notes, modernisation has further alienated many already disillusioned practitioners and added to extensive staff retention and recruitment problems. It has also pushed social work away from many components of welfare provision (counselling, advocacy, group work, assessment, and so on) that it once pioneered or claimed an active role in. Modernisation has it seems also failed to provide many of its claimed benefits – such as increased choice or independence to users or carers. It is important, however, not to overstate the impact of modernisation or earlier neoliberal reforms upon front line forms of ethical practice. Although such policy, legislation or cultural norms are likely to at times significantly restrict the available options to practitioners, there are still aspects of social work in which at least some discretion persists. Bourdieu and Wacquant (1992: 109), for example, note that no system of political or economic governance, however well organised or managed, is ever complete or total. Inevitably gaps appear in most, if not all, systems of governance, and it is here that the 'ethical spaces' which prevail through relations, beliefs, actions or constructive moral praxis, might be generated and promoted:

> Social agents are not "particles" that are mechanically pushed and pulled about by external forces. They are, rather, bearers of capital and, depending on their trajectory and on the position they occupy in the field by virtue of their endowment in capital, they have a propensity to orient themselves actively either toward the preservation of the distribution of capital or toward the subversion of this distribution.

The ethical practitioner may take full advantage of realistic opportunities or 'gaps' in the system to empower the vulnerable user in the political sense of providing support or advice, and avoid wherever possible the trap of following procedure or rules simply for the sake of it.

Past and Present, Ethical Tensions and Modernisation

This book is divided into three main sections, each representing pervasive themes or issues which have influenced past and present practices. In Part I we examine some aspects of child, family and relationship-based social work and social care. The institution – both macro (hospital, school, and so on) and micro (residential and other care providers) – has often and indeed continues to house children in care, and it is such contrasting yet related settings that Paul Michael Garrett and Lorraine Green and Ros Day scrutinise in their respective chapters. Paul Michael Garrett focuses on institutional abuse in Irish Industrial schools over many decades and Lorraine Green and Ros Day critically examine the use of touch, most prominently in residential care settings. Sandwiched between these two powerful and moving explorations of institutional support, neglect or abuse, Kylie Agllias and Mel Gray offer a detailed examination of the family unit as a site of paradoxical moral relations. Their focus is on family secrets, lies and estrangement and they explore how social workers might think through and perhaps support or manage such paradoxes. Following this, in Chapter 3 Gurnam Singh and Stephen Cowden examine the significance of cultural sensitivity for social work practice, forcefully dispelling any simplistic notions that acceptance of and accommodation to difference is unequivocally an ethically 'good thing' whilst simultaneously promoting more Universalist approaches to ethics in social work.

In Part II we look closer at some of the ethical tensions and nuances apparent with social work with adults. Again within the spirit of the book, Kenneth McLaughlin and Sean Cordell ask us to critically reflect upon commonplace assumptions often made: this time with regards to the potentially difficult relationship between the social worker and people with significant mental health needs living outside institutions in community settings. Their specific focus is on the ethicality and efficacy of Community Treatment Orders or CTOs, examined across a number of different dimensions. Following this, John Hopton again provokes our assumptions about mental health, this time questioning implicit negative assumptions or prejudices within social work about the limits of psychiatry, the medical model and medical support. John ultimately argues for an integrated yet flexible social and medical model synthesis which respects and works with the service user's beliefs, needs and preferences. Finally, Richard Ward and Sarah Campbell draw from their ongoing elaborate empirical (qualitative) research into embodiment and dementia within care settings to question the phenomenal rise of ethical regulation and governance within formal research and knowledge creating arenas and discursive domains. They also argue that applied research and practice-based ethics are not as divisible or easily separated as they appear to be.

Part III seeks to analyse some of the many ethical problems generated through the ongoing modernisation agenda and its numerous related yet often paradoxical initiatives such as privatisation and participation. Lynne Wrennall draws from a critical libertarian interpretation of ethics to offer a scathing and detailed critique of sectional interests which she argues have significantly undermined the interests of service users in social care. This chapter draws from eclectic sources to unearth and deconstruct a wide range of suspect ethical challenges to us all, including the promotion of business interests, corruption and implicit neglect within business and market-led social work. Malcolm Carey then looks at some of the ethical implications and challenges of service user and carer participation, and raises doubts about whether statutory social work in particular can in fact undertake ethical participation. There are a number of problems with this embedded culture including not least the reality that social work is in fact forced onto many of its users, including people who are often powerless and significantly disadvantaged (especially women and minority ethnic group members). There are also questions about the apparent democratic claims about wider public participation too; nevertheless, a handful of very good examples of more constructive and ethical participation have emerged. Finally, in the spirit of many of the chapters there are seeds of hope on offer. In this case the resistance of stressed practitioners stands out within Donna Baines exploration of the attempts by workers to grapple with the tensions between their personal sense of social justice and the more sectional interests of managers and the influence of the increasingly neo-liberal infused market which houses the changing Canadian and Australian voluntary sectors.

Our aim in producing this book is to explore in finer detail some of the many moral and ethical implications of the complex, often unpredictable, ever changing and multiply nuanced work that social workers undertake. This in our view is one of the important traits that distinguishes social work as an emotional, political and, in many instances at least, ethical trade. This book therefore cannot and indeed does not seek to cover all of the many areas in which social workers or care mangers ply their often unseen or unappreciated 'invisible' work, but instead attempts to address what we consider at present to be just a few of the most significant and pressing.

References

Althusser, L. (2003) *The Humanist Controversy and Other Writings*. London, Verso.

Banks, S. (2012) *Ethics and Values in Social Work*, 4th edn. Basingstoke, Palgrave Macmillan.

Banks, S. and Williams, R. (2005) 'Accounting for Ethical Difficulties in Social Welfare Work: Issues, problems and Dilemmas', *British Journal of Social Work* 35 (7): 1005–22.

Bauman, Z. (1993) *Postmodern Ethics* Cambridge, Blackwell.

Beckett, C. and Maynard, A. (2005) *Values and Ethics in Social Work: An Introduction*. London, Sage.

Bourdieu, P. and Wacquant, L.J.D. (1992) *An Invitation to Reflexive Sociology*. Cambridge, Polity Press.

Bowles, W., Collingridge, M., Curry, S. and Valentine, B. (2006) *Ethical Practice in Social Work: An Applied Approach*. Crows Nest, New South Wales, Allen and Unwin.

British Association of Social Work (2002) *Codes of Ethics*, http://www.basw.co.uk/Default.aspx?tabid=64 accessed 15/05/2012.

Brown, K. (2006) 'Vulnerable Adults and Community Care' in Brown, K. (ed.) *Vulnerable Adults and Community Care*. Exeter, Learning Matters.

Butler, I. (2002) 'Critical Commentary: A Code of Ethics for Social Work and Social Care Research', *British Journal of Social Work* 32 (2): 239–48.

Carey, M. and Foster, V. (2011) 'Introducing Deviant Social Work: Contextualizing the limits of radical social work whilst understanding (fragmented) resistance in the state social work labour process', *British Journal of Social Work* 41 (3): 576–93.

Cruickshank, B. (1999) *The Will to Empower: Democratic Citizens and Other Subjects*. London, Cornell University Press.

Davies, L. and Leonard, P. (eds) (2004) *Social Work in a Corporate Era: Practices of Power and Resistance*. Farnham, Ashgate.

Dean, M. (2010) *Governmentality: Power and Rule in Modern Society*, 2nd edn. London, Sage.

Downie, R.S. and Calman, K.C. (1994) *Healthy Respect: Ethics in Health Care*. Oxford, Oxford University Press.

Estes, C., Biggs, S., Phillipson, C. (2003) *Social Theory, Policy and Ageing: A Critical Introduction*. Berkshire, Open University Press.

Ferguson, H. (2010) *Child Protection Practice*. Basingstoke, Palgrave.

Foucault, M. (1984) *The Use of Pleasure*. London, Penguin.

Foucault, M. (1986) *The Care of the Self*. New York, Pantheon.

Galpin, D. (2009) 'Transformation: A Future for Social Work Practice?' in Galpin, D. and Bates, N. (eds) *Social Work Practice with Adults*. Exeter, Learning Matters.

Gray, M. (2010) 'Moral Sources and Emergent Ethical Theories in Social Work', *British Journal of Social Work* 40 (6): 1794–811.

Gray, M. and Macdonald, C. (2006) 'Pursuing Good Practice? The Limits of Evidence-based Practice', *Journal of Social Work* 6 (1): 7–20.

Hall, D.L. (1994) *Richard Rorty: Prophet and Poet of the New Pragmaticism*. Albany, State University of New York Press.

Harris, J. and White, V. (eds) (2009) *Modernising Social Work: Critical Considerations*. Bristol, Policy Press.

Houston, S. (2011) 'Engaging with the Crooked Timber of Humanity: Value Pluralism and Social Work', *British Journal of Social Work*, Advanced Access, June 28, 2011.

Hugman, R. (2005) *New Approaches for Ethics in the Caring Professions*. Basingstoke, Palgrave Macmillan.

Humphries, B. (2004) 'An Unacceptable Role for Social Work: Implementing Immigration Policy', *British Journal of Social Work* 34 (1): 93–107.

Jones, C. (1983) *State Social Work and the Working Class*. London, Macmillan.

Kasachkoff, T. (1992) 'Some Complaints about and Defences of Applied Philosophy', *International Journal of Applied Philosophy* 7 (1): 5–9.

King, M. (2008) 'Invited Commentary … on Proposals for Massive Expansion of Psychological Therapies would be Counterproductive Across Societies', *The British Journal of Psychiatry* 192: 331–2.

Meagher, G. and Parton, N. (2004) 'Modernising Social Work and the Ethics of Care', *Social Work and Society* 2 (1): 10–27.

Munro, E. (2011) *The Munro Review of Child Protection – Final Report – A Child Centred System*. London, DfE. https://www.education.gov.uk/publications/standard/publicationDetail/Page1/CM%208062v.

National Association of Social Workers (2011) *Code of Ethics*. Washington, DC, NASW.

Petrie, S. (2009) 'Are the International and National Codes of Ethics for Social Work in the UK as Useful as a Chocolate Teapot?', *Journal of Social Work Values and Ethics* 6 (2).

Pierson, J. (2011) *Understanding Social Work: History and Context*. Maidenhead, Open University Press.

Pollack, S. (2010) 'Labelling Clients 'Risky': Social Work and the Neo-liberal Welfare State', *British Journal of Social Work*, 40 (4): 1263–78.

Pullen-Sansfacon, A. and Cowden, S. (2012) *The Ethical Foundations of Social Work*. Harlow, Pearson Education Limited.

Rorty, R. (1989) *Contingency, Irony and Solidarity*. Cambridge, Cambridge University Press.

Shaw, I.F. (2012) *Practice and Research*. Farnham, Ashgate.

Singer, P. (1979) *Practical Ethics*. Oxford, Oxford University Press.

Singer, P. (ed.) (1986) *Applied Ethics*. Oxford, Oxford University Press.

Singer, P. (1993) *How Are We to Live? Ethics in the Age of Self-interest*. Oxford, Oxford University Press.

Warburton, N. (2004) *Philosophy: the Basics*, 4th edn. Routledge, London.

Webb, S.A. (2006) *Social Work in a Risk Society*. Basingstoke, Palgrave Macmillan.

White, S., Hall, C. and Peckover, S. (2007) 'The Descriptive Tyranny of the Common Assessment Framework: Technologies of Categorisation and Professional Practice in Child Welfare', *British Journal of Social Work* 39: 1197–217.

Part I

Past and Present: Moral Practices with Children and Families

In the first section of the book contributors highlight and analyse some of the different arenas and contexts in and through which social work predominantly with children and their families takes place. Although sometimes considered 'dirty work' with apparent 'social undesirables', social work accommodates a variety of emotionally intense, politically and culturally sensitive and practically essential roles in disparate community environments. In the first chapter Paul Michael Garrett exposes and describes in graphic detail the multifaceted trajectory of long-term institutional abuse of 'poor' and often already abused and neglected children within industrial schools in Ireland. Garrett positions history, social class and politics at the core of practical social work ethics, pinpointing much continuity between the way these children were dehumanised and treated in the past and the way they are represented and responded to now. Again by offering new insights into mostly institutional support, Lorraine Green and Ros Day in Chapter 4 ask us to stop and consider the many ethical dilemmas and complexities surrounding the issue of touch in social work/care. They focus on a range of issues affecting different client groups in varied settings whilst also reviewing extant research and literature on touch and discussing its practical and ethical implications for social work. Both these chapters also contrast the larger 'macro' institution of old with the still common residential 'micro' institutions which have become more prevalent and are represented by the homeless shelter, nursing home, extended living accommodation, and other examples. Such different settings alter the relationships between residents and also staff and perhaps inevitably generate new moral dilemmas, anxieties or forms of sanction or abuse. As well as the intense variety of settings in which social work practice takes place we can also see in this section the many different power relations that persist within and as part of formal or informal care and any subsequent concomitant relationships.

In Chapter 2, Kylie Agllias and Mel Gray focus on family secrets and lies, showing that ethical decision making in social work practice becomes more complex and fraught when it is so intricately tied to deeply personal – even private – beliefs and hidden experiences which might challenge normative ideologies and practices of family, parenting, marriage and motherhood. The chapter also examines ethical dilemmas associated with intergenerational family estrangement in later life, through an ethics of care lens and a focus on relational ethics.

In Chapter 3, Gurnam Singh and Stephen Cowden question whether uncritical cultural sensitivity is always a positive quality or ethically defensible? They explore the dilemmas faced by social workers in responding to issues associated with cultural and religious identities. They challenge the powerful but seemingly flawed orthodoxy which emerged during the 1980s of always seeing cultural differences as benign and positive and warranting accommodation and 'special' treatment, an orthodoxy which has been framed through the lens of 'culturally sensitive' social work practice. These chapters together stress the significance of history and the home, institutions and nuanced relationships between people and professionals: and in particular they highlight the complex care/control binary inherent within social care as well as the labyrinth or sometimes minefield of disparate ethical uncertainties that are perhaps inevitably woven into the delicate yet contested trade of social work.

1 Beyond the Community of Persons to Be Accorded 'Respect'? Messages from the Past for Social Work in the Republic of Ireland

Paul Michael Garrett

Introduction

This chapter's foundational understanding is that the defence of social work ethics is vital. This is especially the case during a period of neoliberalisation when ways of working and relating to others are increasingly subject to market mechanisms and 'care' practices become even more vulnerable to corruption (Harvey, 2005; Wardhaugh and Wilding, 1993). In this context, perhaps what many still perceive as the core social work value – 'respect for persons' – has the potential to become increasingly political and more subversive of dominant hegemonic orders intent on (dis)respecting particular groups and communities.

Sarah Banks (2006, p. xiii) suggests that the focus of professional ethics has been on 'developing lists of principles and how to handle conflict between principles' (see also Banks, 2003; 2004). However, the influence of history and the contexts in which ethical dilemmas occur has been secondary. When workers struggle with issues that transcend their interpersonal relationships with service users, they commonly view their struggles as idiosyncratic or outside the lens of ethics (Weinberg, 2010). This chapter, therefore, seeks to locate history at the core of reflection on practical social work ethics. It will discuss how particular groups, constructed as 'outcasts' at specific historical conjunctures, are symbolically and often spatially located beyond the community of persons to be accorded 'respect'. Here the focus will be on the treatment of 'troublesome', impoverished young people confined to Industrial Schools in the Republic of Ireland in the past.

In the six years spanning 2005–2011, political, public and media discussion on child abuse has dwelt on four reports published after separate inquiries into abuse by Roman Catholic priests and other, largely male, figures in 'caring' roles: (i) a 2005 report examining abuse in the diocese of Ferns (Murphy et al., 2005); (ii) the Ryan Commission's voluminous report (Commission to Inquire into Child Abuse, 2009); (iii) the Murphy Commission report examining complaints of child sexual abuse against a number of Dublin based priests during the period 1975–2004 (Commission of Investigation, 2009). Subsequently, a further fourth (iv) Commission of Investigation (2011) critical report, examining events in the Roman Catholic diocese of Cloyne, was published in July 2011 (see also Garrett, 2013). In what follows, the aim is to concentrate on the Ryan Commission which investigated abuse in Industrial Schools and related institutions.[1] It will begin by surveying some of the key findings featured in the Ryan Report and then move on to illuminate some of the continuities detectable in terms of the responses to 'troublesome' young people in the past and today. In this context it will be argued that social workers and associated professionals should try to foster forms of reflection and ethical practice which incorporate a sense of social history and which are attentive to the specific national domains in which they operate.

---

1   Throughout the discussion, for ease of reference, the Commission to Inquire into Child Abuse (2009) will be referred to as the 'Ryan Report'. In Table 1.1, some rounding up/down was applied by the Commission. The 'gulag' reference is taken from Arnold (2009). In the latter half of this chapter, HSE refers to the Health Services Executive: a quasi-governmental organisation which operates at arm's-length from the elected government and minister with responsibility for health and related services. The setting up of such an agency is a typical neoliberal measure that serves to dilute democratic accountability whilst also facilitating further privatization. Although the necessarily limited space available does not provide for a detailed engagement with their work, the analysis in this chapter is theoretically grounded in the work of Pierre Bourdieu and Antonio Gramsci (see also Garrett 2007a; 2007b; 2008; 2009) and also draws on and reworks some of the material previously featured in Garrett (2012; 2013). Lorraine Green provided me with helpful suggestions which helped me to refine aspects of the chapter.

The Irish 'Gulag': The Ryan Report on the Historical Treatment of the Impoverished and 'Troublesome' Young

The Industrial Schools Act 1868 established Industrial Schools to hold and contain neglected, abandoned and ambiguously 'troublesome' children. They began to expand from the 1920s and already by 1924 there were more children in Industrial Schools in the Free State than there were in all of the Industrial Schools in England, Scotland, Wales and Northern Ireland put together (Raftery and O'Sullivan, 1999). These were run on a day-to-day basis by the Roman Catholic religious orders, but funded by the state. As Skehill (2004, p. 231) suggests, the system 'appears to have been perceived, by some officials within the Department of Education … as a solution to the problems of child care in the country'. Local authorities also appear to 'have endorsed this view and many opted for the easier route of transferring children from the county homes' [former poor law institutions] to the Industrial Schools, rather than seeking out foster parents for them (Skehill, 2004, p. 231). This development was opposed by inspectors responsible for 'boarded-out children' with one suggesting, in the early-1930s, that payments could be given to parents to enable them to maintain children at home rather than committing them to the Industrial Schools (Skehill, 2004, pp. 233–4). Although not heeded, this idea was to emerge yet again – and was to be officially derided – in the 1960s. Furthermore, during the first ten years of partial independence, the 'Rules and Regulations for Industrial Schools', on discipline and punishment, were those of the previous British administration. By then 'Britain had already moved to a greatly reformed system, with short sentences, reduced corporal punishment, strict inspection and accountability' (Arnold, 2009, p. 13). In 1936 the Cussen Report recommended that Industrial School children should be integrated into the community and be educated in national schools. However, over 'the period 1936 to 1970, a total of 170,000 children and young persons … entered the gates of the 50 or so industrial schools' and were to remain, on average, for seven years (Ryan Report, vol. 1, p. 41).

In the mid-1960s, one commentator in surveying the care of those termed – in the vocabulary of the day – 'deprived' children, avowed: 'we would all be very intolerant if the Irish Government kept Aer Lingus [the national airline] cluttered with bi-planes [old fashioned aircrafts], yet many of our institutions are quite as obsolete and the passengers are helpless children' (Hunt in Tuairim London Branch Study Group, 1966, p. 53). More emphatically, a group of social reformers concluded 'too little social legislation has been passed since Ireland won its independence. It is surely strange that we should be content with social legislation passed to us from a government which we threw off' (Tuairim London Branch Study Group, 1966, p. 2). In November 1970, the publication of the Kennedy Report contributed to the abandonment of the Industrial School model (Department of Health, 1970; Raftery and O'Sullivan, 1999, ch. 15).

The Ryan Commission heard evidence from 1,090 men and women who reported being:

> abused as children in Irish institutions. Abuse was reported to the Committee in relation to 216 school and residential settings including Industrial and Reformatory Schools, Children's Homes, hospitals, national and secondary schools, day and residential special needs schools, foster care and a small number of other residential institutions, including laundries and hostels. 791 witnesses reported abuse to Industrial and Reformatory Schools and 259 witnesses reported abuse in the range of other institutions. (Ryan Report, Executive Summary, p. 12)

In terms of the specific types of abuse suffered, more than 90 per cent reported being physically abused while in the Industrial Schools or out-of-home care. They 'frequently described casual, random physical abuse but many wished to report only the times when the frequency and severity were such that they were injured or in fear for their lives. In addition to being hit and beaten, witnesses described other forms of abuse such as being flogged, kicked and otherwise physically assaulted, scalded, burned and held under water' (Ryan Report, Executive Summary, p. 13). Absconders, colloquially referred to as 'runners', were 'severely beaten, at times publicly. Some had their heads shaved and were humiliated' (Ryan Report, Executive Summary, p. 20).

Although no definitive evidence exists relating to the operation of organised 'rings' of abusers, sexual abuse was reported by approximately half of all the witnesses appearing before Ryan's Confidential Committee. 'Acute and chronic contact and non-contact sexual abuse was reported, including vaginal and anal rape, molestation and voyeurism in both isolated assaults and on a regular basis over long periods of time' (Ryan Report, Executive Summary, p. 13). Sexual abuse was 'endemic in boys' institutions [which comprised the majority]. The situation in girls' institutions was different. Although girls were subjected to predatory sexual abuse by male employees or visitors or in outside placements, sexual abuse was not systemic in girls' schools' (Ryan Report, Executive Summary, p. 21).

Detainees were also victims of neglect and emotional abuse. This was 'reported by witnesses in the form of lack of attachment and affection, loss of identity, deprivation of family contact, humiliation, constant criticism, personal denigration, exposure to fear and the threat of harm ...

Witnesses were incorrectly told their parents were dead and were given false information about their siblings and family members' (Ryan Report, Executive Summary, p. 13). Given the scope of this abuse it is hardly surprising that many witnesses had to deal with its impact throughout their lives:

> Witnesses ... described lives marked by poverty, social isolation, alcoholism, mental illness, sleep disturbance, aggressive behaviour and self harm. Approximately 30% of the witnesses described a constellation of ongoing, debilitating mental health concerns, for example, suicidal behaviour, depression, alcohol and substance abuse and eating disorders, which required treatment including psychiatric admission, medication and counseling. (Ryan Report, Executive Summary, p. 14; see also Carr et al., 2010)

Significantly, there was a constant flow of knowledge about what was occurring within the Industrial Schools although this was apt to be disregarded by the State and the evidence of brave and vocal survivors of the system was suppressed (see Tyrrell, 2006). This was because those who 'spoke out' tended be marginalised and lacking the power to define and name abusive practices within the wider public domain. There were great difficulties presented for dissenting and oppositional voices because of the power of the Roman Catholic Church and the social standing and status – what Bourdieu theorises as forms of 'capital' – of priests, nuns and other associated religious figures. Related to this, State 'officials often labelled those who broke this silence as cranks and troublemakers' (Holohan, 2011, p. 147).

Within the Industrial Schools, to differing degrees depending on local and situational relationships, there tended to be a 'culture of obeying orders without question' (Ryan Report, vol. 2, p. 80). This factor retains significance today because of the complex interplay of authoritarianism, obedience and compliance that continues to characterise the institutional ambiance of present-day organisations in Ireland. For example, the largely politically tame – Nyberg Report – purportedly examining the causes of the Irish banking crisis – detected the pervasive authoritarian atmosphere which helped to silence critical perspectives at odds with the 'official' and accepted opinions, within the banking sector and beyond: 'Domestic doubters were few, late and usually low-key, possibly because it was thought that expressing contrarian views risked sanction' (Commission of Investigation into the Banking Sector in Ireland, 2011: viii). For Nyberg and his colleagues, a 'main lesson is the need to make sure, both in private and public institutions, that there exist both fora and incentives for leadership and staff to openly discuss and challenge strategies and their implementation. It must become respectable and welcome to express professionally argued contrarian views' (Commission of Investigation into the Banking Sector in Ireland, 2011: ix–x).

Historical testimony indicates that the inspections of Industrial Schools conducted by the Orders responsible for running the institutions – so-called 'visitations' – were more thorough than those undertaken by the Irish government. In the early 1960s, a secret report on Artane Industrial School requested by John Charles McQuaid (Roman Catholic Archbishop of Dublin and Primate of Ireland, 1940–1973) also confirmed the evidence of pupil complainants. The relevant section within the Department of Education – the Inspectorate of Reformatories and Industrial Schools which occupied a lowly place in the Department's bureaucratic hierarchy – constantly failed to act in a competent and decisive way. That is to say, the 'State had access to records and allegations of abuse, yet it failed to respond to such allegations. Officials did not reply to or lost letters, did not return telephone calls or told direct lies about their involvement' (Arnold, 2009, p. 102). When 'religious staff abused, the matter tended to be dealt with using internal disciplinary procedures and Canon Law. The Gardaí [police] were not informed. On the rare occasions when the Department was informed, it colluded in the silence' (Ryan Report, Executive Summary, p. 23).

'Expertise' is also likely to have had an impact on public perceptions because 'experts' were seemingly able to authoritatively provide a 'scientific' rationale for what amounted to barbarism (see also in this context, Bauman, 1989). In short, they functioned as 'primary definers' and explained to the public the alleged character deficits and mental shortcomings of those confined (Hall et al., 1978, p. 221). They were able, therefore, to help to solidify dividing practices that delineated the 'good and bad, normal and pathological' and a 'specific constellation of relations' (Chambon, 1999, p. 68). Dr Anna McCabe, for example, (responsible for medical – and often general inspections – of the Schools from 1939–1965) described the detained children as 'terrorists' (Ryan Report, vol. 4, p. 29). Other spheres of 'expertise' also served to bolster the notion that those detained should be *appropriately* regarded as pariahs in need of tough treatment. A Professor of Logic and Psychology at the prestigious University College Dublin – and also a priest – argued that the educational backwardness of Industrial School inmates resulted from an innate inability, bad blood, and poor family circumstances (Arnold, 2009).

'Expertise' may also have influenced how the Courts regarded the children and young people who faced committal to Industrial Schools. All over Ireland 'committals took place without the "inquiry" demanded by the law … proceedings were perfunctory' (Arnold, 2009, p. 175). The Irish Society for the Prevention of Cruelty to Children (ISPCC) Inspectors furnishing the 'evidential' basis for the committal was rarely questioned. Known as 'cruelty men', they were usually recruited from retired police and army officers and were answerable to a local committee of volunteers:

'there was no proper monitoring or supervision of Inspectors, so [they] may have been overly zealous in sending children' to Industrial Schools (Ryan Report, Executive Summary, p. 18). The training of these Inspectors only commenced, in fact, in 1968.

Containing, Regulating and Exploiting the Poor: Industrial Schools as a Class Project

Poverty was a vital and pivotal factor leading to the incarceration of children in Industrial Schools. Moreover, many of these children were likely to have suffered abuse within the familial environment (Ferguson, 2007). Their bodies were cheapened and rendered more vulnerable to exploitation. These children were mostly, but not exclusively, from the families of the urban and rural poor and this could have contributed to their being especially vulnerable to abusive and criminal practices: the 'predatory nature of sexual abuse including the selection and grooming of socially disadvantaged and vulnerable children was a feature of the witness reports' pertaining to 'special needs services, children's homes, hospitals and primary and second-level schools'. Children with impairments of sight, hearing and learning were also 'particularly vulnerable to sexual abuse' (Ryan Report, Executive Summary, 2009, p. 26).

Sixty-seven per cent of witnesses referred to in the Ryan Report stated that their parents' occupational status was unskilled (See also Table 1.1).

Table 1.1   Occupational status of witnesses' parents – male and female industrial and reformatory schools (Ryan Report, vol. 3, p. 21)

Occupational status	Males	%	Females	%	Total witnesses	%
Professional worker	3	1	6	2	9	1
Managerial and technical	4	1	4	1	8	1
Non-manual	14	3	15	4	29	4
Skilled manual	23	6	22	6	45	6
Semi-skilled	50	12	23	6	73	9
Unskilled	277	67	253	67	530	67
Unknown	42	10	55	15	97	12
Total	413	100	378	100	791	100

In official circles, these families were regarded with contempt and from the early years of the new state, only established in 1922, the 'impoverished child was viewed as a burden' (Holohan, 2011, p. 188): as 'other' and as potentially contaminating the hegemonic Irish Republican ideal of petty bourgeois civility and propriety. In 1921, shortly before independence, the minister for local government and future President of the Executive Council of the Irish Free State, W.T. Cosgrave, voiced the opinion that

> People reared in workhouses, as you are aware, are no great acquisition to the community and they have no ideas whatsoever of civic responsibilities. As a rule their highest aim is to live at the expense of the ratepayers. Consequently, it would be a decided gain if they all took it into their heads to emigrate. When they go abroad they are thrown on their own responsibilities and have to work whether they like it or not. (in Ryan Report, vol. 5, p. 11)

James Dillon, a Fine Gael member of Dáil Éireann – the Irish parliament – repeatedly raised the issue of what he termed the 'scandal' of the Minister for Education shovelling children into Industrial Schools, arguing that 'none of these children are the children of rich people. No rich person would ever be treated this way' (in Holohan, 2011, p. 189). Witnesses reported:

> being subjected to ridicule about their parents and families, most often in public, in the course of being abused. The sons of lone mothers, "orphans" or "conventers" were reported as particular targets for such abuse, being told that their mothers were "sinners", "slags" and "old whores" who did not want them or could not care for them. Others reported hearing their families described as "scum", "tramps" and "from the gutter". Witnesses admitted to institutions in the context of family difficulties reported being subjected to the constant denigration of their parents. Witnesses recalled being constantly told their parents were "alcoholics", "prostitutes", "mad" and "no good". (Ryan Report, vol. 3, p. 107; see also Garrett, 2000a; 2000b)

In the early 1960s, the Irish Association of Civil Liberties wrote to the Department of Education maintaining that the grants provided to Industrial Schools should, instead, be diverted to financially hard-pressed parents. This proposal was, however, ridiculed as a 'pipe dream' – the money given to parents would only result in more frequent visits to 'the public house or more intensive study of the "runners in the last"' (in Skehill, 2004, p. 286). Indeed, this illustrates the disdain felt for the socially marginalised by primary definers even during a period which began to witness the gradual evolution of more liberal attitudes.

The social class dimension to the abuse of children is very apparent throughout the five volumes of the Ryan Report. The Daingean Reformatory, for instance, was the only boys' reformatory for most of the period examined and it was managed by, but not owned by, the Oblates of Mary Immaculate. Here the physical abuse 'was extreme' and ritualised floggings and beatings were inflicted even for minor transgressions. Sexual abuse was also common (Ryan Report, Executive Summary, 2009, p. 7). Tellingly, in their evidence to the Inquiry, the 'Oblates stated that the typical social class of the pupil was urban working class. The boys were mainly from the larger Irish cities of Dublin, Cork and Limerick … Of the complainants who gave evidence to the Committee, many had ended up in Daingean for trivial offences that owed more to poverty than criminality' (Ryan Report, vol. 1, p. 620). Moreover, the 'low status of poor children in Irish society was reflected in the low status of those members of the religious orders who worked in the schools. This in turn reflected the low status of the Reformatory and Industrial Schools Branch within the Department of Education' (Holohan, 2011, p. 199).

Industrial Schools need also to be perceived as *employing*, as well as incarcerating institutions which were embedded within local economies. They employed local lay people and used the children confined to carry out profit-making labour. The word 'School' was a 'misnomer' because as the former Goldenbridge resident, Christine Buckley (2009) and many other witnesses argued, the main emphasis was on manual work with minimal emphasis on academic education apart from Irish and religion (Ryan Report, vol. 2, p. 47). There is evidence 'particularly in girls' schools that children were removed from their classes in order to perform domestic chores or work in the institution during the school day' (Ryan Report, Executive Summary, 2009, p. 24).

Artane Industrial School was the largest Industrial School in the State. In 1962, just five of the 413 inmates were offenders (Arnold, 2009, p. 39). Here the 'trade shops and the farm constituted a substantial business enterprise of which the farm brought in a large yearly income' (Ryan Report, vol. 1, p. 106). Children, as well as being the victims of sexual and physical abuse, were often components in what a Christian Brother referred to as processes of 'mass production' (Ryan Report, vol. 1, p. 197). Furthermore, the detainees were *unpaid* labourers:

> Child labour on farms and in workshops was used to reduce the costs of running the Industrial Schools and in many cases to produce a profit. Clothing and footwear were often made on the premises and bakeries and laundries provided facilities to the school and in some cases to the general public. The cleaning and upkeep of girls' Industrial Schools was largely done by the girls themselves. Some of these chores were heavy and arduous and exacting standards were imposed that were difficult for young children to meet. In girls' schools also, older residents were expected to care for young children and babies on a 24-hour

basis. Large nurseries were supervised and staffed by older residents with only minimal supervision by adults. (Ryan Report, Executive Summary, 2009, p. 25)

In Dublin, Goldenbridge Industrial School for girls, revealed as a place with a 'high level of physical abuse', was renowned for rosary bead production. As the Ryan Report notes this 'industry was conducted in a way that imposed impossible standards on children and caused great suffering to many of them. It was a School that was characterised by a regime of extreme drudgery, both in terms of the rosary bead making ... and the daily workload of the children' (Ryan Report, Executive Summary, 2009, p. 8; see also Fahy, 1999). When discharged, Industrial School detainees were then directed to gender specific low-waged sectors with boys 'generally placed in manual or unskilled jobs and girls in positions as domestic servants' (Ryan Report, Executive Summary, 2009, p. 24).

The remaining part of the chapter will focus on contemporary Ireland and briefly examine how current practices in relation to those we might term young 'outcasts' can be compared to those confined in Industrial Schools in the past. That is to say, it is vital, when seeking to explore social work values, to interrogate how *current* micro practices might still contain significant residues of historical practices that have been condemned as oppressive, even barbaric.

In the Shadow of the 'Gulag': The Contemporary Treatment of 'Troublesome' and Impoverished Young People in Ireland

In contemporary Ireland, it is clear that the treatment of young prisoners continues to replicate that of the detainees in Industrial Schools. According to Irish prison chaplains, the way that young prisoners – those aged 16 to 21 – are 'managed' in the much criticised St. Patrick's Institution raises particular concerns. This is the largest facility in the State for young offenders and national and international bodies have repeatedly condemned the deplorable conditions there over the past 25 years. Those 'young people detained in St. Patrick's Institution are [like inmates in Industrial Schools in the past] not allowed to wear their own clothes (unlike every other prisoner in every other prison)' (Irish Prison Chaplains, 2010, p. 19). As the chaplains summarise, St. Patrick's Institution 'is a "warehouse" for young people ... It is a demoralising, destructive and dehumanising experience, with few redeeming features' (Irish Prison Chaplains, 2010, p. 20; see also Wardhaugh and Wilding, 1993).

Similarly, asylum seekers are rigidly segregated with 52 direct provision centres established in April 2000 and almost 6,000 asylum seekers are still living in them for more than three years. These are privately operated establishments with contracts with the Reception and Integration Agency (RIA): residents are given €19.10 each week to live on and provided with a shared room and meals in 'hotel-style' accommodation. A person waiting for their asylum claim to be decided by the state has no right to work (see also Arnold, 2012). Of even greater concern, many unaccompanied children seeking asylum went missing from state care over the past decade. Importantly also, a 2004 amendment to the constitution provided that children born on the island of Ireland to parents who were both non-nationals would no longer have an automatic and constitutional right to Irish citizenship.

Continuing anxieties also exist about the practice of placing children in adult psychiatric wards. At least 100 children under the age of 18 were admitted to adult psychiatric facilities in 2010 'despite a commitment by the Health Services Executive – HSE to phase out the practice'. An inspector of mental health services 'described the practice of admitting children to adult centres as 'inexcusable, counter-therapeutic and almost custodial in that clinical supervision is provided by teams unqualified in child and adolescent psychiatry' (see also '100 children placed in adult psychiatric units', *The Irish Times*, 7 October, 2010, p. 2; Bonnar, 2010).

Specifically in terms of children, the Health and Information and Quality Authority (HIQA) reported that staff in one-third of the state's residential centres had not been properly vetted and the children placed there were at unnecessary risk. Similarly, many foster carers have not been vetted. The HIQA has also called on the HSE to immediately cease using one of its three secure units for troubled and vulnerable young people – Ballydowd – due to concerns over the safety of child residents. This was echoed by the HIQA in subsequent reports which expressed 'grave concerns regarding the safety for children' within one of the other units, Coovagh House in Limerick (Health and Information Quality Authority, 2010a; 2010b; 2010c).

During 2010 the deaths of children and young people 'in care' and the failure of the HSE to produce robust and reliable data emerged as a key issue (see Table 1.2). The incompetence of the HSE can be interpreted as part of an historically embedded culture of inertia, secrecy and disrespect not only for the specific dead children and young people but, more expansively, for those often troubled families in contact with social services. Indeed, the Irish state is revealed in its most transparent and brutal form, in its actions and inactions, and specifically in its failure to produce accurate information on the death of children in 'care' and contact with social workers.

**Table 1.2   Deaths of children and young people
in 'care' reported by the media**

These have included:

Kim O'Donovan (15) found dead, after a suspected drugs overdose, in city centre bed-and-breakfast accommodation (August 2000)

Tracey Fay (18) found dead in a disused coal bunker after injecting herself (January 2002)

Shane Hafford (16) died in an apartment in Drogheda near to the children's home in which he had been placed (April 2003)

David Foley (17) died of an overdose three years after voluntarily seeking care from the state (September 2005)

Melissa Mahon (14) was killed while she was in HSE care. A man was found guilty of her manslaughter in May 2009 (September 2006)

Michelle Bray (14) died after inhaling the contents of a deodorant can (January 2007)
William Colquhoun (18) in residential care when he died (July 2008)

Christopher O'Driscoll (17) discovered in a derelict house in Cork having died from pneumonia exacerbated by drug-taking (May 2009)

Danny Talbot (19) in the care of the HSE died following a suspected drugs overdose (Summer 2009)

Daniel McAnaspie (17) originally from Dublin went missing in February 2010, when in the care of the HSE, and was later found in a ditch in Co. Meath having been stabbed to death (May 2010) (see also Ingle, 2010)

In March 2010 it was reported that the HSE had not published a single report on the death of a child in state care since it was formed in 2005. Moreover, no independent child death review system was in place until that same month, when the Minister for Children established an expert group to investigate the deaths of children in the 'care' system over the last decade. This Group was then criticised by the Ombudsman for Children (OfC) because of its lack of statutory powers and independence. At this time, a senior HSE official told the Public Accounts Committee that 20 children had died in state care over the previous decade. However, the Minister for Children told Dáil Éireann that the number was 23 ('HSE ordered to speed up reporting of deaths of children', *The Irish Times*, 5 March 2010: 1). Soon, though, reports began to emerge which suggested that the true figure was far in excess of this number.

The palpably incompetent and secretive HSE compounded problems by refusing to hand over the relevant files to the independent panel set up by the Irish government. This prompted the Minister for Children to seek legal advice on how to deal with what was – supposedly – an executive agency of the state: the publication of the Health (Amendment) Bill 2010 was, therefore, meant to respond to the HSE's intransigence. It was also reported that the Ombudsman and Information Commissioner (O&IC) and OfC were both finding their work hampered by the 'excess of legalism' in the HSE ('HSE failure to produce records of deaths "bizarre"', *The Irish Times*, 28 May 2010: 7). In an unprecedented intervention, the O&IC charged the HSE with 'ill-founded legalism matched only by a lack of common sense' (see also O'Reilly, 2010, p. 13).

Revealing the inadequacy of information retrieval systems across the HSE, which had not been satisfactorily addressed during the so-called 'Celtic Tiger' period, a senior manager in the agency stated that assembling numbers on the deaths of children was difficult because it involved checking manual records and relying on the local knowledge of social workers. ('HSE to give number of child deaths in State Care', *The Irish Times*, 28 May 2010, p. 7). At length, however, the HSE announced that 37 children had died in state care in the 10 years from 1 Jan 2000 to 30 April 2010 – that is to say, a 60 per cent increase on figures it had previously provided: eighteen of these deaths were attributable to what were termed 'unnatural causes'. At the time, the Minister for Children remained critical of the HSE for taking 10 weeks to hand over the figures he requested in March. Furthermore, the HSE was still to provide information on deaths related to children 'known to' (or in contact with) the HSE (e.g. child protection system) ('37 children died in State care in 10 years', *The Irish Times*, 29 May 2010, p. 8). It was later announced that at least 188 young people who were in care or in contact with social services had died over the past decade. This new figure was based on a wider definition of deaths to include children who were known to social services, or young people aged 18–21 who were receiving 'after-care' services. However, a senior HSE official said the number could still rise further if social work teams around the country found evidence of further deaths ('Child deaths in care or in contact with services now at 188', *The Irish Times*, 5 June 2010, p. 1). Even in terms of the figures produced, it was startling that the numbers of dead children and young people had escalated from 20, to 23, to 37 to 188 in the space of a few weeks. In December 2010, it was revealed that the number of dead children had risen to 199, 11 more than was announced by the HSE in June ('HSE revises figures for deaths of children', *The Irish Times*, 9 December 2010, p. 3): two of these children had been in public care and seven were known to child welfare services. This figure was subsequently to have been revised downwards – to 196 –

by a report from an Independent Child Death Review Group in June 2012 (Shannon and Gibbons, 2012).

More broadly, a 'change agenda' is now emerging following the coming to power of a Fine Gael/Labour coalition in 2012. The 'challenges' inherited from the previous Fianna Fail administration include the lack of a 'national framework for service delivery; no proper data collection; no standard approach to assessing risk and referring cases; no effective interagency working between agencies funded by the public. What we have found, in one word, is a disgrace' (Department of Children and Youth Affairs (DCYA), 2012). The government claims, therefore, it is intent on pursuing the 'most radical reform of child welfare and protection services ever undertaken in the State' (DCYA, 2012). These reforms include: setting up of a new Child and Family Support Agency; aiming to introduce 'mandatory reporting' for suspected child abuse; giving the *Children First* guidance to agencies on responding to child abuse statutory affect; holding, in November 2012, a referendum on a constitutional amendment giving recognition to the paramount interests of the child; introducing new national standards for the protection and welfare of children (Heath Information and Quality Authority (HIQA), 2012). All of these initiatives are likely, however, to failure because of economic imperatives and the overriding commitment to intensified neoliberation (Allen, 2012).

Conclusion

The Republic of Ireland is not the only country encountering difficulties in maintaining a robust system of child welfare and child protection, but the way in which the problem is emerging is also nationally specific and needs to be located conjuncturally and in relation to other developments within the troubled jurisdiction (Garrett, 2012). The argument in this chapter, however, is that for social workers and associated workers to work ethically, particularly with socially marginalized groups, there needs to be attentiveness to past practices and ways of seeing and acting. Those in Industrial Schools, in the past, were frequently a key focus for the intervention of the state, yet they were invariably perceived as lying beyond the community of persons to be accorded respect. Indeed, the treatment which they received has led Quinn to argue that it furnishes evidence of 'an explicit breach of the Republican principle of the inherent equality of all citizens [which] was supposed to be the chief distinguishing feature between the envisioned Republic and our former political attachment' (in Holohan, 2011, p. 221).

Indeed, the state has functioned to structurally embed processes of (dis)respect and the modes of positioning particular groups *outside* the Republican 'community'. What is more, it could be argued that social workers have, as agents of the state, at times colluded with such processes or failed to resist them. This is evidenced by, for example, the actions of the ISPCC which was implicated in children being sent to Industrial Schools ('ISPCC notes regret over committing children', *The Irish Times*, 23 May 2009, p. 7). However, it is also vital to recognize the power structural forces have and exercise, and their success in silencing and containing potential 'whistleblowers'. Attitudes towards whistleblowers have traditionally been 'hostile, and informing has been perceived as having traitorous qualities within Irish culture. "Informers" are regarded as weak of integrity and character. Those that did complain have traditionally been condemned as informers by Irish society, rather than being commended for their acts of citizenship. The implications of revealing such truths can be professionally and personally costly' (Byrne in Holohan, 2011, p. 227). Both the Organisation for Economic Cooperation and Development (OECD) and the Council of Europe body, the Group of States against Corruption (Greco), have criticised the Government's failure to introduce legislation that would protect public officials and private sector workers who report wrongdoing.

In the latter part of the chapter it was argued that there are clear connections which can be established in terms of how some children and their families were treated in the past, and the way they are treated in Ireland today. Given this situation, social workers and social work educators might reflect more on how the professional value base might be rendered more meaningful, especially when, as at present, a number of communities are being subjected to further attacks on account of cuts in welfare benefits and services introduced by a ruling Fine Gail/Labour coalition administration (Children's Rights Alliance, 2013). Thinking about how society works and how a ruling bloc maintains control, within particular national frameworks, might lead social workers to reflect on how they engage with the ethical tensions which are invariably connected to the exercise of power. To what extent do social workers collude with projects which diminish, stigmatise and exploit users of services, while invoking their alleged 'empowerment' (see also Rose, 2000)? Such questioning might further direct attention to the use of language within micro-engagements involving social workers. Far from being an exercise in what is often caricatured as 'political correctness', such questions have the potential to delve into how power relations operate through language and culture. For example, words such as 'underclass' and phrases such as 'welfare dependency' are reflective of this dimension. In powerful ways they are rooted in historical and contemporary discourses circulating around official concerns about the poor and potentially politically rebellious (Garrett, 2002; see also Pearson, 1975, ch. 6).

Engaging in such oppositional activity is, of course, a far from easy task because those in positions of structural power (and invested with the power of naming and defining) seek to maintain hegemony and identify what is permissible and what should be 'closed down'. Within academic institutions, educators are often constrained because programmes have curricula that is predetermined and mapped out by central 'authorities' and 'experts'. This is not to argue that there are no 'spaces' for a more critical engagement within social work education. In fact, hegemony is 'not a state of grace which is installed forever ... [it is] not a formation which incorporates everybody' (Hall in Fischman and McLaren, 2005, p. 430, emphasis added).

It needs to be stressed, however, that there should not be an exclusive preoccupation with words, because there is also a need for a more orthodox left politics that seeks to construct progressive coalitions for social and economic change (within, for example, trade unions, political parties and professional associations). Within the Republic of Ireland, such strategies are now vital, not only to promote – with recourse to the professional lexicon – 'respect for persons', but because beyond this, there is a need to create a different set of social and political possibilities founded on total opposition to a destabilized and vengeful capitalism.

Further Reading

Tyrrell, P. (2006) *Founded on Fear*. Dublin: Irish Academic Press: A remarkable testimony of the abuse suffered in an Industrial School in the west of Ireland. Tyrrell's manuscript was completed in the 1960s, but was never published at the time. In April 1967 his charred remains were discovered on Hampstead Heath in London. He appears to have committed suicide by setting himself on fire and it took a year to establish his identity. See also the extended review (Garrett, 2010).

Holohan, C. (2011) *In Plain Sight: Responding to the Ferns, Ryan, Murphy and Cloyne Reports*. Dublin: Amnesty International Ireland: A good, if at times, poorly assembled collection of papers on these four reports. The book is fairly unique and important in that it seeks to make the connection between the abuse of children and class exploitation.

Garrett, P.M. (2004) *Social Work and Irish People in Britain: Historical and Contemporary Responses to Irish Children and Families*. Bristol, Policy Press: A book which partly concentrates on the treatment of another (dis)respected and 'troublesome' population, Irish 'unmarried mothers'.

References

Allen, K. (2012) 'The model pupil who faked the test: Social policy in the Irish crisis', *Critical Social Policy*, 32 (3), pp. 422–40.

Arnold, B. (2009) *The Irish Gulag*. Dublin: Gill and Macmillan.

Arnold, S. (2012) *State Sanctioned Child Poverty and Exclusion: The case of children in state accommodation for asylum seekers*, http://www.irishrefugeecouncil. ie/wp-content/uploads/2012/09/State-sanctioned-child-poverty-and-exclusion.pdf

Banks, S. (1995) *Ethics and Values in Social Work*. London: Macmillan.

Banks, S. (2003) 'From Oath to Rulebooks: A critical examination of codes of ethics for the social professions', *European Journal of Social Work*, 6 (2), pp. 133–45.

Banks, S. (2006) *Ethics, Accountability and the Social Professions*. New York: Palgrave.

Bauman, Z. (1989) *Modernity and the Holocaust*. Cambridge: Polity.

Bonnar, S. (2010) *Report for the Mental Health Commission on Admission of Young people to Adult Mental Health Wards in the Republic of Ireland*, http:// www.mhcirl.ie/News_Events/Report_on_Admission_of_Young_People_ to_Adult_MH_Wards_.pdf

Buckley, C. (2009) 'A Long Journey in Search of Justice for Victims of Abuse'. *The Irish Times*, 19 May, p. 14.

Carr, A., Flanagan, E., Dooley et al. (2010) 'Adult Adjustment of Survivors of Institutional Child Abuse in Ireland', *Child Abuse & Neglect*, 34, pp. 477–89.

Chambon, A.S. (1999) 'Foucault's Approach: Making the Familiar Visible' in A.S. Chambon, A. Irving and L. Epstein (eds) (1999) *Reading Foucault and Social Work*. New York: Columbia University Press.

Children's Right Alliance (2013) *Report Card 2013*, http://www.childrensrights. ie/sites/default/files/submissions_reports/files/ReportCard2013_ ExecSumm.pdf

Commission of Investigation (2009) *Report into the Catholic Archdiocese of Dublin*. Dublin: Department of Justice, Equality and Law Reform.

Commission of Investigation (2010) *Report into the Catholic Diocese of Cloyne*. Dublin: Department of Justice, Equality and Law Reform.

Commission of Investigation into the Banking Sector in Ireland (2011) *Misjudging Risk: Causes of the Systematic Banking Crisis in Ireland*, http:// www.irishtimes.com/focus/2011/nyberg/index.pdf

Commission to Inquire into Child Abuse (2009) *Commission to Inquire into Child Abuse Report*. Dublin: Stationary Office.

Department of Children and Youth Affairs (DCYA) (2012) Minister Frances Fitzgerald TD publishes Report of the Independent Child Death Review

Group 2000-2010, press notice, 20 June, http://www.dcya.gov.ie/viewdoc. asp?DocID=2175

Department of Health (1970) *Reformatory and industrial schools system report 1970 chaired by District Justice Eileen Kennedy*. Dublin: Stationary Office.

Ferguson, H. (2007) 'Abuse and Looked After Children as "Moral Dirt": Child Abuse and Institutional Care in Historical Perspective', *Journal of Social Policy*, 36 (1), pp. 123–39.

Fischman, G.E. and McLaren, P. (2005) 'Rethinking Critical Pedagogy and the Gramscian and Freirean Legacies: From Organic to Committed Intellectuals or Critical Pedagogy, Commitment, and Praxis', *Cultural Studies/Critical Methodologies*, 5 (4), pp. 425–47.

Garrett, P.M. (2000a) 'The Abnormal Flight: The Migration and Repatriation of Irish Unmarried Mothers', *Social History*, 25 (3), pp. 330–44.

Garrett, P.M. (2000b) 'The Hidden history of the PFIs: The Repatriation of Unmarried Mothers and their Children from England to Ireland in the 1950s and 1960s', *Immigrants and Minorities*, 19 (3), pp. 25–44.

Garrett, P.M. (2002) 'Social Work and the "Just Society": Diversity, Difference and the Sequestration of Poverty', *Journal of Social Work*, 2 (2), pp. 187–210.

Garrett, P.M. (2007a) 'Making Social Work more Bourdieusian: Why the Social Professions should critically engage with the work of Pierre Bourdieu', *European Journal of Social Work*, 10 (2), pp. 225–43.

Garrett, P.M. (2007b) 'The Relevance of Bourdieu for Social Work: A Reflection on Obstacles and Omissions', *Journal of Social Work*, 7 (3), pp. 357–81.

Garrett, P.M. (2008) 'Thinking with the Sardinian: Antonio Gramsci and Social Work', *European Journal of Social Work*, 11 (3), pp. 237–50.

Garrett, P.M. (2009) 'The "Whalebone" in the (Social Work) "Corset"? Notes on Antonio Gramsci and Social Work Educators', *Social Work Education*, 28 (5), pp. 461–75.

Garrett, P.M. (2010) '"It is with Deep Regret that I Find it Necessary to Tell my Story": Child abuse in industrial schools in Ireland', *Critical Social Policy*, 30 (2), pp. 292–306.

Garrett, P.M. (2012) 'Adjusting "our Notions of the Nature of the State": A political reading of Ireland's child welfare and child protection crisis' *Capital & Class*, 36 (2), pp. 263–81.

Garrett, P.M. (2013) 'A "Catastrophic, Inept, Self-serving" Church?: Re-examining three reports on child abuse in the Republic of Ireland', *Journal of Progressive Human Services*, 4 (1), pp. 43–65.

Hall, S., Critcher, C., Jefferson, T., et al. (1978) *Policing the Crisis: Mugging, the State and Law and Order*. Houndsmill: Macmillan Education.

Harvey, D. (2005) *A Brief History of Neoliberalism*. Oxford: Oxford University Press.

Health Information and Quality Authority (2010a) *Ballydowd Special Care Unit* (Inspection Report 410), 31 August.

Health Information and Quality Authority (2010b) *Coovagh House Special Care Unit* (Inspection Report 590), 15 December.

Health Information and Quality Authority (2010c) *Gleann Alainn Special Care Unit* (Inspection Report 589), 15 December.

Health Information and Quality Authority (2012) *National Standards for the Protection and Welfare of Children*, http://www.dcya.gov.ie/documents/ChildProtectionWelfareStandards.pdf

Holohan, C. (2011) *In Plain Sight: Responding to the Ferns, Ryan, Murphy and Cloyne Reports.* Dublin: Amnesty International Ireland.

Ingle, R. (2010) 'The Short life of Daniel McAnaspie', *The Irish Times, Weekend Review*, 22 May, p. 1.

Irish Prison Chaplains (2010) *The Irish Chaplains' Annual Report*, http://www.catholicbishops.ie/2010/11/29/irish-prison-chaplains-annual-report-2010/

Murphy, F.D., Buckley, H. and Joyce, L. (2005) *The Ferns Report*. Dublin: Stationary Office.

O'Reilly, E. (2010) 'In Camera Rule Must Not Obscure Child Rights', *The Irish Times*, 1 June, p. 13.

Pearson, G. (1975) *The Deviant Imagination*. London: Macmillan.

Raftery, M. and O'Sullivan, E. (1999) *Suffer the Little Children: The Inside Story of Ireland's Industrial Schools*. Dublin: New Island Books.

Rose, N. (2000) 'Government and Control', *British Journal of Criminology*, 40, pp. 321–39.

Shannon, G. and Gibbons, N. (2012) *Report of the Independent Child Death Review Group*, http://www.dcya.gov.ie/documents/publications/Report_ICDRG.pdf

Skehill, C. (2004) *History of the Present of Child Protection and Welfare Social Work in Ireland*. Lewiston: Edwin Mellon Press.

Tuairim London Branch Study Group (1966) *Some of Our Children: A Report on the Residential Care of Deprived Children in Ireland*. London: Tuairim.

Tyrrell, P. (2006) *Founded on Fear*. Dublin: Irish Academic Press.

Wardhaugh, J. and Wilding, P. (1993) 'Towards an Explanation of the Corruption of Care', *Critical Social Policy*, 13 (1), pp. 4–32.

Weinberg, M. (2010) 'The Social Construction of Social Work Ethics: Politicizing and Broadening the Lens', *Journal of Progressive Human Services*, 21, pp. 32–44.

2 Secrets and Lies: The Ethical Implications of Family Estrangement

Kylie Agllias and Mel Gray

'Everybody has something they don't want the world to know. Everybody. For some people, it's something embarrassing. Maybe even humiliating. For some, it's something ... worse. To save my family I did some desperate things years ago. I made hard choices. For me it was something worse' (Stephen White, *Missing Persons*, 2005, p. 336). What if a client[1] were to tell you what that 'something worse' was and what if that 'something worse' related to a missing person which was all over the media? What if he told you in confidence, knowing you were bound by a code of ethics not to divulge client secrets? Not to break client confidence? This chapter concerns the complexity of ethical decisions when working with 'family secrets' or 'the hidden side of family relationships' encountered commonly in cases of family estrangement, extramarital affairs, adopted children, and domestic violence situations, for example. Ethical decisions in social work become more complex and fraught when they are intricately tied to deeply personal – private or hidden experiences – and deep-seated convictions about why the client acted in the way he did. In such situations, pervasive ideas about family, parenting, marriage, and parenthood make this an area fraught with difficulty since client behaviour often goes against the grain of common expectations or sociocultural norms. All or most of us have lived in and are part of a family and, when we factor in our own experiences – of loyalty, betrayal, connection, and rejection – within the family, it becomes extremely difficult to remain 'objective' with our clients. Yet, that is what our professional values demand – confidentiality, objectivity, or at least, impartiality – the ability to make rational, sound, fair judgements and decisions. Situations where competing interests, conflicting stories, and

---

1 Though clients are simultaneously service users or vice versa, we prefer to retain old usage of the term 'client' to denote that the issues about which we are writing in this chapter take place within the context of a client-worker relationship.

multiple perspectives must be considered are made even more complex when the social worker is all too aware of the psychological damage that can ensue for family members.

This chapter differs from some of the others in that it does not deal with a particular field of practice, like mental health or child protection. Social workers encounter and work with families in all fields of practice and the issue of family estrangement is far more common than we realise. Perhaps it is most often encountered in work with the elderly when people tend to rely more on their family for support. Social workers are all too familiar with cases where the isolated elderly person has lost all contact with their family. When they dig deeper, they all too often find that relationships deteriorated over a long period of time before contact was completely severed and often the estrangement began in a bitter feud, domestic violence, abuse, or a painful divorce. This chapter provides an overview of the nature of family estrangement, which often begins with 'secrets and lies' as our title suggests. More specifically, it examines value issues and ethical dilemmas associated with intergenerational family estrangement in later life, from an ethical perspective.

Family Secrets

> A secret is something hidden … [or] … "unexpressed" or, as is more often the case … shared selectively. All families have secrets that they hide from the world and one another: "the keeping (and breaking) of secrets appears to be a core activity in … bonding members together and in excluding – or … [distancing] – other members". (Smart, 2011, p. 540)

Some secrets may be preludes to pleasant surprises, while others might be private and essential in some way and, perhaps, best kept hidden (Smart, 2009). However, invariably a time comes when a family member feels the need to share their secret. Many family secrets – particularly the ones discussed in this chapter – are intricately interwoven with silence, guilt, shame, embarrassment, regret, and stigma and whether they might be functional and dysfunctional is not always easy to determine. Imber-Black (1998) claims 'dangerous secrets most often make us feel shame, while truly private matters do not' (p. 21). Rather than having anything to do with privacy, she associates secret-keeping with deliberate concealment to keep the family intact. From a systems perspective, as long as the secret is kept, the family unit will remain the same. Secrets bridge the gap between the private reality and public face of the family (Smart, 2011). For example, the secret of an illegitimate child, a father's alcoholism, child abuse, an abortion, or a family member's mental illness might be concealed to avoid judgement and stigmatisation. Sometimes secrets are shared by and 'known to' all family members, yet are kept concealed outside the confines of the family to protect a family member or the family's reputation. For example, in this sense, an alcoholic father might become 'untouchable' and his alcoholism might remain 'unspoken' about. As long as the family holds onto this secret and keeps its pact, the father's alcoholism will remain concealed and family interactions will adapt to shield him from public scrutiny (Ashton, 2006; Kroll, 2004; Menees and Segrin, 2000).

So within the family, on the one hand, secrets might be kept to protect individuals and others from harm or to alienate or reduce the power of one or more members. In the case of infidelity, for example, the secret might serve to protect the unfaithful party while, at the same time, decreasing the faithful partner's ability to make an informed decision about whether or not to remain in the relationship (Butler, Harper, and Seedall, 2009). Family members are highly likely to refrain from revealing a family secret, such as domestic violence, when they fear that disclosure might meet with an aggressive response (Afifi and Steuber, 2010). Imber-Black (1998) asserts that family members who are not privy to a secret often sense that something is amiss and feel anxious, suspicious, doubtful, and distant. On the other hand, living with a secret, and particularly one that the individual does not wish to keep, or bear alone, can, ironically, increase the person's power, while they, at the same time, feel obliged to reveal or keep the secret, shame at so doing, and weighed down by the burden of telling or not telling someone about it.

Family secrets are sometimes kept from one generation to the next and form part of the family's history such that 'remnants of the past adhere to … present actions, as well as … future aspirations' (Sucov, 2006, p. 25). Indeed, family secrets, estrangements, and communication patterns may persist across generations, with historical secrets still impacting on current families (Smart, 2009). Despite the overly simplistic, mainly Western construction of the biological nuclear family, all families comprise members beyond the boundaries of the immediate familial enclave. Members continue to be referred to as family after death and 'even in the absence of contact or affective involvement' (Bedford and Blieszner, 1997, p. 526). This is especially so if secrets emerge from trauma and oppression. For example, Holocaust survivors, prisoners of war, refugees, and Indigenous Peoples may harbour secrets to survive violence and trauma in the first instance, and later, in an effort to move forward and protect future generations, they might try to forget past trauma.

Family Secrets Raise Complex Ethical Questions for Social Workers

Wood (2001) outlines how social work theory and practice *vis á vis* the family has changed since its origins in the late nineteenth century. Early social work was centred largely on the family but, in the 1970s and 1980s, the family therapy movement usurped social work's role in this area elevating therapeutic work with families to a specialisation requiring specialist training and expertise, As Wood (2001) notes:

> The majority of scholarly accounts describing the history of family therapy ignore the contributions made by early social workers to the development of family theory and practice ... despite this lack of acknowledgement, there does exist substantial historical evidence that the social work profession laid vital foundations for systemic thinking and practice with families. (p. 15)

This was partly a result of a crisis in the profession regarding social casework as the main *modus operandi* as radical social workers resisted the individualisation and psychologisation of people's problems and the focus on clinical social work:

> Due to this apparent lack of fit with the prevailing methods of social work, family casework, and later, family therapy, came to be seen by many in social work as a further sub specialty of clinical social work, rather than as a field of practice and a potential practice method. (Wood, 2001, p. 25)

In the end, 'while social work struggled with finding a place for the further development of family social work theory, the rapidly growing domain of family therapy quickly colonised this field of practice, giving little credit to the ground already laid by social workers' (Wood, 2001, p. 28). Instead social work became a systems-oriented generalist profession working at multiple levels of intervention using diverse practice methods ranging from individual, group, community, and policy work.

At the same time, advances in the social sciences were leading to new conceptualisations of the family: 'the changing nature of family life [was] push[ing] people to negotiate *new moral codes or principles*' (Smart, 2004, p. 401 emphasis added) in working with families. As social conventions and mores change so too does the profession in responding to new issues and problems. Family estrangement might be just such an issue which might question conventional social work practice founded on open communication and engagement with clients. For the most part, social workers are taught that open communication with – and between – family members is important to help them develop insight, solve problems, maintain close ties, and feel valued. Poor family functioning or problem behaviours are often associated with rigid belief systems, family taboos, strict rules about conformity, and inadequate communication between family members. Indeed, research has shown that keeping secrets can affect individual well-being and contribute to poor family relationships (Afifi and Steuber, 2009; Frijns and Finenour, 2009; Smart, 2009). So how might a social worker approach situations where families are reluctant to talk about their secrets?

The social worker's natural inclination would be to bring everything out into the open but are 'family secrets' best kept hidden or in what sorts of situations might it be important that they be revealed? There are times when social workers know that bringing issues of violence and abuse into the open has the potential to cause more harm than good. The natural inclination is to consider the consequences for the family. But, who decides what's best in these situations? Are there any rules to guide social workers and what moral or ethical issues are involved? Codes of ethics provide non-contextualised, general principles and we know that social workers frequently do not advert to them because they find them unhelpful in particular situations such as we are discussing here (McAuliffe, 1999). How then does the social worker decide what to do when a client reveals a family secret in confidence and keeping that confidence will bring harm to others?

From a utilitarian perspective the social worker would want to ensure her actions and decisions were beneficial to as many family members as possible and she would want to follow a least harms approach (Robinson and Reeser, 2000). These ethical considerations would require her to decide whose interests were paramount and, if necessary, to break confidentiality to protect children, for example, or, if required, to share information with fellow professionals as routinely happens, especially if there were concerns of risk or danger to the client or other individuals. While confidentiality is an important value in social work, complete or absolute adherence rests on the individual social worker's judgement as to how best to proceed.

What does the social worker do when the client wants help in making a decision as to whether or not to disclose a family secret? Typically these types of family secrets involve decisions about whether to divulge the information to another family member, and how this might be done with minimal harm. Examples might be when a couple has kept their daughter's adoption a secret, or a mother being afraid to tell her son that his father is in prison, or a husband hiding the fact that he lost his job three months ago. In these instances, someone's self-determination is being compromised because another person is trying to shield them from hurt or pain. They might be seen as behaving paternalistically in such situations. Does the person who is being shielded in this situation have a right to know or are they better off not knowing and who decides what's best for them? The person trying to decide whether or not to disclose a well-kept secret would have to consider the consequences not just for the other person but for themselves as well. How might the other person respond? Are some 'secrets' unforgiveable, some disappointments too hard to forget? What would the social worker do in a marital counseling situation when a client reveals, in confidence, that he is having an affair and he doesn't want his wife to know? Must confidentiality be upheld? What of his wife's right to know? We can see, even in the questions we ask, the dominant deontological and consequential ethical perspectives we tend to use in social work in asking about rights, duties, obligations, responsibilities, and consequences. Clearly, complex ethical dilemmas always leave the social worker feeling pushed and pulled between competing interests and conflicting stories. They are made even more complicated by ideas about family in society, and our personal experiences of family and family life.

Ideologies of Family

Social, cultural, and political ideologies about marriage, family, gender roles, and childrearing are learnt early in life, usually in our 'natural' family or family of origin (Mannheim, 1959, in Everingham, Stevenson, and Warner-Smith, 2007). While many of us will not always adhere to dominant sociocultural norms, for the most part, we will have developed – and internalised – beliefs about the family that conform to prevailing ideologies, which *inter alia* see mothers as the primary caregiver; fathers as providers; siblings as dependable; couples as faithful; adult-children as caregivers for older generations; and grandchildren as a source of great happiness. The dominant motif is the united, close family enjoying togetherness, and sharing common values, beliefs, and attitudes about family life and acceptable behaviour. Conflict, disagreement, betrayal, infidelity, estrangement, and rejection are seen as dysfunctional, abnormal, and perhaps even pathological. In other words, clients' – and indeed practitioners' – attitudes and responses to family secrets are culturally, politically, and socially embedded. Being mindful of this, the client and the social worker can begin by thinking through their feelings about and attitudes towards family secrets from the perspective of the ideological influences that have shaped their thoughts about them. They might then, for example, consider whether estrangement happens for good reason, whether or not reconciliation between the estranged parties is feasible or even desirable, or whether things are best left as they are.

Values and Beliefs about Families

Besides social constructions of family and our own personal experiences of family life sit our values and beliefs about how individuals or families ought to behave. The very nature of work with families involves the ability to shift the focus from individual family members to the family as a whole. Nowhere is this clearer than when dealing with family secrets, for keeping or breaking secrets can have wide-reaching consequences. What especially comes under the microscope in family estrangement is the ideal of the cohesive family. Sometimes individuals have to estrange from their families for their own survival, especially in violent or abusive situations. Sometimes families become so enmeshed that individuality is lost. There might be sound reasons for keeping family secrets or estrangements which fly in the face of the motif of the unified, cohesive family. In this regard, mindful of the ethic of recognition, we would want to avoid using stigmatising labels like 'antisocial' or 'dysfunctional' family which are common in the social policy discourse (Barrett and MacIntosh, 1982; Garrett, 2007).

Personal Experiences of Family

Coexisting with socially constructed ideals, and values and beliefs about family are our personal experiences of love, loyalty, connection, conflict, betrayal, and rejection within the family. The very fact that all social workers have, themselves, lived in a family makes it imperative that they remain cognisant of the influence of these experiences on their practice. They must consider and reflect upon their own beliefs about what it means to be a family and their own experiences of secretiveness, silence, betrayal, rejection, estrangement, social stigma, and so on, for these will have a knock-on effect in working with families.

Family Estrangement: Values, Ethics and Moral Considerations

Family estrangement 'is the physical distancing and loss of affection between family members, often due to intense conflict or ongoing disagreement. A person may be active in the estrangement, by leaving or dismissing the family, or they may be cast out by one or more members of the family' (Agllias, 2011a, p. 107). Initially it might seem incongruent to conceptualise family estrangement in the realm of 'family secrets', because the estrangement of a family member often leaves an emptiness that is impossible to hide.

However, the development of estrangement and the experience of living without a family member are intimately bound to secrets, silence, and stigma. Recent research suggested that many older people considered that secrets or the withholding of information by a third party (most often the other parent) contributed to their adult-child's estrangement (Agllias, 2011b). Some suggested that their adult-child's capacity to fully understand family dynamics had been distorted when information about domestic violence, mental illness, or abuse within the family had been withheld. Many felt silenced by the estranged party, who refused contact and also refused to express their reason for estranging in the first place. The majority felt silenced and disenfranchised by a society that did not recognise, and indeed judged, parents estranged from their children negatively. This perceived – and actual – stigma resulted in the perpetuation of secret-keeping, and these parents often minimised, avoided, and lied about the status of their relationship with their adult-child in social situations (Agllias, in press).

How might value theory and the literature on ethical decision making in social work assist social workers confronted by the kinds of ethical issues discussed in relation to family secrets? Some approaches have been mentioned above. Before examining a few case studies, let us look briefly at the various ways in which we might view the area of family secrets and family estrangement from an ethical perspective. There are a variety of ethical perspectives that are not always in agreement with one another but which, nevertheless, help us expand our thinking on ethical issues, viewing them from all angles, as it were. Let's examine these:

1. The dominant deontological perspective would be concerned with rules and principles in social work relating *inter alia* to respect for persons, self-determination, and confidentiality, and might look towards ethical codes and the myriad ethical decision-making frameworks to assist in deciding what to do (Banks, 2006, 2008; Congress, 2010; Dolgoff, Loewenberg, and Harrington, 2009; McAuliffe, 1999, 2010; Reamer, 2001). Immanuel Kant is the *prima facie* deontological thinker whose universalist-rationalist approach has been widely embraced by social work. Some practitioners find this approach too constraining, believing what's right or wrong depends crucially on the situation or circumstances we are in. These kinds of judgments lead us to be more lenient when we think people's actions can be justified, even when they are morally wrong, such as stealing food when one is starving or spiting on someone who has been especially mean to you. In this case, disclosing something a client has told you in confidence might be quite justified if someone might be harmed by your silence.

2. A consequential perspective might pay special attention to the consequences of particular decisions or actions. A particular

consequential perspective known as utilitarianism might seek to do or decide what will benefit the majority of people in the situation (see Chapter 1). It would seek to minimise harm and maximise the well-being of as many people involved (Robinson and Reeser, 2000). In the situation of family secrets, it could lead to the breaking of confidentiality if all the family members were suffering as a result of the confidant's behaviour.

3. A virtue ethics perspective would be concerned with the moral disposition or motivation of those involved and be especially attentive to doing the right thing – doing what is morally right, or acting according to the virtues, that is making decisions or taking actions that contribute to well-being (Clark, 2006; Gray and Lovat, 2007; Houston, 2003; McBeath and Webb, 2002; Morelock, 1997). It might, however, contradict the rule-based deontological perspective *vis á vis* the premise of maintaining confidentiality central to our discussion here and would then present an ethical dilemma. As already noted, we are more inclined to think that the right thing to do depends on the circumstances rather than the rules.

4. A relational ethics of care perspective, while associated with feminist ethics, has progressed to a political theory about the nature of care in society and whose responsibility it is to care for others (Featherstone, 2001, 2010; Gray, 2010a; Hugman, 2005; Meagher and Parton, 2004; Orme, 2002, 2008; Parton, 2003). In analysing the notion of care, it distinguishes between what it means to give and receive care and to care for others. In the kind of cases being considered in this chapter, what it means ethically to care will be affected by social norms associated with gendered family roles and responsibilities. This is where feminist theory has contributed important insights about dominant assumptions like women should take major responsibility for caring for their families. This would lead to a mother who cuts off her children being seen in a negative light with rejecting children being seen as antisocial or neglectful.

5. This could then lead to reflections around Levinas' ethics of responsibility which is concerned primarily with our responsibilities and duties towards others (Tascón, 2010). Levinas was a foremost theorist of the ethics of overturning the entire edifice of Western ethics, centring on the freely choosing subject to one bound by the call of the other and the duties this entails. It draws on deontological ethical theory which it grounds in relationships. Hence, like the ethics of care, it is sometimes also referred to as 'relational ethics' and asks questions about issues of ethical responsibility towards others.

6. A discursive or discourse ethics, which draws on the work of Jürgen Habermas, is based in communication or our dialogical relationships.

By dialogical is meant a situation in which we would ordinarily talk through our problems applying our reasoning and logic to reach a solution, taking all the information and circumstances into account. For Habermas the only way to reach morally binding decisions is through communication and intersubjective engagement or as we usually say through conversing with others, sharing ideas, and discussing the implications. His discourse ethics differs from Kant's universalist-rationalist approach by emphasising the intersubjective, interactional components of our encounters (Hayes and Houston, 2007; Houston, 2010; Lovat and Gray, 2008). There is a tendency in all of us to think that most problems can be solved if we can talk them through with others. Yet family estrangement is an area where this just cannot happen. People have been cut off often without explanation and nothing they can do or say will alter what has happened. There is a finality to these situations which presents an ethical conundrum defying our normal way of thinking about conflict resolution.

7. The particularist ethical approach is characteristic of a postmodern ethics that debunks the universal rules and principles of a deontological ethics, believing each situation must be judged on a case-by-case basis (Rossiter, 2006; Rossiter, Prilleltensky, and Walsh-Bowers, 2000). It is commonly perceived that this leads to a highly relativistic form of ethics where people can make up the rules as they go along since there are no rules we can all agree on or that apply to every situation. Drawing on Bauman's *Postmodern Ethics*, Gray (2010b) examines its links with Levinas' ethics of responsibility and corrects misconceptions about an anything-goes relativism in postmodern ethics. In the kind of situations being discussed here, a postmodern ethics would lead to considerable flexibility in how people's decisions and behaviours were perceived, with particular contexts and issues being important considerations. In other words, the best course of action would depend on the particular case and each case – or situation – would be judged on its merits.

8. There are various social perspectives, such as feminist, anti-oppressive, and antiracist practice, and issues of human rights and social justice, that have important ethical implications based on issues of gender, race, ethnicity, culture, and religion, which would require that attention be paid to these factors in cases of family estrangement (Gray and Webb, 2010). Here it might be a matter of dispelling myths such as women who reject their children are immoral or that poor people don't take as good care of their children as rich people. In such situations the social worker would take great pains to show that this phenomenon can easily affect all people everywhere. No-one is

particularly immune because of their gender, race, ethnicity, culture, social status, or religion.

9. On the matter of religion, attitudes towards family estrangement might be affected by people's religious beliefs about family and gender roles and responsibilities within them. Social work's value system tends to be largely Judaeo-Christian in origin (Payne, 2005) and many of the faith-based services in which social workers are employed tend to be Christian in nature (Gilligan, 2010; Whiting, 2010). However, most religions have a long history of altruism and caring, and as social work spreads to non-Western contexts, it encounters diverse spiritualities and religions. These might be important considerations when people are trying to deal with the trauma and loss of estrangement. Religious sanctions might add another layer of complexity to social stigma and misrecognition.

Estrangement poses value and ethical considerations particularly in later life. While most service provision for the aged is underpinned by person-centred care, social inclusion agendas increasingly position intergenerational family members as critical to the older person's care, support, social life, and decision-making processes towards the end of life. In some systems families are consulted about care plans for older people going into residential care, but an absence of family can cause a dilemma for workers. Should they abide by the older person's wishes not to contact the adult-child and risk complaints or litigation at a later point? One care worker describes the typical response in her workplace:

> Whilst we all believe that family should be part of the consultation, there are a lot of fragmented families out there. Often I ask "would you like me to contact your family or anyone else?" Often the clients say "no we don't talk to our son or daughter". I will document that that was their choice. So if there was ever a Ministerial then it's clear that it was the client's wish not to have their child as part of their Care Plan. (Ageing Services Learning and Research Centre, 2009, p. 119)

In this case the worker decided that the clients' rights to confidentiality and self-determination were the priority. However, her statement also recognises the possibility that some adult-children may not be happy if they were later to discover they had been excluded from the decision-making process. This poses the question, then, how might this worker have decided upon this course of action? Is her response universal or are there times when she responds differently? What other information might she consider when making such a decision? What conclusions might she have drawn about the nature of the child's absence that has led her to favour the older person's rights over the adult-child's? How might these ideas intersect with social and personal ideologies about adult-children's responsibilities to parents in old age or might her decision be made on the basis of organisational directives that give weight to the 'clients' wishes? How might this situation be complicated if a third party were involved? Let's examine Case Study 1 to reflect on your response to a more complex scenario.

Case Study 1

Jocelyn, aged 75 years, had lived in a residential aged care facility for seven years. She had been physically estranged from her adult-children for over 30 years. She had not spoken to her siblings, nephews, and nieces for the past 20 years. Jocelyn told the social worker that she did not want anyone to contact her family members under any circumstance and that she wanted to die alone. She made it quite clear that if her children could not visit throughout her life, she certainly did not want them on her deathbed. She also asked the care staff to keep her whereabouts private. She asked not to be told if any of her children tried to contact her. These wishes were clearly documented on her file and staff members were made aware of them. However, the social worker noticed that she would sometimes talk about how lucky other residents were to have family in their lives. Recently the Care Facility was contacted by a woman searching for the whereabouts of a woman called Jocelyn Davies, who claimed to be her niece. The woman said that she had fond memories of Jocelyn throughout her childhood, and had recently begun to wonder what had happened to her aunt.

Working from a deontological perspective, the social worker was mindful of the client's wishes in this instance and her right to make her own decisions and have her wishes fulfilled. But leaving things there did not sit well with the social worker's intuition that Jocelyn was using a tough love approach to prevent herself from being hurt again. She had long ago given up any attempt to see her children again but the social worker was sure the appearance of her niece on the scene was a good thing. Had the social worker had that conversation with Jocelyn, mindful of the dialogical ethics approach, she would have been able to discuss the pros and cons of reconnection and mutually form strategies that would keep Jocelyn safe while giving her the choice of whether or not she wanted to see her niece. For the social worker, doing what she intuitively felt and acting in terms of her virtues – to act with integrity according to her values of openness and honesty – rather than not tell Jocelyn her niece had asked to see her, was the 'right thing to do'. In weighing the pros and cons in this particular case, the social worker would be enabling Jocelyn to consider the consequences of her original decision not to see her niece and to think about the possible outcomes of changing that decision. The social worker would then have a clear conscience that she had 'allowed' Jocelyn to make her own decisions in the matter – self-determination had been upheld and an ethic of care exercised.

We can see from this situation that there are several members of the family potentially affected by Carol's decisions, and these do not include any family members of whom the social worker is unaware at this stage of the assessment, e.g., Pauline's nuclear family members. There may be a number of competing interests and, as with the prior case, the social worker felt

---

Case Study 2

The hospital social worker was requested to meet with Carol, a 71-year old woman diagnosed with terminal cancer, to discuss discharge and palliative planning. Carol usually lives alone with her 36-year-old son, Thomas, who has a physical and mild intellectual disability. They live a secluded life with few visitors or outings. During Carol's recent hospitalisation, Thomas was housed in respite care. Reports from respite carers suggested that Thomas was highly distressed during this period and continually asked for his sister, Pauline. This was a shock to the social worker who could find no record of Carol's daughter on clinical files. When she asked about her daughter, Carol said that she and Thomas had been physically estranged from Pauline for seven years due to a dispute about a loan. When discussing plans for Thomas' future care, Carol revealed that she had decided it would be Pauline's duty to care for Thomas after her death. Carol had regularly reminded Thomas that he would be living with Pauline in the future, but this was not an arrangement she had ever discussed with Pauline. Carol made it very clear that she did not want any contact with her daughter, nor did she want anyone else to contact her before her death. She stated that it was unnecessary to consider any alternative care arrangements for Thomas, because she knew Pauline would take care of him. The social worker's initial reaction was surprise that Pauline had decided on arrangements for her son's care without consultation with her daughter, and felt concerned that these arrangements would not be fulfilled after her death. She felt most concerned that Thomas' reunification expectations might be unfulfilled at the time of his mother's death and possibly create a difficult transition to residential care.

hamstrung by considerations of client autonomy and confidentiality. The social worker was also a little bit peeved that Carol had never mentioned her daughter. She felt that she had established a trusting relationship with her and the fact that Carol had not been totally honest jarred. She also thought that Carol's decision was totally unrealistic and not fair on her son and she wanted not only to do the right thing by all involved but to be able to act in a way that was consistent with her image of herself as a virtuous person. She discussed this with her supervisor who raised the question of whether it might be possible that Carol was acting virtuously by respecting her family's wishes not to see her, for whatever reason. Carol was a recovered alcoholic who had gone through a divorce that was traumatic for her children and possibly their only protection was to cut off their mother even to the point that it meant not seeing their brother again. Surely having to do that says something about the extent of the pain they all had endured. What would be the point now of opening old wounds in an elderly lady's life? But the social worker felt a duty of care not only to Carol but also to her son and what guarantee was there that he would be well cared for once his mother died if plans were not being put in place in anticipation of this?

From an ethics of care perspective, this case also shows the predominant values in society that women are primarily responsible for caring for their children, even in adulthood. Feminists have highlighted this gendered notion of care and the power relations inherent in situations such as this (Gilligan, 1982). Might the social worker have viewed Carol's predicament differently from an ethic of care perspective? Would she have thought, for example, to explore whether Carol's second son was in a position to care for his brother? As it happened, the social worker contacted Carol's daughter after her death and found she was not, in any way, in a position to care for her disabled brother. Being aware of the strong pull towards female family members' responsibility for care would have led her to consider other options. She might have considered Thomas's existing support network and options beyond this gendered notion of care.

So deep is the idea of self-determination entrenched in the social work mindset that it is hard to go against a client's wishes even when one's ethical disposition points strongly in that direction. In both these cases there is an unknown third party involved whose interests remain a mystery. There is too a family history of which the social workers involved had a very patchy knowledge based on what the client in each instance had revealed to them. In both cases the social workers were aware that families were complex entities and each, like the individuals involved, had a unique identity. What right really did the social workers have to interfere in these instances? Was the social workers' ethical disposition of any importance? Did it not complicate a rather clear case from a deontological perspective that the clients' wishes should be respected? In social work we tend to favour these 'clear guidelines' approaches as they let us off the hook to some extent but often our emotions pull us in another direction. These reactions in us provide the perfect signal that we are on ethical ground and a moral dilemma is brewing. They are our early warning signals. As shown above, social workers have a range of ethical perspectives on which to draw and they need always to remain mindful that where ethical decisions are concerned, 'there are no answers, only choices' (Gray and Gibbons. 2007).

Conclusion

The area of family estrangement presents many contradictions to our understanding of family and its importance in people's lives. It teaches us to be far more aware when families are going through traumatic experiences surrounding abuse, divorce, or conflict that, if not appropriately handled, estrangements will ensue further down the line. What is hard to accept about such situations is that these might ensue even with the best and most appropriate interventions. It is even harder to accept that estrangement in some cases is a good thing and people cutting off family members might indeed be a virtuous act, best in the long term for all involved. We are taught that families provide the best environments in which to raise children yet families are often fraught with as many dangers as the proverbial minefield. Situations such as those described in this chapter lend themselves to deontological solutions and highlight why that ethical approach is dominant in social work. It is almost as though the other approaches act as a background helping us to appreciate the importance of ethics and morality, yet still fuelling our intuition that following the rules or principles produces the right consequences for all involved. A broader knowledge of ethical perspectives and the ethical implications of much of our decision making in social work assists us in gaining a deep understanding of family estrangement and the complex emotions of pain and loss, guilt and shame, anxiety and regret, sadness and longing, and so on. The ability not to judge people's past behaviour is essential to an empathic understanding of the finality of the loss associated with estrangement, and accepting that sometimes secrets must be kept at all costs.

Further Reading

Gray, M., and Webb, S.A. (eds) (2010) *Ethics and Value Perspectives in Social Work*. Basingstoke: Palgrave: This agenda setting text explores a broad range of value perspectives and their impact on and contribution to social work thinking about ethics. It draws on international authors to present new perspectives, such as Islam and New Age.

Scales, S., Potthast, A. and Oravecz, L. (eds) (2010) *The Ethics of the Family*. Newcastle upon Tyne: Cambridge Scholars: *The Ethics of the Family* is an interdisciplinary book that introduces the concept of family through an ethical lens. It then provides a number of essays featuring key ethical issues that affect families, including marriage, conception, parenting and child protection.

Sucov, E. (2006) *Fragmented Families: Patterns of Estrangement and Reconciliation*. Jerusalem: Southern Hills Press: This book offers a theoretical exploration of family estrangement for family members and human services workers. It focuses on estrangement related emotions and responses as well as pathways to reconciliation or acceptance.

References

Afifi, T.D. and Steuber, K. (2009) 'The Risk Revelation Model (RRM) and Strategies used to Reveal Secrets', *Communication Monographs*, 76, 144–76.

Afifi, T.D. and Steuber, K. (2010) 'The Cycle of Concealment Model', *Journal of Social and Personal Relationships*, 27(8), 1019–34.

Ageing Services Learning and Research Centre (2009) *Re-ablement of Older People in North Coast NSW*. Southern Cross University.

Agllias, K. (2011a) 'No Longer on Speaking Terms: The Losses Associated with Family Estrangement at the End of Life', *Families in Society: The Journal of Contemporary Human Services*, 92(1), 107–13.

Agllias, K. (2011b) *Every Family: Intergenerational Estrangement between Older Parents and their Adult-children*. PhD, School Humanities and Social Sciences, University of Newcastle, Australia.

Agllias, K. (forthcoming) 'The Gendered Experience of Family Estrangement in Later Life', *Affilia: Journal of Women and Social Work*. Accepted 11 July 2012.

Ashton, J. (2006) 'Alcohol's Tragic Family Secret', *Sign of the Times*. Retrieved June 16, 2012 from http://www.signsofthetimes.org.au/items/alcohol-s-tragic-family-secrets

Banks, S. (2006) *Ethics and Values in Social Work* (3rd edn). Basingstoke: Palgrave.

Banks, S. (2008) 'Critical Commentary: Social work ethics', *British Journal of Social Work*, 38, 1238–49.

Barrett, M. and MacIntosh, M. (1982) *The Anti-social Family*. London: Verso.

Bedford, V.H. and Blieszner, R. (1997) 'Personal Relationships in Later-life Families', in S. Duck (ed.), *Handbook of Personal Relationships*. Chichester, West Sussex: John Wiley and Sons Ltd., 527–39.

Butler, M.H., Harper, J.M. and Seedall, R.B. (2009) 'Facilitated Disclosure versus Clinical Accommodation of Infidelity Secrets: An early pivot point in couple therapy: Part 1: Couple relationship ethics, pragmatics and attachment', *Journal of Marital and Family therapy*, 35(1), 125–43.

Clark, C. (2006) 'Moral Character in Social Work', *British Journal of Social Work*, 36, 75–89.

Congress, E. (1999) *Social Work Values and Ethics: Identifying and Resolving Professional Dilemmas*. Belmont, CA: Wadsworth.

Dolgoff, F., Loewenberg, F. and Harrington, D. (2009) *Ethical Decisions for Social Work Practice* (8th edn). Belmont, CA: Thomson, Brooks Cole.

Everingham, C., Stevenson, D. and Warner-Smith, P. (2007) 'Things are Getting Better All the Time'?: Challenging the narrative of women's progress from a generational perspective', *Sociology*, 41(3), 419–37.

Featherstone, B. (2001) 'Where To for Feminist Social Work?', *Critical Social Work*, 2(1). Retrieved 10 May 2008 from: http://www.uwindsor.ca/units/socialwork/critical.nsf/982f0e5f06b5c9a285256d6e006cff78/fe61dbdb7d2330de85256ea800646086!OpenDocument

Featherstone, B. (2010) 'Ethic of Care', in M. Gray and Webb, S.A. (eds), *Ethics and Value Perspectives in Social Work*. Basingstoke: Palgrave, 123–41.

Frijns, T. and Finenour, C. (2009) 'Longitudinal Associations between Keeping a Secret and Psycho-social Adjustment in Adolescence', *International Journal of Behavioural Development*, 33, 145–54.

Garrett, P.M. (2007) 'Making "Anti-social Behaviour": A fragment on the evolution of "ASBO politics" in Britain', *British Journal of Social Work*, 37(5), 839–56.

Gilligan, C. (1982) *In a Different Voice: Psychological Theory and Women's Development*. Harvard, MA: Harvard University Press.

Gray, M. (2010a) 'Moral Sources: Emerging ethical theories in social work', *British Journal of Social Work*, 40(6), 1794–811.

Gray, M. (2010b) 'Postmodern Ethics', in M. Gray and Webb, S.A. (eds), *Ethics and Value Perspectives in Social Work*. Basingstoke: Palgrave, 197–214.

Gray, M. and Gibbons, J. (2007) 'There are No Answers, Only Choices: Teaching ethical decision making in social work', *Australian Social Work*, 60(2), 222–38.

Gray, M. and Lovat, T. (2007) 'Horse and Carriage: Why Habermas's discourse ethics gives virtue a *praxis* in social work', *Ethics and Society*, 1(3), 310–28.

Gray, M. and Webb, S.A. (eds) (2010) *Ethics and Value Perspectives in Social Work*. Basingstoke: Palgrave.

Hayes, D. and Houston, S. (2007) 'Lifeworld, System and Family Group Conferences: Habermas' contribution to discourse in child protection', *British Journal of Social Work*, 37, 987–1006.

Houston, S. (2003) 'Establishing Virtue in Social Work: A response to McBeath and Webb', *British Journal of Social Work*, 33, 819–24.

Houston, S. (2010) 'Discourse Ethics', in M. Gray and Webb, S.A. (eds), *Ethics and Value Perspectives in Social Work*. Basingstoke: Palgrave, 157–77.

Hugman, R. (2005) *New Approaches in Ethics for the Caring Professions: Taking Account of Change for Caring Professions*. London: Palgrave Macmillan.

Imber-Black, E. (1998) *The Secret Life of Families*. New York: Bantam Books.

Kroll, B. (2004) 'Living With an Elephant: Growing up with parental substance misuse', *Child and Family Social Work*, 9, 129–40.

Lovat, T. and Gray, M. (2008) 'Towards a Proportionist Social Work Ethics: A Habermasian perspective', *British Journal of Social Work*, 38, 1100–14.

Mannheim, K. (1959) 'The Problem of Generations', in K. Mannheim (ed.), *Essays on the Sociology of Knowledge*. London: Routledge.

McAuliffe, D. (1999) 'Clutching at Codes: Resources that influence social work decisions in cases of ethical conflict', *Professional Ethics: A Multidisciplinary Journal*, 17(3–4), 9–24.

McBeath, G. and Webb, S.A. (2002) Virtue Ethics and Social Work: Being lucky, realistic, and not doing one's duty. *British Journal of Social Work*, 32, 1015–36.

Meagher, G. and Parton, N. (2004) 'Modernising Social Work and the Ethics of Care', *Social Work and Society*, 2(1), 10–27.

Menees, M. and Segrin, C. (2000) 'The Specificity of Disrupted Processes in families of Adult Children of Alcoholics', *Alcohol and Alcoholism*, 35(4), 361–7.

Morelock, K.T. (1997) 'The Search for Virtue: Ethics teaching in MSW programs', *Journal of Teaching in Social Work*, 14(1/2), 69–87.

Orme, J. (2002) 'Social Work: Gender, Care and Justice', *British Journal of Social Work*, 32, 799–814.

Orme, J. (2008) 'Feminist Social Work', in M. Gray and Webb, S.A. (eds), *Social Work Theories and Methods*. London: Sage.

Parton, N. (2003) 'Rethinking Professional Practice: The contributions of social constructionism and the feminist "ethics of care"', *British Journal of Social Work*, 33, 1–16.

Payne, M. (2005) *The Origins of Social Work: Continuity and Change*. Basingstoke: Palgrave.

Reamer, F. (2001) *The Social Work Ethics Audit: A risk management tool.* Washington, DC: NASW Press.

Robinson, W. and Reeser, L. (2000) *Ethical Decision-making in Social Work.* Boston, MA: Allyn and Bacon.

Rossiter, A. (2006) 'The 'Beyond' of Ethics in Social Work', *Canadian Social Work Review*, 23(1–2), 139–44.

Rossiter, A., Prilleltensky, I. and Walsh-Bowers, R. (2000) 'A Postmodern Perspective on Professional Ethics', in B. Fawcett, Featherstone, B., Fook, J. and Rossiter, A. (eds), *Practice and Research in Social Work.* London: Routledge, 83–103.

Siporin, M. (1982) 'Moral Philosophy in Social Work Today', *Social Service Review*, 56(4), 516–38.

Siporin, M. (1983) 'Morality and Immorality in Working with Clients', *Social Thought*, 9(4), 10–28.

Smart, C. (2004) 'Changing Landscapes of Family Life: Rethinking divorce', *Social Policy and Society*, 3(4), 401–8.

Smart, C. (2009) 'Family Secrets: Law and understandings of openness in everyday relationship', *Journal of Social Policy*, 38(4), 551–67.

Smart, C. (2011) 'Families, Secrets and Memories', *Sociology*, 45(4), 539–53.

Sucov, E.B. (2006) *Fragmented Families: Patterns of Estrangement and Reconciliation.* Jerusalem: Southern Hills Press.

Tascón, S. (2010) 'Ethics of Responsibility', in M. Gray and Webb, S.A. (eds), *Ethics and Value Perspectives in Social Work.* Basingstoke: Palgrave, 142–56.

White, S. (2005) *Missing Persons.* New York: Signet Paperback.

Wood, A. (2001) 'The Origins of Family Systems Work: Social workers' contributions to the development of family theory and practice', *Australian Social Work*, 54(3), 15–29.

3 Is Cultural Sensitivity Always a Good Thing? Arguments for a Universalist Social Work

Gurnam Singh and Stephen Cowden

Introduction

The requirement for social workers to be sensitive to cultural difference has now become accepted as an essential component of best practice – indeed, social workers failing to display sensitivity to cultural differences would most likely be seen to be in contravention of most professional ethics frameworks. However, closer scrutiny as to exactly how and to what degree one should display cultural sensitivity in practice reveals a complex set of ethical and philosophical dilemmas for social workers; and this is the main focus of this chapter. Specifically, we argue that the largely uncritical acceptance of the concept of 'celebrating diversity' as an inherently 'good thing', has undermined Universalist approaches to ethics within social work. That is not to say that assertions of the function of social work are not based on universal principles; the problem lies in the way that these are often proffered alongside intimations to cultural relativism. A good illustration can be found in the definition of social work offered by the *International Federation of Social Workers* which argues that whilst 'The holistic focus of social work is universal, the priorities of social work practice will vary from country to country and from time to time depending on cultural, historical, and socio-economic conditions' (IFSW, 2000, Para 5). Whilst the IFSW is perhaps not as guilty as some, it is precisely this kind of dualistic thinking that seeks to cover all possibilities that we argue has led to confusion amongst practitioners, particularly when working with service users from different cultural, religious or ethnic backgrounds.

We begin the chapter by exploring the linked and opposing ideas of 'cultural relativism' and 'universalism', which we suggest provide the underpinning philosophical foundations for arguments for and against cultural sensitivity. In brief, cultural relativism represents the idea that each identifiable culture group and its practices can and should be judged by its own norms, whereas universalism seeks to base its principles on the identification of overarching aspects of all human cultures. Whilst one could approach the problem from a purely philosophical perspective, we suggest that to fully comprehend both sides of the argument one needs to situate the analysis in the broader historical struggles of minorities for social justice. In doing so, we offer a consideration of the way the discourse associated with cultural sensitivity developed out of anti-racist struggles from the 1970s; struggles that identified both the way processes of racialisation were built upon deep-rooted 'white European' assertions of cultural superiority (Said, 1978, 1994; CCCS, 1982) and attempts to develop an alternative positive affirmation of non-white minority culture, which has in the social work literature been conceptualised as 'black perspectives' (Ahmad, 1990; Singh, 1992; Robinson, 2009). However, our account of this notes the way in which what was essentially a critique of power, became transmuted into an orthodoxy in which the celebration of cultural and religious differences came to be seen as an end in itself; in other words historic struggles by oppressed minorities from former European colonies for equality and justice became reduced to a problem of tolerance and 'managing diversity'.

In this chapter we address these problems both theoretically and also through a case study. We conclude the chapter by arguing that while recognising cultural difference forms a crucial basis for maximising communication, building trust and negotiation, within this, there is a more fundamental moral duty to develop an approach that is capable of offering a universal ethics whilst at the same time avoiding the kinds of cultural pathology that have historically characterised the experience of minoritised service users. Here we consider the work of Martha Nussbaum and her attempt to establish a Universalist framework that avoids some of the pitfalls of cultural imperialism.

Universalism, Cultural Relativism and Social Work

The debate between universalism and relativism is quite an old and extensive one and to some extent maps across the two major approaches to ethics; the 'deontological', based on a fixed and universal rules based approach, and the 'teleological', which emphasises the contextual nature of ethical decision making (Pullen-Sansfacon and Cowden, 2012). As Healy

(2007) points out these conflicting perspectives lie 'at the heart of the heated debates in the arena of human rights, where they are often labelled as the Universalist and cultural relativist positions' (2007:12). Whilst debates surrounding these two divergent perspectives can be located within a much broader sweep of history, the emergence of a public policy approach from the 1970s that sought to accommodate plurality of cultural standpoints known popularly as 'multiculturalism' (Singh and Cowden, 2011) led to a renewed impetus surrounding debates about how best to respond to the needs of minority groups. Whilst the intention of this policy was to foster respect for different cultures and therefore to give minorities a sense of belonging, as Malik (1996) notes, it actually led to collusion between the (racist) state and opportunistic religious and cultural organisations in the guise of self-appointed community leaders. By offering financial and political support for different communities to develop projects to address their specific cultural needs, not only did these policies undermine the anti-racist movement that struggled for the much bigger prize of justice and equality, it actually encouraged segregation and inter-ethnic conflict.

Within the relatively short history of social work this tension was manifest through two specific approaches. The first and arguably predominant tradition up until the late 1970s is rooted in the Enlightenment tradition and is based on a Universalist understanding of human functioning. In this context, universalism can be defined as constituting both a set of beliefs and moral imperatives underwritten by the idea that despite outward differences, all human beings share a broad set of fundamental needs, hopes and desires. These sorts of commitments to safeguarding and maintaining equality were very much in keeping with the aims and aspirations of the post-war welfare state.

Specifically in relation to minorities, the predominant social work approach of this period can be characterised as one of 'cultural assimilation'. Though well intentioned, in seeking to enable migrants to 'fit into' the majority culture, this approach largely resulted in the pathologising of minority clients based often on crude racial stereotypes (Singh, 1992). Such pathologising historically resulted in the positive strengths of black families of, for example, surviving the trauma of migration, discrimination and disadvantage being underemphasised. On the other hand, conceptions of minority cultural forms as being overly structured and therefore incapable of respecting individual rights (e.g. extended Asian patriarchal families) or lacking structure and therefore at risk of failing (e.g. black single parent families) became overemphasized. As Williams (1996) notes: 'The characterization of individuals, families or communitites being to blame for their deprivation because of their way of life, their culture, has long been part of common-sense ideas in social work (1996: 68). In doing so the complexity of family life experienced by minorities seeking to retain dignity and self respect in the face of rapid transition, widespread racism and social exclusion became, as Gambe et al. (1992: 26) noted, 'reduced to simplistic, catch all explanations, such as "endemic cultural conflict"'.

It was in the face of such pathologisation of minority cultures that a new approach emerged which, amongst other things, sought to emphasise the positive aspects of minority cultural life. Associated with the *postmodern turn* within the social sciences, this approach is based on a cultural relativist framework as the basis for determining human need and action.

The UK Health Professions Council's *Standards of Proficiency for Social Work* (2012) encompasses both of these traditions, often in quite contradictory ways. For instance Standard 2.7 outlines the need for social workers to 'understand the need to respect and uphold the rights, dignity, values and autonomy of every service user and carer'. The demand to 'uphold the rights' of an individual represents a Universalist aspiration, whilst the demand to 'uphold the values' of an individual, points toward a relativist position. While on the surface this may appear laudable, the problem resides in how one understands the requirement to uphold the 'values of every service user and carer', particularly in situations where those values themselves are anything but accommodating of individual rights and freedoms. For example, should a social worker uphold the values of racist service users and carers?

A central problem here lies in the imprecise nature of the concept of 'respect', which has broadly speaking two distinct meanings. One conception builds on the well-established concept of 'tolerance'. Historically speaking, the idea of tolerance came to the forefront in European societies following the Reformation in the sixteenth century when it was seen as a means of ending the bloodshed between difference religious denominations (Grell and Scribner, 2002). Essentially, the idea of tolerance was a response to the need to establish social cohesion through a combination of pragmatism and idealism. Hence, this constituted a conditional acceptance of difference in the short term, with the longer-term aim being one of assimilation through the development of common values and culture.

It was the sense that tolerance represented a kind of cultural imperialism by stealth that led to the turn to 'cultural relativism'. This was first articulated by the anthropologist Franz Boas over 100 years ago, and in suggesting that there was nothing absolute about human civilisation or culture and that cultural plurality was a fundamental feature of humankind (Boas, 1974), was seen as challenging Enlightenment notions of human progress. In sociology, the principle is sometimes practised to avoid cultural bias in research, as well as to avoid judging another culture by the standards of one's own culture. For this reason, cultural relativism has been considered an attempt to avoid ethnocentrism or the tendency for people to negatively judge others on the basis of an assertion of a perceived superiority of one's own cultural identity.

In relation to social work, from the 1990s, assertions of cultural relativism are most clearly evident within the influence of postmodernism which sought to present culturally and morally relativistic approaches as a major step forward against the oppressive predominance of modernist conceptions of social work. Jan Fook, an advocate of this perspective, argues that given the fragmented nature of knowledge and the multiple ways in which one might construct meaning, an emphasis on a diversity of approaches and perspectives becomes crucial (Fook, 2002: 23). Like much of the rhetoric of the cultural diversity/sensitivity based approaches, this sounds inclusive and progressive on the face of it. However, an embrace of multiple perspectives easily runs the risk of disarming social workers who are invested with the task of making ethical judgements and interventions based upon this. This is particularly the case when it comes to exercising moral judgement about the actions and behaviours of 'cultures' other than one's own. It is one thing to talk about the value of different realities, but which realities are we talking about. It is in this way that culturally relativist arguments – although not exclusively the product of postmodernism, but which have been given a massive boost by it – have contributed to the quagmire of confusion in which much social work theory and practice is currently mired (Herz, 2012).

Alongside the ethically confused nature of these arguments, we also want to make some practical political points about the impact which cultural relativism has had on social work. The main beneficiaries of these ideas at an organisational level have been religious organisations and discourses, since this language has allowed them move into the space previously occupied by 'modernist' universalism and secularism. In an earlier piece of work looking in more detail at the way this has happened we noted that:

> … a general consensus within contemporary public policy has emerged in which an uncritical engagement with "faith communities" has ceased to be seen as problematic, and where being sensitive to faith-based "difference" is seen as an end in itself. (Singh and Cowden, 2011: p. 347)

One can see examples of this policy in the government support for a rapid expansion of faith based schools, and in the form of the preventing violent extremism (PVE) agenda, where we have seen significant sums of money being specifically ring fenced for Muslim faith groups to develop their provision.

The key point here is while religious groups and indeed fundamentalist groups may not be the kind of 'diverse approaches' that Fook (2002) and other proponents of postmodernism in social work envisaged, these groups have been without doubt one of the main beneficiaries, and opposition to their increasing influence has in part been stymied by the predominance of postmodernist ideas. Ironically, in the UK at a time when minorities have been suffering most in terms of the economic crisis, and where far right extremism and hostility to minorities and Muslims in particular are on the rise (Amnesty International, 2009), we now also have the presence of powerful minority groups, almost entirely defined in terms of faith allegiances, being regularly feted by Government departments. It is almost as though the anti-racist movements that emerged out of the minority experience in the 1970s never existed (Singh and Cowden, 2012). Indeed, as Gilroy (1990) noted over two decades earlier in his essay provocatively entitled *The End of Anti-racism*, it was the policies of successive governments from the mid 1980s that sought to define the problem of racism in cultural terms that resulted in a mirroring of the very categories upon which racist stereotypes and ideologies were constructed in the first place.

It is in this light that we seek to pose the question of whether focusing on culture is always a good thing. Given that such a perspective could be considered somewhat contentious, it is also important for us to be absolutely clear about what we are not arguing for. We are not seeking to argue that social workers should go back to an updated version of what was termed the 'colour blind' approach where professionals were encouraged to see clients as individuals only (Dominelli, 2008). Nor are we advocating that social workers should be intolerant to cultural differences. On the contrary, our argument is 'cultural differences' must always be understood as arising out of particular material conditions. Thus the way to develop a genuine understanding of people, in the situations where social workers encounter them, requires a dialectical approach that allows us to see the dynamic relationship between human agency and social structure as the basis for practice interventions. Hence, such an approach seeks to articulate the ways in which cultural identities and discourses of 'otherness' are produced and reproduced through and from structures of oppression, power and privilege; and it in this sense that we argue in favour of Universalist approaches.

A Brief History of Social Work and Cultural Sensitivity

Having set out our broader philosophical position, we now want to turn to the specific history of social work and consider how the idea of 'cultural sensitivity' has become so embedded within social work. In doing so we want to argue that, whilst problematising the idea, it is important to simultaneously acknowledge the ways in which anti-racist struggles, both within and outside of social work, have historically been intimately linked with a critique of the hegemonic associations of cultural pathology, family dysfunctionality and minorities, as a basis for justifying racist practices (see Singh, 1992, 1999 and 2002). Hence, both in the ways that the problems of black and minority ethnic (BME) clients and communities were understood and worked with, we now have well documented critiques of what was in effect a form of social work underpinned by a profound *cultural imperialism*; where the role of welfare and education professionals was seen as one of enabling children and families from 'immigrant' backgrounds to overcome their 'culturally backward' ways and assimilate into the more civilised world of the dominant British culture (Dominelli, 2008).

These approaches were of course not only found in social work, but were part of the whole way the relationship between BME communities and the British state was articulated in post war Britain (CCCS, 1982). Ultimately, with what might be seen as new forms of cultural imperialism (contrasted to the more direct form inherent in the colonial policies of the British and other European empires from the eighteenth to twentieth centuries) we saw major social tensions emerging between BME communities and the state and this was nowhere manifested more than in the relationship between these communities and the police (Hall et al., 1978; Bowling et al., 2003). In 1981 these tensions revealed themselves in riots, which occurred across predominantly black areas in several British cities – St Paul's in Bristol, Moss Side in Manchester, Toxteth in Liverpool and Brixton and Tottenham in London. The Government's response at the time was to commission what came to be known as the *Scarman Report* which concluded that BME communities were indeed subject to institutional racism on a large scale and that public authorities had a key role in addressing this issue. Along with the Police Service and Education, the social work professional, which at the time had few black staff, became a key site for the unfolding of the anti-racist challenge (Singh, 2004).

It was in this context that the predominant ethical stance adopted by social work practitioners came to broadly support the rights of minority groups to assert different cultural values. The social work literature of this period was characterised by a concern with developing a critical praxis in working with BME services users, one that was sensitive to the various manifestations of power and powerlessness and cultural diversity (Cheetham, 1981; Ahmed et al., 1986; Devore and Schlesinger, 1991; Robinson, 2009). Often, the starting point and arguably the main strength of this approach was its emphasis on complex psychosocial processes as a basis for connecting individual behaviour to wider socio-cultural and material processes. For instance, in debates surrounding the placement of black children in care, Barn (1993) has demonstrated, in an analysis of over 500 cases, deep rooted problems both in the way black children were inappropriately entering the system and then in the widespread racism and dehumanisation they encountered in and through it.

The emergence of anti-racist initiatives in social work thus took place in a context of a politicised black community which had fought off both attacks from the far right on one hand and challenged institutional racism on the other (see CCCS, 1982; Gilroy, 1987a, 1987b; Sivanandan, 1990 and 1991). McLaughlin also notes that social work's taking up of these ideas was additionally facilitated by the adoption of 'equal opportunities' policies by left wing Labour-led Local Authorities which had significant influence throughout the 1980s in inner city areas of Britain (2005: 286). Looked at from the vantage point of today it is clear that as this radicalism has subsided, the space once occupied by secular black and anti-racist organisations has gradually come to be replaced by groupings which are defined by ethnic and faith based allegiances. The fertile soil in which these organisations grew was, as we have noted earlier, tilled and watered by postmodernist discourses of difference, and their influence in social work is presently manifest through the growing prevalence of books concerned with culture, faith and spirituality (see for example, Graham, 2002; Gilligan and Furness, 2009, Gray and Webb, 2010, Crabtree, Hussein and Spalekv, 2008). Indeed it would appear that the idea of faith and the culture based around that have now become the predominant mode of expression for multicultural social work. Gilligan and Furness' work typifies this trend in its claim that:

> We would argue that those involved in a profession such as Social Work need to recognise the likely, but not always obvious significance of religion and belief to many service users and colleagues. We suggest that Social Workers need to be ready and open to explore these subjects with people and to recognise that they may be significant sources of personal values, of serious dilemmas, of motivation and support, and of anxiety in relation to issues very relevant to Social Work practice. (2009: 4)

While this book is clearly opposed to religious absolutism and to the abuses of power carried out within religious institutions, its language of 'understanding' embodies a sense of faith as essentially benign. Hence for Gilligan and Furness an increasing level of religious identification, which they cite as part of the rationale for their work (2009: 15–18), is presented as though it were simply something for social workers to be more 'aware of'. Our concern with this approach is that it is completely silent on the historical, ideological and material conditions in which religious identities and the social relations which accompany them are being produced, asserted and in many cases imposed. The sense in which this is presented simply as a 'given' has, we would argue, major implications for women, disabled and gay people particular those within BME communities at the present time.

Chetan Bhatt has argued that this inability to talk about the 'will to power' inherent in the rise of religious identification is made possible through what he calls a 'mesmerising culturalism' which has allowed 'the embedding of a ubiquitous cultural-communitarian orthodoxy across varied intellectual, political and policy fields' (Bhatt, 2006: 99). Simply put, he suggests that diversity policies throughout the late 1990s cleared the path for the assertion of religion as the most important dimension of cultural identity. Bhatt details the ways in which a number of highly reactionary fundamentalist groupings managed to secure considerable influence over the cultural representation of particular minority communities by situating themselves within this language of cultural sensitivity and difference. This is related to the way 'culture' comes to be defined, within the faith-awareness literature in social work, as something which happens in a context which is seen to be entirely separate from wider social, political and economic issues. It is also interesting to note that it is the culture of minority groups which are seen most to envelop and enclose their members – as Bhatt notes while 'today, we are all cultural subjects', it remains the case that 'some of us are more culturally imbued than others' (Bhatt, 2006: 100). Indeed the social work literature on these matters, for all its concern with identity, says almost nothing about respecting the cultural identities of white majority populations. If respecting cultural sensitivity is such a good thing, why is it so unlikely that one would encounter such a suggestion?

Related to this injunction to 'respect culture', one also finds a preoccupation with 'tolerance'. The social theorist Slavoj Žižek has been one of the few to ask why this term has such significance and influence at the moment:

> Why are so many problems today perceived as problems of intolerance, rather than as problems of inequality, exploitation or injustice? Why is the proposed remedy tolerance, rather than emancipation, political struggle or even armed struggle? The immediate answer lies in the liberal multiculturalist's basic ideological operation, the "culturalisation of politics". Political differences – differences conditioned by political inequality or economic exploitation – are naturalised and neutralised into "cultural differences"; that is into different "ways of life", which are something given, something that cannot be overcome. They can only be "tolerated". (2009: 119)

The point here is that this discourse of 'tolerance', like the confused cultural relativist arguments on which it is based, acts to obfuscate dealing with things that might be otherwise seen as abuses of power. For example, the suggestion that Asian families choose to look after their elders justifies not developing services, or that violence is in some sense a 'normal' aspect of Black family life, and thus not protecting children appropriately. Our concern here is that the imperative to be 'respectful' to the other's culture, can create a situation of almost wilful blindness toward oppressive relations, particularly towards women and children, which come to be naturalised and rendered beyond criticism through the often conjoined category of 'culture' and 'religion'.

Cultural Sensitivity and Neo-Liberalism

We have noted so far that culturally relativist arguments, particularly those associated with postmodernism, have presented 'multiple ways of knowing and constructing meaning' (Fook, op. cit.) as something which challenges the dominance of modernist universalism, again suggesting that the recognition of cultural difference is self-evidently good. When it comes to thinking about the way this agenda of 'respecting culture' has inserted itself as the dominant version of multicultural social work we also need to ask who are the beneficiaries of these policies?

We have outlined elsewhere how in a very short period in the aftermath of 9/11 we have seen not just increasingly forceful demands for recognition and influence from within all major religions, but in the context of neo-liberal state policy, increasing receptiveness by the state to faith based community, welfare and educational initiatives (Singh and Cowden, 2011). In contemporary policy and rhetoric there are almost surreal contradictions in the way in which minority 'cultures' are discussed. On one hand it is entirely typical to hear Islamic identities and movements blatantly pathologised and presented without question as a 'threat to democracy'. The news that it was home-grown Islamist militants who had bombed London on 7/7 prompted a wave of concern and liberal soul-searching about the way cultural sensitivity may have contributed to or even caused these actions. Hence within the new rhetoric, migrants who wanted to enter Britain needed to stop living in the specificity of their cultural and religious ghettoes and start learning how to be British. Yet on the other hand in the context of the state seeking to divest itself of its social responsibilities in education, health and social care, a faith based social policy and social care agenda is being extensively promoted. This contradictory discourse compounds the sense of uncertainty and confusion that we see within contemporary social work. What now follows is a case study, which seeks

Case Study: The Ali Family

The Ali family are asylum seekers who have recently arrived in the UK from Somalia. Along with Mr and Mrs Ali, there are five children ranging from the ages of two to thirteen. They have a strong Muslim identity, speak little English and communicate mostly in their mother tongue Swahili. They are presently being helped by a charity which befriends and advises refugees and asylum seekers on welfare related matters. Mrs Ali has been attending a drop in session once a week and her case has been assigned to Adila, a social work student in her final placement. Adila's manager, John, felt that of all his students, with her African and Muslim background and the fact that she spoke Swahili, Adila would be most sensitive to Mrs Ali's cultural needs.

At their first meeting Mrs Ali's main concern was to discuss how she could change benefit payments from her husband's bank account of his wife's as he has retained control of all monies, leaving her without enough money for the family's needs. Concerned by how isolated Mrs Ali is, Adila begins regular weekly visits to Mrs Ali. Over time she notices how much Mrs Ali looks forward to her visits but also how uncomfortable, and even hostile, Mr Ali is toward her presence. On one visit when Mrs Ali was alone in the flat, Adila was completely taken aback when Mrs Ali burst into tears. When she asked what the matter was, Mrs Ali asked her first to promise her that she would not tell anyone as this information would bring shame to her and isolate her even further from her husband's family, who already had a very negative view of her. Caught in the emotion of this moment Adila gave this assurance. Mrs Ali then explained that she had for some time suffered regular beatings from her husband, but that these had recently become much worse as a consequence of their thirteen year old daughter Fozia's refusal to wear a headscarf. Mr Ali has justified these beatings to her failure to bring Fozia up as a good Muslim. Mrs Ali also informed Adila that her husband's family were encouraging these beatings as they blamed her for allowing Fozia to become 'corrupted by Western values'.

to consider these issues in context. Please note, to maintain confidentiality, all names are fictitious.

In this instance we see a social work student allocated a case on the basis of cultural identification, and yet it is this very cultural identification, and Adila's awareness of Mrs Ali's vulnerability, that has created a number of dilemmas for her:

- The first issue and ethical dilemna concerns Adila's personal integrity – if she reports Mr Ali to the police or other authorities, she is breaking her word to Mrs Ali.
- The second concerns the response those authorities have toward Asylum Seekers, whose legal status in the UK remains precarious. If Mr Ali was convicted by the police for his violence to his wife, it is entirely possible within existing Immigration legislation and policy that he could be deported back to Somalia.
- The third revolves around how questions of gender and women's rights can be balanced against question of cultural and religious prescriptions of women's roles and duties.
- The fourth concerns Fozia and the kind of expectations she will have as a young woman growing up in the UK, against cultural and religious conceptions of 'honour' and 'dignity'.

The first priority in seeking to deal with this situation is to understand it as a complex and dynamic exchange concerning the denial of rights and opportunities. Specifically, one needs to focus on patriarchal violence, racism and the personal traumas which are caused by wars and other geo-political conflicts, whose impact is primarily but not exclusively, on populations originating from the former European colonies. This is not to say that culture is unimportant; on the contrary, discerning the way culture is produced and reproduced in time and space is critical to understanding why people act the way they act, and the ways in which they might rationalise and normalise certain behaviours. If social work is anything it is about reading culture, but this must not be in a shallow sense. The key lesson is that external expressions and assertions of cultural identity always reveal deeper processes associated with struggles, with loss and separation, as well as manifestations of symbolic power and tangible violence, legitimacy and privilege.

In seeking to resolve these dilemmas it is necessary to decouple principles of human rights from the imposition of a 'white' Western cultural frame, or any other dominant framework for that matter. In other words one is seeking to combine principles of universalism with the insights developed by anti-racists about avoiding the kinds of ethnocentric practices that Devore and Schlesinger (1991) are at pains to point out. Whilst not an easy task, we think that the work of the moral philosopher, Martha Nussbaum and her conception of *capabilities* can be of particular relevance in this regard (Nussbaum, 2011). Used extensively in the field of 'development studies', this approach has yet to be taken up within social work. In collaboration with the Nobel prize winning economist Amartya Sen, Nussbaum sought to develop an approach to universalism that avoids the pitfalls of both cultural relativism on the one hand and cultural imperialism on the other (Nussbaum and Sen, 1993). Deeply concerned with the plight of minorities, the starting point for the *capabilities approach* is the view that human development, traditionally seen purely in terms of economic growth, needs to incorporate other dimensions of life.

Rooted in the Aristotelian notion of the 'good life', the key to this approach is to delineate a theory of 'social good' or 'well being' that resides primarily but not only within the individual. A 'good life' is not derived from the accumulation of material resources alone but from being able to develop opportunities resulting from a set of fundamental political entitlements or what she refers to as *central human functional capabilities*. Her aim, according to Charusheela, is 'to ground a specific conception of the core features of human experience that lets us identify the basic functionings that we will agree are universal, that is, essential for each individual to have in their capabilities set, regardless of their social location or cultural background' (2008: 5). In this sense, she offers a challenge to dominant claims that people may make to defend traditional cultural assertions on such matters as the role of women and the welfare of children. She argues that assertions of tradition and culture are 'simply the view of the most powerful members of the culture' and once this is understood one begins to think of traditional values in a completely different way (2011: 107).

Stemming initially from her work on women and human development Nussbaum identifies ten *human capabilities* which she argues can be applied in a universal way. These can be summarised as: avoiding premature death, having good health, being able to move freely, being able to cultivate one's imagination, being allowed to love, being able to develop critical reflection about one's life, having dignity for self and others including non-human species, being able to play and having control over one's environment (Nussbaum, 2010). She warns against adopting the model in a rigid manner and suggests that the list should be viewed as flexible, open-ended, and that the abstract principles will need to be interpreted for specific situations. She also sees the list as available for appropriation by both secular and religious groups in their own way.

The key point of Nussbaum's argument is that she believes that much of what passes as 'authentic culture' is simply hegemonic (i.e. powerful, ideologically-based assumptive truth) and therefore is an incomplete basis for knowing what minorities and oppressed groups in general may think and desire. In contrast the *capabilities approach* is a self-conscious normative framework built on an awareness of the existence of widespread cultural differences that invites critique and revision, and hence it cannot be seen as 'colour blind'. Further, given that the practical implementation of the framework is always more 'messy' than what can be delineated in the abstract, the abstract generality of the framework deliberately allows implementation into particular places and contexts. For example, taking the issue of 'freedom of speech', there is recognition that there may be different contexts in which this will be precisely defined and implemented. Because the approach focuses on 'capabilities' and not 'functioning', it allows the individual to develop what Nussbaum terms 'a zone of freedom' (2011: 110). And so in this sense the capabilities approach is not seeking to offer a prescription for life but a basis for determining how somebody can be enabled to live their life to the fullest. Similarly, given the statements are primarily offered for broader political ends aimed at securing rights for oppressed groups, there is no judgement made of the veracity of religious beliefs as such. Importantly this then offers respect for expression of diversity and religion in particular, whilst at the same time allowing a principled challenge to oppressive beliefs, whatever their genesis. It in this sense that Nussbaum argues that paradoxically, the best way to defend diversity is precisely to argue for universal capabilities, such as freedom of conscience, belief and expression.

The challenge that Nussbaum offers for the social work professional is clear; whilst paying attention to the way in which minority group identities and cultures may become constructed over time, professionals also need to deploy critical insights into the way cultural identities are not only formed but 'enforced' within a complex web of power relations. In this regard, cultural identity is not seen as something that is to be either preserved or destroyed, but to be tested and engaged with, from a concrete universalist reference point such as the *human capabilities* framework.

Whilst we recognise much work needs to be done to thinking through the implications that Nussbaum's theory has for social work, we finish our discussion by offering a brief comment on the value this framework has for social work by applying it to the case study above. Our initial dilemma concerned Adila's professional integrity. The reality is that the lack of an intervention in this situation has the potential to lead to highly adverse consequences for the well-being of the entire family, so Adila must act. While she needs to be aware of issues of culture, language and religion, she needs to interpret these through the realisation of the profound levels of change and disorientation the whole family will be experiencing. In this sense, both Mr and Mrs Ali need to be worked with on an understanding of the multiple levels of trauma they have experienced, both in terms of why they have had to leave their country of origin, as well as the anomie of becoming 'asylum seekers' in another country. The key issue here for the social worker is not to work with the family to reconstruct their previous cultural order, but rather to enable the family to engage in a transformative process whereby they develop a new identity. This does not have to be seen, as it so often is, as built around a negation of Islam or being Somalian, but is about situating the universal capabilities which Nussbaum identifies into a particular situation. In saying this it is crucial to bear in mind that questions of women's rights and gender roles need to be seen not as Western constructs, but as universal constructs upon which cultural and religious identities can, and will continue to be, created. It is in this sense, as we have argued elsewhere, that social workers need to see themselves as *transformative intellectuals* (Singh and Cowden, 2009). This involves Adila utilising a range of pedagogical strategies to enable, as Nussbaum suggests, the capability of developing critical reflection about one's life and enabling her to develop her own voice or extend her capacity to express her freedom of speech.

Conclusion

The main thrust of this chapter has been to explore the limits of cultural relativism and in doing so assert the need for social work to develop and articulate a clear Universalist standpoint. We have pointed out that the emergence of demands for a cultural relativist approach are reflected both in the critiques made by minorities of cultural imperialism and ethnocentrism, and also link with postmodernist assertions of the contingent nature of reality. Interestingly, taken to their extremes both positions, relativism and universalism, become untenable; to assert that reality is wholly fluid is in itself to adopt a form of absolutism. It is also deeply ironic that many of the beneficiaries of these culturally relativist arguments are groups that advocate various forms of religious absolutism. In order to find a way through these paradoxes and problems we have sought to outline the capabilities approach developed by Nussbaum. The distinctive quality of her arguments for Universalist approaches is her idea that irrespective of cultural differences, of which there are many, it is possible for human beings to identify a set of fundamental political entitlements as the basis for making moral and ethical judgements. Whilst we have only taken initial steps in elaborating this approach here, we hope to have indicated the relevance this can have for social work and clearly much more work is needed on this.

If one accepts that culture is a prerequisite for any kind of human exchange, in the final reckoning, the issue is not about whether or not we should adopt a cultural perspective, but how one can avoid drifting into a cultural relativism which discounts the possibility of making judgements about others. We argue that in seeking to respect cultural diversity, there is also a moral imperative to celebrate aspects of our common humanity. Even if for a complex set of reasons not always expressed, this is to be most readily found in the deep-rooted aspirations that all human beings have for freedom from oppression, as Slavoj Žižek asserts:

The formula of revolutionary solidarity is not "let us tolerate our differences"; it is not a pact of civilisations, but a pact of struggles which cut across civilisations, a pact between what, in each civilisation, undermines its own identity from within, fights against its oppressive kernel. What unites us is the same struggle. (2009: 133)

Further Reading

Nussbaum, M.C. (2011) *Creating Capabilities: The Human Development Approach*. Cambridge, MA: Belknap/Harvard University Press: Although surprisingly little reference of her work is made in social work, as one of the most preeminent moral philosophers of our time, Martha Nussbaum has written widely on human development and the ethics of social justice. This book provides an accessible summary to Nussbaum's work which directly addresses the tensions associated with respecting cultural diversity and traditions whilst recognising the growing impact of universal human rights based culture.

Singh., G. and Cowden, S. (2011) 'Multiculturalism's New Faultlines: Religious Fundamentalisms and Public Policy', *Critical Social Policy*, 31(3), August 2011, pp. 343–64: As well as reviewing the direction of multicultural social policy over the past this piece offers a critical examination of the tensions that have emerged amongst policy makers, activists and professionals surrounding the (re)emergence what can be termed the 'faith agenda'. Using the case of Shabina Begum, a Muslim schoolgirl who demanded to wear the jilbab to school, the paper is interested in understanding the curiously paradoxical place of religion and faith based groupings in the contemporary multicultural polity.

Yuval-Davis, N. (2011) *The Politics of Belonging: Intersectional Contestations*. London: Sage Publications: This book offers a critical examination of the related issues of culture, identity, religion and State with a particular emphasis on questions of gender. In doing so it offers a contemporary framework for addressing the tensions related to issues of cosmopolitan versus parochial identities. The way in which it links these to questions of both 'care' and 'autonomy' make it particularly relevant for social work.

References

Ahmad, B. (1990) *Black Perspectives in Social Work.* London: Venture Press.

Ahmed, S., Cheetham, J. and Small, J. (eds) (1986) *Social Work with Black Children and Their Families*: Child Care Policy and Practice Series. London: Batsford/BAAF.

Amnesty International (2009) *State of the Worlds Human Rights.* Amnesty. org.uk. http://www.amnesty.org.uk/news_details.asp?NewsID=18219 [Accessed on 16 September 2012]

Barn, B. (1993) *Black Children in the Public Care System.* London: British Agencies for Adoption and Fostering.

Bhatt, C. (2006) 'The Fetish of the Margin: Religious Absolutism, Anti-Racism and Postcolonial Silence', *New Formations,* 59, pp. 98–115.

Boas, F. (1974) [1887] 'The Principles of Ethnological Classification', in George W. Stocking Jr. (ed.), *A Franz Boas Reader.* Chicago: University of Chicago Press.

Bowling, B., Parmar, A. and Phillips, C. (2008) 'Policing Minority Ethnic Communities', in T. Newburn (ed.), *Handbook of Policing.* Cullompton, UK: Willan Publishing, pp. 528–55, http://eprints.lse.ac.uk/9576/1/Policing_ethnic_minority_communities_(LSERO).pdf [Accessed 1 February 2012].

CCCS (1982) *The Empire Strikes Back: Race and Racism in 70's Britain.* London: Hutchinson.

Charusheela, S. (2008) 'Social Analysis and the Capabilities Approach: A limit to Martha Nussbaum's Universalist Ethics', *Cambridge Journal of Economics,* doi:10.1093/cje/ben027, pp. 1–18, http://phil.unlv.edu/charusheela-nussbaum-final-cje.pdf [Accessed 30 January 2012].

Cheetham, J. (ed.) (1981) *Social Work and Ethnicity.* London: Allen and Unwin.

Cowden, S. and Pullen, A. (2012) *The Ethical Foundations of Social Work.* London: Longman-Pearson.

Crabtree, S.A, Hussein, F. and Spalekv, B. (2008) *Islam and Social Work: Debating values, transforming practice.* Bristol: Policy Press.

Devore, W. and Schlesinger, E.G. (1991) *Ethnic-sensitive Social Work Practice.* New York: Macmillan Publishing Company.

Dominelli, L. (2008). *Antiracist Social Work* (3rd Edition). Basingstoke: Palgrave Macmillan.

Fook, J. (2002) *Social Work: Critical Theory and Practice.* London: Sage.

Gambe, D. (1992) *Improving Practice with Children and Families: A Training Manual.* London: CCETSW.

Gilligan. P. and Furness, S. (2009) *Religion, Belief and Social Work: Making a Difference.* Bristol: Policy Press.

Gilroy, P. (1987a) *There Ain't no Black in the Union Jack.* London: Hutchinson.

Gilroy, P. (1987b) *Problems in Anti-racist Strategy*. London: Runnymede Trust.

Gilroy, P. (1990) 'The end of anti-racism'. *Journal of Ethnic and Migration Studies*, 17(1), pp. 71–83.

Graham, M. (2002) *Social Work and African-Centred Worldviews*. London: Ventura Press.

Gray, M. and Webb, S. (2010) *Ethics and Value Perspectives in Social Work*. London: Palgrave Macmillan.

Grell, R.O. and Scribner, B. (2002) *Tolerance and Intolerance in the European Reformation*. Cambridge: Cambridge University Press.

Hall, S. (1992) 'The Question of Cultural Identity', in S. Hall, D. Held and T. McGrew (eds), *Modernity and its Futures*. Cambridge, UK: Polity Press in Association with the Open University, pp. 273–316.

Hall, S., Critcher, C., Jefferson, T., et al. (1978) *Policing the Crisis: Mugging, the State and Law and Order*. London: Macmillan.

Healy, L.M. (2007) 'Universalism and Cultural Relativism in Social Work Ethics'. *International Social Work*, 2007, 50(1), pp. 11–26.

Herz, M. (2012) '"Doing" social work: Critical considerations on theory and practice in social work'. *Advances in Social Work*, 13(3), pp. 1527–8565.

Health Professions Council (2012) *Standards of Proficiency for Social Work*, http://www.hpc-uk.org/assets/documents/10003B08Standardsofproficie ncy-SocialworkersinEngland.pdf [Accessed 17 September 2012].

IFSW (2000) International Federation of Social Work: Definition of social work, http://www.ifsw.org/f38000138.html [Accessed 30 January 2012].

Malik, K. (1996) *The Meaning of Race: Race, History and Culture in Western Society*. London: Macmillan.

Mullaly, R.P. (2006) *The New Structural Social Work: Ideology, Theory and Practice*. Oxford: Oxford University Press.

McLaughlin, K. (2005) 'From ridicule to institutionalization: Anti-Oppression, the State and Social Work'. *Critical Social Policy*, 25(3), pp. 283–305.

Nussbaum, M.C. and Sen, A. (eds) (1993) *The Quality of Life*. Oxford: Clarendon Press.

Nussbaum, M.C. (2000) *Women and Human Development: The Capabilities Approach*. Cambridge: Cambridge University Press.

Nussbaum, M.C (2011) *Creating Capabilities: The Human Development Approach. Martha C. Nussbaum*. Cambridge, MA: Harvard University Press.

Robinson, L. (2009) *Psychology for Social Workers: Black Perspectives on Human Development and Behaviour*. London: Routledge.

Singh, G. (1992) *Race and Social Work: from Black Pathology to Black Perspectives*. Race Relations Research Unit: University of Bradford.

Singh, G. (1999) 'Race' and The Child Protection System' in Violence Against Children Group (eds), *Child Abuse and Child Protection: Placing Children Centrally*. London: Pavilion Publishing.

Singh, G. (2002) 'The Political Challenge of Anti-racism in Health and Social Care', in D. Tomlinson and W. Trew, *Equalising Opportunities, Minimising Oppression*, London: Routledge.

Singh, G. and Cowden, S. (2009) 'The Social Worker as Intellectual', *European Journal of Social Work*, 12(4), December 2009, pp. 479–93.

Singh, G. and Cowden, S. (2011) 'Multiculturalism's New Faultlines: Religious Fundamentalisms and Public Policy', *Critical Social Policy*, 31(3), August 2011, pp. 343–64.

Sivanandan, A. (1990) *Communities of Resistance – Writings on Black Struggles for Socialism*. London: Verso.

Sivanandan, A. (1991) 'Black Struggles Against Racism', in *Northern Curriculum Development Project, Setting the Context of Change: Anti-racist Social Work Education*. Leeds: CCETSW.

Williams, F (1996) 'Racism and the Discipline of Social Policy: A Critique of Welfare Theory', in D. Taylor (ed.), *Critical Social Policy: A Reader*. London: Sage, pp. 48–76.

Žižek, S. (2009) *Violence*. London: Profile Books.

4 To Touch or Not to Touch? Exploring the Dilemmas and Ambiguities Associated with Touch in Social Work and Social Care Settings

Lorraine Green and Ros Day

Introduction

In early years child care, primary school education and in residential children's homes, some, particularly male staff, go to extraordinary lengths to avoid being alone with or touching children. These workers consequently often showcase their constant visibility and 'safe practice' in order to avoid potential, feared allegations of inappropriate conduct (Cameron, 2001; Green and Parkin, 1999; Jones, 2004; Owen and Gillentine, 2011; Piper and Smith, 2003). In most social work (SW) and social care settings (SC), many already abused and multiply disadvantaged service users are often deprived of touch and are 'touch hungry' (Lynch and Garrett, 2010) or have previously been violated through abusive touch. They therefore may respond by avoiding touch completely or search for it covertly or in ways that place them at further risk of exploitation. Alternatively, they may impose touch on others in an aggressive or socially unacceptable manner. In one residential children's home studied by one of the authors the teenage boys often accessed touch through initiating 'play fighting' with other children and staff but when this was banned they devised other inventive and covert ways of meeting their touch needs:

What happens with the lads is now they can't get close to you by horseplay, is they will give you a dig on the arm or tap or brush against you. It's a way of getting contact but not being seen as soft. (Male residential worker, cited in Green, 2005)

Another residential worker interviewed by Green who worked in a different residential home recounted initially being very unsure about what kinds of sexualised touch behaviour between residents were normal and acceptable.

When I first started here one lad kept on grabbing another between the legs and the younger lad didn't like it. However, when I asked the manager what to do she just ignored it. And I kept on asking myself is it normal for 12- and 13-year-old lads to be grabbing each other between the legs and I just didn't know what to do. (Female residential worker cited in Green and Masson, 2002: 160)

In the research on residential care cited above, although the prime focus was on sexuality and sexual exploitation, ethical dilemmas and issues associated with touch were numerous and pertinent examples included: sexually abusive staff grooming children through affectionate apparently platonic touch which then slowly and subtly became sexual; touch being used by staff to dominate, control and sometimes restrain teenage residents; teenage boys touching female staff in ways the staff perceived as sexual and intimidating; younger children placed in residential care because they had very sexualised behaviour which foster carers could not accommodate, subjecting other residents and staff to unwanted sexualised touch; teenage boys using play fighting to both meet their touch needs and assert their dominance over other boys and girls; residents having sex with other residents and being vulnerable to the advances of predatory outsiders because they craved the physical contact or were unable to say 'no'; male staff vigorously avoiding any form of supportive touch with female residents for fear of false allegations. Although this research focused on children's homes, it is not only residential care where touch and the body are pertinent. The 'care and control of client bodies, particularly disenfranchised bodies lies at the heart of social work's disciplinary activities' (Tangenberg and Kemp, 2002: 9). Many clients come to the attention of social workers when their bodies are seen to be out of control; for example drug users, adults with physical illnesses and disabilities and maltreated children. Alternatively, social work intervenes when bodies have to be restrained or forcibly removed. This might occur with a mental health section, the removal of a child at risk or a distressed child or adult with learning disabilities 'acting out'.

The topic of touch is therefore an ever-present but often taboo and rarely appropriately addressed topic within SW. This chapter explores the importance of and the dangers associated with touch within SW/SC, including the ethics and prohibitions surrounding it, concentrating predominantly on touch between workers and service users. The chapter begins by citing some real-life scenarios in order to illuminate the breadth and depth of touch issues in SW and SC, many of which are discussed later. It then reviews the available research on touch and SW, despite a paucity of touch literature in SW and in most disciplines. Following this extant multidisciplinary literature involving touch is then analysed. The second section analyses psychological and clinical research on touch, attachment and emotional bonding and its implications. Differential, normative touch practices according to culture, age, gender and other factors are also evaluated. Sociological and philosophical conceptualisations of touch are then introduced. The final section justifies the use of considered touch in social work and social care according to different moral philosophy perspectives and reviews the literature previously examined in relation to its relevance to SW. It then returns to some of the ethically problematic case examples mentioned in the first section, suggesting possible responses.

Social Work, Social Care and Touch

> Bodies are always thoroughly entangled processes ... defined by their capacities to affect and be affected ... (and) there are forms of bodily memory which lie outside a subject's conscious reflections ... and trauma (which) can be transmitted across generations and enacted through bodily forms of knowing. (Blackman and Venn, 2010: 9/18)

The preceding quote was chosen to premise the section dealing with social work literature and to frame the following, real-life examples of touch issues in social work and care. These are numbered for easy reference as they are discussed at different points in the chapter.

1. A sexually abused nine-year-old girl who is in a residential children's home keeps on climbing onto the laps of the male residential workers and rubbing herself against them. They are horrified and immediately push her off telling her she is dirty.
2. A social worker sits with a traumatised female service user whose husband has a terminal illness. The social worker intuitively feels she should put her hand on the woman's arm to comfort her but is scared of how she might react.
3. A new foster carer asks the social worker for advice on how she should show affection to her foster children. The social worker stresses that she should not treat them as her own children in case they have been

abused and she must always show affection in a way that protects her from allegations, but other than that gives her no guidance.

4. A young, gay, HIV-positive man tells his social worker that no one will ever love him or want a relationship with him ever again. The social worker wants to gently lie his hand on the man's shoulder to convey acceptance and understanding but feels he will violate professional boundaries.

5. An isolated elderly Italian lady with mental health difficulties always sits so close to the social worker on the only settee in the flat that she is actually touching her. The social worker feels discomforted by this but does not know what to do.

6. A social worker is working with a disadvantaged single parent with three young children. The mother loves her children but is unable to express any physical affection towards them. They are always running up to strangers in the street and chatting to them and hugging them.

7. Four teenage boys live in a children's home with mostly male residential workers. They try to initiate play fighting with each other and the workers but this is not allowed because it often degenerates into violent fights. One of the workers describes the way the boys often deliberately brush against him to get physical contact because this is the only acceptable masculine way they can procure touch.

8. A frustrated woman with learning disabilities and little verbal communication starts throwing around furniture at the day centre she attends, placing herself and the other service users at risk. The workers immediately restrain her.

9. A social worker is transporting two young children to a supervised contact visit with their father. He walks with them to the car holding both their hands. He then picks up the youngest one and puts him securely into the child seat whilst also physically helping the older one to fasten the seat belt.

Such scenarios may seem common but all involve ethical dilemmas and ambiguities and there is little in terms of SW education, training, literature, research evidence or codes of conduct to advise or guide social workers (Lynch and Garrett, 2010; Strozier et al., 2003). This deficit is interesting since communication is a key and contested aspect of the SW role (see for instance Koprowska, 2008 and Laming, 2003). Communication literature and teaching tends to cover language first and then gestures, facial expression and eye contact (i.e. the visual), rather than touch, although occasionally touch is referred to in teaching materials regarding cultural differences (e.g. Thompson, 2011: 169). This lack is consistent with the general cultural privileging of the visual over the other senses (Van Dongen and Elema, 2001), and of the mind and intellect over the body. Even the one book written on social work and the body surprisingly contains no reference to touch within it (Cameron and McDermott, 2007). The quote that preceded the aforementioned examples, however, underlines the importance and complexity of bodily communication and flags up how trauma may semi-consciously or unconsciously be communicated bodily rather than linguistically, an important fact to be aware of when working with service users who often have been repeatedly abused and marginalised.

The minimal social work and social care research conducted which relates to touch, will now be analysed, but the studies examined here mostly involve small-scale qualitative research with purposive or self-selected samples. These studies are, despite this, useful in that they often involve phenomenological and hermeneutic understandings about a poorly researched area and flag up areas and questions for further research. The eight social work interviewees who participated in a recent small-scale qualitative study asserted touch practices with children, initiated by the children or used for safety reasons, (as in Example 9), were the most appropriate forms (Lynch and Garrett, 2010). They acknowledged touch could additionally express empathy, reassure service users and help build relationships but they were wary those types of touch might be misinterpreted. They were also unequivocally emphatic that touch should never be deployed to gratify the social worker's own emotional needs, although this level of emotional self-awareness may be difficult to find especially when social workers are under stress.

Rees and Pithouse's (2008) research focused on the private worlds of foster carers and involved a purposive sample of ten foster families in South Wales. They, in stark contrast to the situation in residential care, found most of their foster carer respondents were prepared to either spontaneously, or in a more planned self-conscious manner, cuddle, hug and physically reassure children and that the notion of 'symbolic' care and nurturing was very important to those children. This is an interesting finding, given that the advice given to foster carers (such as in Example 3), about treating foster children not as your own is often fairly standard advice. Steckley's (2011) research on physical restraint in children's homes involved 78 in-depth interviews, including vignette scenarios, with children and residential workers across 20 different self-selecting establishments in Scotland. Steckley found that fear of false allegations often led to staff avoiding affectionate or supportive physical contact with children. Physical restraint was the most accepted common form of staff/child touch, with some children appearing to deliberately engineer a restraint to elicit touch from staff, despite the children also talking of the physical pain endured during some restraints. Children also differentiated between staff they felt were sadistic when they restrained them and others who they respected and trusted because they were gentle.

In Green's earlier research in children's homes which was predominately about sexuality, sexual abuse and gender, the importance of touch manifested itself in many different ways (Green, 1998; 2000; 2001; 2005; Green and Masson, 2002; Green and Parkin, 1999). Green's research involved ethnographic fieldwork in two children's homes, documentary analysis of newspaper reportage of staff/child abuse in care homes and agency documents, and over a hundred semi-structured interviews. These interviews were conducted with residential workers and children both inside and external to these homes and with ex-residents and other pertinent personnel such as HIV workers, aftercare workers, social workers and external managers from a range of other settings across the country. Many of the often already abused and neglected teenagers or adult ex-residents disclosed being prepared to trade in sex for physical affection and sometimes material goods such as cigarettes and money either with their peers or with exploitative outsiders. The following is an excerpt of a conversation between a young adult male ex-resident and the researcher where he recounts the sexual encounters he had with a teenage girl who had lived in the same children's home.

> One young girl had been sexually abused. She'd lost her little finger because she had refused to give her stepfather a blow job and he had chopped it off. I became very attracted to her physically and she was very sexually learned. She used to say I'll give you a blow job for a packet of fags and I don't think I ever refused.
>
> (Q) "Did she get anything out of sex with you?"
> (A) "Yes because of her fags."
> (Q) "Did she get anything else out of it?"
> (A) "No, not at all." (Green and Parkin, 1999: 179)

Many children also manifested very unclear boundaries between platonic and sexual touch affection. Current and former residents were often unable to clearly articulate why they had sex with other residents but appeared to see it as either something they were unable to say no to, a fleeting form of companionship and physical contact, or in some cases, more notable with males, a form of conquest.

> It [sex] was an easy commodity, so it did go on. I think a lot of kids did it … because they needed somebody [whether] it was for five minutes or the whole night you needed somebody. Everybody does and that was the only way we had with each other. (Female ex-resident cited in Green, 2000)

> Sex was absolutely nothing to do with feelings, love and emotions. It … made me feel good … the conquest was probably the most important thing looking back. The lads used to compare notes about how far we'd got with particular people. You just went from one to another. (Male ex-resident cited in Green and Parkin, 1999: 178)

The earlier example (7) of teenage boys covertly brushing against male workers in an attempt to procure touch in a macho way also came from this research, as did young children trying to engage with workers in sexualised ways, but workers responding in a horrified manner because they had had no training to deal with such personally and professionally challenging behaviour (1). Restraint practices were common, as in Steckley's research detailed above, but any kind of affectionate or reassurance touch was stringently avoided because of fear of allegations, particularly between male workers and female residents. Little concern was shown about men modelling and demonstrating appropriate caring and affectionate behaviour to girls and boys who had little idea or experience of what this might be. One pertinent example of touch avoidance was provided in an interview by a male residential worker who was doing a night shift alone.

> One night after all the other staff had gone home unbeknownst to me one of the girls got drunk and I was told she was ill in the toilet. So I went in there and she looked as if she was unconscious … and she only had this really flimsy top and bed shorts on. I thought I can't leave her there but if I touch her I might be in bother. And I know it's not very fair but I had to knock two of the other girls up in the early hours of the morning and ask them to carry her up to bed. (Green and Parkin, 1999: 183)

Many of the residential workers interviewed for this particular research project (Green, 1998; 1999; 2001; 2005) also said that if ever teenage girls were upset they would never talk to them alone in their bedrooms but would converse from outside in the corridor. Similar behaviours and fears exist with male teachers and male volunteers, particularly in primary schools (Neuberger, 2008; Piper and Smith, 2003) and with children's sports coaches (e.g. Lang et al., 2010). Not only do such actions restrict trusting and 'intimate' communication, rendering it limited and superficial, they absolutely foreclose any possibility of supportive touch between the two people concerned. The artificial subdivision of the public and private spheres, with residential care settings being both part of large *organisations* where people work (sometimes acting in loco parentis as corporate or state parents) and the *homes* of children and adults, also creates confusion and ambiguities about appropriate behaviour. Therefore, acceptance of public sphere rules such as 'no touch' tends to predominate over private sphere rules which would encourage touch and affection (Green and Parkin, 1999). This may well explain why in 'private' foster homes, affectionate and reassuring physical touch is more accepted than in 'public' children's homes and schools.

Ferguson (2011) argues for the central importance of touch, particularly with younger children in child protection work, asserting that if workers engage physically with children, their assessments are likely to be more accurate. In relation to the Peter Connelly (Baby P) case (Laming, 2009), Ferguson implicitly suggests that if the social worker had physically wiped the cream off the child's face, thereby revealing the injuries hidden beneath, (this visit occurring a few days before Peter's death), rather than asking someone else to do it, who then failed to return, the tragedy could possibly have been avoided. Ferguson (2011) traces child protection back to the early twentieth century when child protection officers failed to touch children linked to fear not only of physical contamination because of the squalor and 'dirtiness' of their houses, clothing and bodies, but also due to 'moral' pollution and fear of the 'other'. Ferguson subsequently argues, although overt feelings of disgust and contamination fears seemed less acceptable in social work from the 1970s on, (presumably when ethics of *respect for persons, non judgementalism* and *individualisation* became widely accepted), they still linger on unacknowledged, impacting on practice. Ferguson cites the example of many professionals failing to touch or intervene with Victoria Climbié (another child who died at the hands of her carers). The fact she was smelly, unkempt, incontinent, black and 'foreign', spoke a different language, wore a wig and was alleged to have scabies, appear to have contributed to this multi-professional failure to respond appropriately. Similarly, media accounts of Peter Connelly emphasised the dirty conditions he lived in and the fact he had nits. Anthropological understandings of purity and impurity, taboo, disgust and pollution may give theoretical clarity to these ideas (Douglas, 1966 and Dumont, 1970 deal with such issues).

Fears of the 'other' and of moral and material contamination are, however, not the only reasons social workers fail to touch service users today. In the 1970s it was acceptable and 'good practice' to pick up children, play with them and comfort them and this is still the case in some other countries such as South Africa (Lynch and Garrett, 2010). In today's neo-liberal Western risk societies we attempt to prevent any adverse occurrences by taking as few risks as possible (Beck, 1992; Douglas, 1992) and this has led to teachers being unprepared to even apply a plaster to a child's scratched arm. 'No touch' formal or informal policies/rules are often standard in many SW and SC organisations (Pemberton, 2010) despite no evidence that false allegations are rising over time (Piper, 2006). These pertain particularly to heterosexual men and girls, but the taboos are even stronger around openly gay men alone with boys, or men whose sexuality is unknown or who are heterosexual but are seen to be 'effeminate' by other workers and therefore assumed to be gay (Green, 2005). This is not to undermine the terrible consequences false allegations can lead to or to disregard how some male workers working with children feel continually under surveillance and suspicion. However, if all males working with children always defensively distance themselves, this presents men as both physically and emotionally unavailable, and creates a paranoid climate. Social work organisations therefore seem to be privileging their ability to protect themselves from feared allegations over the care, development and attachment needs of the service users they are ostensibly there to support. It is also possible that this situation has assumed the mantel of a moral panic (Ungar, 2001) which occurs when a certain issue is reported, sensationalised and exaggerated by the media and various high status commentators to the point people's fear of it becomes disproportionate to its actual likelihood. This links to McLaughlin's (2008) thesis on risk-averse cultures that exaggerate abuse/neglect and promote a pathological fear of the other, including of colleagues, thereby instilling a negative general view of human nature whilst encouraging service user dependency on professionals.

This poses the question as to whether 'safe' and 'ethical' *professional* practice coincide or conflict? Does safe practice mean ensuring the worker is unlikely to be accused of abuse but only through subverting the norms of good social work/care practice which involves assessing needs and supporting, empowering and enabling vulnerable individuals? It is undoubtedly true that unfounded allegations often cause great anguish, but they are much rarer than often assumed. Green (1998) furthermore suggested that the upset experienced in cases of unfounded allegations was often more linked to the punitive manner in which workers were dealt with organisationally than the actual allegation itself. The risks of and the subsequent low probability adverse event we are trying to pre-empt and prevent also has to be weighed against what is lost through defensive practice, as Munro (2011) has also argued more generally of current child protection practice. Perhaps open discussions about touch, sexuality and appropriate boundaries and a preparedness to engage with reassurance or affectionate touch with some service users, teenagers in care being a prime example, could avert some of the tragedies. It is therefore clearly important that social welfare workers are aware of the literature on touch and can take this into account when deciding when and if to engage with touch practices. The following sections therefore review the extant, but fairly minimal, multidisciplinary literature on touch, relating them to SW and SC. After this, it will be ascertained how helpful this literature might be for resolving ethical dilemmas and ambiguities surrounding touch.

Touch, Attachment and Emotional Bonding

Touch is the first sense we acquire in the uterus and the last we lose. Our skin, through which we receive and process touch, is also our largest sensory organ. Positive attachment behaviours have been shown throughout life to involve affectionate and intimate touch which bonds individuals together (Takeuchi et al., 2010). Children from deprived orphanage situations have consistently suffered multiple, sometimes irreversible, psychological, social and neurological problems (Maclean, 2003), but disentangling the effects of touch deficit or abusive touch from other deprivations suffered is complex. The emotional importance of touch is also demonstrated in our language, language which we commonly use but rarely analyse (Montagu, 1971). 'Out of touch' and 'tactless' are negative terms, suggesting an inability to take into account or connect with someone's feelings or a misapprehension of a situation, whereas if someone is 'touched' by something it means the experience contains deep emotional resonance. Various studies have also verified the existence of 'touch hunger' whereby individuals may be deprived of sufficient positive human touch but their reactions to this may vary from avoiding intimate touch completely to searching for it in the most inappropriate ways and situations (Field, 2001).

Ecologically valid social-psychological research studies suggest the most cursory of touches, such as a librarian brushing against someone's hand when returning their card, are likely to predispose the borrower favourably to them (Fischer et al., 1976). People are more likely to be compliant with suggestions, for example in relation to medication adherence (Chang, 2000; Guegen et al., 2010) or the purchase of an item, such as a car (Erceau and Guegen, 2007) and trust and like people more if they are touched by them. This issue however, is much more complex and multifaceted than the experiments above initially suggest. Aside from the disputed morality of deliberately manipulating touch to obtain desired outcomes, where someone is touched, who by and within what context are vital considerations. One study reported being touched by a co-worker on the face as the most offensive touch interaction most people could conceive of and being touched on the shoulder by an unknown person as the least offensive (Lee and Guerro, 2001).

In traditional Freudian-influenced psychoanalysis touching patients was proscribed because of its assumed relationship with sexual feelings. Reservations were expressed about positive or negative transference. This refers to the un- or semi-conscious patient's displacement of negative, positive, aggressive, affectionate or sexual feelings from their origins (such as birth parent or partner) onto the therapist. However despite this concern, much literature suggests planned and well-thought out psychotherapeutic touch can be positive and healing for children and adults (McNeil-Haber, 2004; Phelan, 2009). Bick, furthermore, claims that a secure self and a sense of containment can only be achieved through extensive skin to skin touch contact with a caregiver (Bick, 1987) and touch deficit may also contribute to children failing to thrive (Le Breton, 2003). Such claims and research help reinforce the argument for the use of 'holding' and nurturing touch in psychotherapy, psychoanalysis and possibly in SW too but with many provisos and cautions. The next section also shows how touch norms vary greatly according to cultural, individual and societal differences.

Ritual Greetings and Gender, Age, Culture and Status Differences with Touch

People from diverse cultures often greet each other differently. In Italy a kiss on the cheek and a hug is routine whereas in Japan a formal bow with no touch is normal. In Southern Europe people are more touch-orientated regarding greetings and departures than elsewhere in Europe, such as the UK (Remland et al., 1995). Touch practices will also vary according to the nature of the relationship, the context, cultural norms, age, gender, social class and sexual orientation (Derlega et al., 1989; Dibiase and Gunnoe, 2004; Guthrie and James, 2007; Willis and Dodds, 1998).

In early research, men were found to initiate touch with women more than women with men (Henley, 1973). This was attributed to men generally possessing more power than women and viewing touching women as an automatic right, although later research has produced mixed findings (Fuller et al., 2010), possibly because of increasingly equalised relationships between the sexes. Higher status individuals such as managers, however, still touch *their* lower status subordinates more than vice versa (Heaphy, 2007). Homophobia and the often associated enactment of powerful masculinities (such as those found in politicians, corporate businessmen and sporting heroes) and less powerful but sanctioned heterosexual and virulently homophobic masculinities, such as the apparently hard macho physically and mentally strong working-class man (Connell, 1995), consolidate patriarchal power. They therefore reinforce status divisions between men and other men and men and women. These heterosexist, but powerful masculine performatives and prescriptions, have in some cultures, effectively debarred men from touching other men affectionately but platonically (Derlega et al., 1989; Floyd, 2000), presumably for fear of stigmatisation through emasculation and homophobic violence. In one Polish study a man touching another unknown man's arm, whilst making a request, diminished the chances of that request being fulfilled (Dolinski, 2010). This may partially explain the example (9), given at the beginning of the chapter, whereby teenage boys in children's homes instigated play fights with each other and brushed against workers to gain touch. Women are also likely to touch each other more than men because their friendships are often less competitive and involve more open intimacy and trust (Derlega et al., 1989; Green, 2010). Recent laboratory research showed that decoding the emotional content of touch when other cues, such as vision and voice tone, are absent could be done at higher than chance estimates for happiness, sympathy, sadness, anger, disgust, gratitude, fear and love (Hertenstein et al., 2009). When this research was later re-analysed in relation to gender it was found women scored better at this than men (Hertenstein and Keltner, 2011) and they also repeatedly perform better on general measures of interpersonal sensitivity (Hall et al., 2000; Rossop and Hall, 2004). This may be because women have traditionally occupied most paid and unpaid caring roles in society and through socialisation and culture have become skilled at both conveying meaning through touch and interpreting it.

In nursing research in hospitals, patients have often been found to subjectively and objectively respond positively to supportive touch. However, in one study where a nurse touching a patient was measured to see how far it decreased stress measures, evaluated through self report and heart rate and blood pressure, positive effects were only found in female patients. The authors hypothesised that men interpreted being touched as denoting dependency and emasculating them (Whitcher and Fisher, 1979). In other research when GPs, as opposed to nurses, touched patients on the forearm this touch was received favourably by both sexes (Guegen et al., 2007) but more by male patients. The fact that these particular men were not in a hospital setting and therefore potentially less vulnerable could have been important, alongside the more elevated status of a GP vis-à-vis a nurse. Positive touching such as baby massage as a means of bonding with an infant and the use of alternative touch therapies in pain management and hospices are noteworthy here as seemingly unproblematic examples. There therefore seems to be an issue emerging of touch and age or touch and status, as well as gender issues related to touch here, but the inter-relationships between them require further research.

Social Constructionism and Mind/Body Dualism

The preceding sections evaluated mostly positivistic, experimental, clinical and psychological research. However, sociological and philosophical literature communicates more nuanced and less definitive understandings of embodiment that are subjectively and historically located. Most sociologists repudiate the Cartesian model of mind/body dualism, whereby historically and through medical and media discourse, body and mind are seen as separate spheres rather than mutually interactive and conjoined.

The mind is therefore frequently privileged over and demarcated from the debased body which is seen as unreliable, leaky and uncontained and being driven by physical needs and urges. Sociology also asserts more socially constructed views of the body, rejecting biologically determinist explanations. Although some sociologists see the body as completely determined or inscribed upon by culture – *hard constructionism* (e.g. Butler, 1993; Foucault, 1979) many others integrate both mind and body into their explanations – *soft constructionism* (Shilling, 1993; Turner, 1986). Touch is also different from our other senses. Merleau-Ponty's phenomenology of the body demonstrates how even if we de-privilege the body versus the mind, we do not *have* a body or *own* a body, we *are* a body, *our* body and that body is the mediator through which all our senses and feelings are experienced. Consequently when we touch someone we also touch ourselves and are therefore are quite literally embodied and connected with them yet separate at the same time.

To illustrate how the biological, the social and the psychological need to be incorporated when dealing with touch, physiological research claims there are portions of the skin that when touched in a particular way or with a certain textural feel, such as velvet (Francis et al., 1999), invoke pleasurable effects. Touch associated with reduced stress in early childhood has also been found to elicit a positive response in later life (Reite, 1990). We also possess other skin receptors which register pain. However, if someone has received initially pleasurable skin touches followed by or merged with abusive or exploitative touch, then similar 'pleasant' touch at a later period in time may invoke ambivalence or even repulsion. Even when no such past experiences are evident, touch with no sexual intention may be received sexually or touch with sexual connotations may not be read as such, for example, in relation to the corporal punishment of children (Green et al., 2002). Some individuals also engage consensually in sadomasochistic sexual relationships because of the pleasure gained from that infliction of pain in that particular context. So personal as well as cultural and gendered readings alongside biology are important regarding how we enact, physically experience and interpret touch.

Touch as 'Body Work' and 'Emotional Labour'

Sociology is also increasingly focusing on *body work* in health and SC as well as in consumer industries. This is paid work which involves engaging with the bodies of others (for example, surveillance, diagnosis, handling, treating etc.) and often involves touch. A beautician performs body work as does a nurse, doctor or a care worker who washes, dresses and feeds a disabled person. Many of the jobs involving body work are stereotyped as women's jobs because women are seen to be naturally 'closer' to the body and more caring (Twigg, 2000). In contrast, traditional masculinity is based around notions of physical and psychological invulnerability. This makes care work, particularly that involving touch, affection and nurturance more challenging for many men. This may be another unstated reason, other than fear of false allegations as to why many men avoid supportive touch in care work. Additionally, the ageing body, as well as disabled, sick and deviant bodies, such as those of drug takers and homeless people, which social workers and care workers often interact with, are stigmatised, devalued and associated with dirt, decay, deficit and decrement (Twigg et al., 2010) as well as moral pollution. There is also the additional stigma attached to so called 'dirty work' with 'social undesirables' (Hughes, 1958; Pinker, 1971). Another reason why ageing and infirm bodies are maligned in a contemporary late modern society may be because of the value we place on science, rationality, youth, beauty and the individual. This exists alongside views of the body as a lifelong project (Giddens, 1991) we can engineer and 'improve' throughout life through processes such as body building, plastic surgery, dieting, tattooing and make up. When this becomes less possible because of age or illness, it threatens the over-elevated significance we place on the individual, their life and on the power of science to resolve all problems.

This also helps to explain why people may be filled with disgust at the thought of or during the experience of engaging with other's bodies in the course of their paid work, as highlighted by Ferguson earlier in relation to child protection, 'dirty' houses and working class children. In research with experienced nurses on psycho-geriatric long-term wards, many reported feeling repulsed at some physical tasks, such as cleaning up faeces, but were gentle with their patients, never forgetting they were people who had feelings (Van Dongen and Elema, 2001). Although in some sense these nurses were separating the person out from their physical body, they were not treating the body or person as abject or object. In an ethnographic study of care workers, they conversely focused primarily on ensuring their clients' bodies were fit for 'show' or 'window dressing' in the communal areas in the nursing home. They thereby objectified and dehumanised the elderly people (Lee-Trewick, 1997). Goffman's work (1963) on public performances and the private sphere also suggests that the body has to be more managed in public as opposed to private spheres.

Much body work therefore involves *emotional labour*, although separating out emotions from physical labour can, albeit unintentionally, reinforce Cartesian mind-body splitting by elevating the emotional and therefore the mind over the corporeal (Wolkowitz, 2002). Although emotional labour may not involve body work, body work invoking touch in SW and SC often incorporates emotional labour. This involves *expressing* unfelt but occupationally or organisationally required emotions (empathy, fondness, respect, aggression etc.) or sometimes, (as in the case discussed above of experienced nurses) *suppressing* one's actual emotions in one's work to affect another's emotional state. When the worker's expressed emotions are false this is known as *surface acting* but when experienced as genuine, *depth acting*. Social workers are expected to express empathy, acceptance and respect towards all their service users, although some research such as Pithouse's (1987; 1995) ethnography in child care suggests that derision and fear is also common in child protection. Other research, e.g. Carey (2009) conversely suggests although social workers are increasingly encouraged to conduct formal assessments and work in very impersonal and formalised ways with service users, some still resist professional and organisational dictates to be formal, distant and professional. Social workers are therefore continually engaged in emotional labour, heightened by the very nature of the work itself which is saturated and veined through with trauma and uncertainty. In statutory situations, such as those experienced in emergency child protection, workers may need to adopt a more authoritarian and confident impression when they may feel stressed and uncertain. Touch may also be involved in these statutory roles, for example in removing a child from a family or sectioning someone under the Mental Health Act 2007 in Britain. Both social workers and care workers therefore have a great deal of, often unacknowledged *negative* power, over very vulnerable people and can deploy it through offering or withdrawing emotional comfort or through restraint or comfort touch. In one local authority Green researched the only statutory training for children's residential care workers at the time (1996) was a course on 'control and restraint', thereby giving the implicit message that these settings were more about containment than care and development and that only 'negative' touch was permissible.

Body work, is, furthermore, explicitly gendered, racialised and classed. Workers such as residential workers in care homes, hospital cleaners and porters, who often assume jobs closer to the body, are disproportionately likely to be black, foreign – often immigrants from poorer countries – and/or female and working class. These workers are therefore commoditized and financially exploited for their body and emotional work (Wolkowitz, 2002) but rarely receive anything but the most basic forms of generalised training. In research with nurses working on an elderly psychiatric ward, many commented they were denigrated because they did 'bed and body work' which was perceived as dirty, unskilled work, even though they viewed themselves as skilled and experienced professionals. The way workers are treated may have a knock-on effect because if you are disrespected and devalued you may consequently become desensitised to other's needs. Communication mismatch regarding touch is, furthermore, likely if workers come from a different country with different touch norms or, demonstrate, for example, prejudicial attitudes towards gay people, women and children.

Class, culture and age are therefore important for touch practices as are one's bodily and emotional public control as the section below on embodiment and habitus further demonstrates.

Embodiment, 'Habitus' and Touch

Elias (1979) traces from the Middle Ages onwards, the ways in which an increasing distaste and disdain for overt emotions or displays of bodily need or habits, became both socially acquired and psychologically internalised through *the civilizing process*. This led to those who were less able to control their bodily functions, such as a disabled dribbling adult or an elderly person with failing limbs and incontinence issues, becoming devalued and stigmatised. If such theorising is applied to and understood in the context of the low status, limited training and poor pay care work receives, and managerial directives which often emphasise the regulation and satisfaction of physical needs above psychological ones, (and frequent insufficient resources for both), one consequence may be the service users whom care workers 'care' for being treated as abject and their living flesh as 'object bodies', as so many ongoing scandals sadly testify.

People's own view of their bodies and bodily practices are also influenced by their socialisation and culture. Bourdieu (1984, 1990), through French research, demonstrates how the different social classes acquire completely different tastes, habits and ways of presenting themselves bodily – *habitus*. The different social classes are therefore literally differently embodied, *body hexis* representing a form of crystallised body memory impacting on our intuitions, predispositions and common sense (Throop and Murphy, 2002) although each class will experience its communication rituals, tastes and feelings as intuitively natural. Mauss (1973) similarly uses the term 'bodily techniques' to explain how in different societies and historical time periods walking, talking, running, gait, posture and caring mobilise the body differently. Mauss therefore argues social norms and *prestigious imitation* invoke body work as an education. This directs people's activities along certain routes, whilst blocking or discouraging others, creating certain physical rituals and practises. One example might be how experts and cultural ideologies affected parental child touch practices in the twentieth century in the UK and the US. The 1940s, for example, represented the 'no touch' period but by the 1950s Benjamin Spock and other theorists on child rearing completely reversed this trend, encouraging parents to cuddle and physically engage with their children to encourage optimum emotional and social development (Halley, 2007).

Touch and its Relevance for Understanding and Dealing with Touch Situations in Social Work and Social Care

The literature above collated the most important multidisciplinary insights relating to touch practices and explored their relevance for SW and SC. In brief, it found touch could be reassuring, healing, soothing, caring and important for attachment and bonding as well as potentially being constraining, oppressive, aggressive and hostile. Touch was also an indicator of dominance and control but intentions and receptions of touch did not always accord with each other. This might be particularly the case with many of social work's service users who inhabit the margins of society and have long-term experiences of abuse, violence and neglect. Age, culture, gender, race/ethnicity and social class were also found to be key arbitrators of touch, as was the context and individuals' past experiences. In social and educational settings with children, gargantuan fears of false allegations, through malice or misinterpretation, led to many 'no touch' policies which were more about protection of the workers and the organisation than the needs and support of the children. Similarly, in some care settings touch was seen as purely instrumental in terms of washing, cleaning and dressing 'object' bodies. Sociological literature also illustrated the problems with adopting mind/body dualism and SW and SC work were theorised as constituting particular forms of emotional labour and body work.

Ethically, whether or not social workers or SC workers should ever use touch with service users, either to restrain them, or to comfort or reassure, or for other reasons, is a decision no amount of experimental, evidence-based practice literature could help a worker to make. This is because a multiplicity of different understandings and evidence need to be considered as well as ethical considerations and tacit knowledge. Just because something 'works' or is effective, as some of the psychological experiments on touch and compliance and consensus showed, does not mean it is morally justifiable. A Kantian perspective focuses on the development of universally applicable moral rules for conduct, regardless of outcome. It would therefore assert that if it is moral to support and reassure a vulnerable service user through touch, this is the only acceptable behaviour possible, regardless of whether such behaviour may be misinterpreted or manipulated. From a consequentialist and/or utilitarian perspective, if supportive touch practices are likely overall to benefit more service users than disadvantage them, even if the occasional worker is wrongly accused of abuse or impropriety, again they would be justified. From an ethics of care stance, workers have an obligation of care to their clients stemming from the mutuality of the care relationship, which might result in a worker deciding touch practices are appropriate in certain situations. These moral approaches are, however, far more complex than depicted here. They do not give us sufficient guidance to make unequivocally 'right' decisions in complex individual cases, particularly in the risk-averse, harsh, practice environments social workers currently practise in. In these environments 'value' often has to be demonstrated by punitive measurable performance indicators and resources are increasingly stretched. Risk related work, in which the employee will not unusually be expected or may need to respond to events rapidly, is not likely to permit adequate *time* to reflect carefully upon the moral implications of specific responses. There is also the possibility that if touch became more prevalent and accepted within social work, this may be exploited by a small minority of staff.

Social work is also increasingly becoming subsumed under the health rubric and therefore accordingly influenced by 'evidence based practice', linked health research methodologies such as randomised controlled trials and systematic reviews and a medical model agenda (Barnes, Green and Hopton, 2006). The increasingly hostile, distrusting and fearful response of actual and potential service users to social work intervention (Canvin et al., 2007; Smith, 2001; Wrennall, 2010) also currently occurs in a climate where statutory UK social work has become routinised, technologised, managerialised and predominantly focused on control, surveillance and high risk child protection practices (Broadhurst et al., 2010; Wastell et al., 2010). This 'risk society' based social work leads to the defensive, tick box and form-heavy, proceduralised and robotic back-covering practices, which have been acknowledged in part by Munro (2011). Social workers therefore become fearful of using discretion and exercising professional skills and service users frequently register defensiveness and express negativity at the mere presence of a social worker. Such developments, if they can legitimately be called such, do not bode well for the relationship-based and social justice aspects of social work. They also mitigate against social workers understanding and taking on board sociological, phenomenological, holistic and nuanced conceptions of touch and the body rather than simply adhering to 'what works' (quickly and cheaply), or what is procedurally indicated and defensible, regardless of the ethical considerations.

We will now conclude by briefly returning to some of the exemplar ethical dilemmas mentioned earlier and suggest possible ways of optimum working, although simultaneously conceding it may be very difficult and risky to work in such ways, even if they present themselves as the most ethical and just ways of working. With the sexually abused child, who was imposing sexualised touch on the residential workers (1), this situation suggests ongoing skilled therapeutic work is necessary with this child. They need to be helped to understand that affectionate touch is not always sexualised (that sexualised touch is not appropriate between adults and children) and that they do not have to behave in sexualised ways to gain affection and attention. Touch work and other work with this particular child would need to be planned and involve support, education and supervision for the workers too. But to throw a child off one's lap and show disgust when that child has previously been encouraged and rewarded for such behaviour is unethical and rejects and confuses them further, whilst simultaneously leaving them open to further abuse. Similarly, the mother who could not show physical affection to her children requires supportive emotional and educational work to be done with her to meet her needs. She needs help with parenting and to understand that her children need physical affection/reassurance and what dangers might ensue if they continue to be deprived of it (6). With the traumatised HIV-positive man (4), research shows people with HIV/AIDS often have a very negative, contaminated view of their body (Chapman, 2000), so putting a hand on this man's arm to reassure him or convey acceptance could be positive, depending upon the individual, the relationship, the context and setting. A similar evaluation would be needed with the woman whose husband is terminally ill (2). With the teenage boys in the residential home who viewed only unacknowledged and covert touch (in terms of their needs) as acceptable (7), the situation is complex and would require much sensitivity. The boys' only defence may be that charade of masculinity and the male workers may also ascribe to similar masculine performatives. With the social worker holding the small children's hands as they walk to the car and strapping them in the car seats (9), this situation might be interpreted as ethically unproblematic because touch is used pragmatically for safety purposes. However, professionals must understand touch is never just pragmatic and is always interpreted and received in some way. One child who is 'touch hungry' may experience such holding of hands either positively or perhaps negatively because they are so unused to it. Another child's experience of being put in a car may have been linked with past sexual abuse so they again may react in unexpected ways to that touch experience.

To conclude, although the issue of touch raises many ethical and practical questions within social work and care settings, exacerbated by minimal education and training, a paucity of relevant literature, 'no touch' policies, limited resources and defensive cultures in many settings, it is an issue of huge importance. This chapter clearly justifies organisations and policy makers paying much more attention to issues of touch in the public sphere, particularly when the present and future well-being of many vulnerable people is at stake and many service users now live in settings that are operated with the profit motive in mind. Organisations and minimally trained and unsupported staff, as well as qualified workers, may shy away from or legislate against positive touch between workers and service users. History, however, suggests they would be wiser to openly confront and sensitively discuss and deal with such issues rather than adopting a defensive and blinkered stance. A string of ongoing scandals regarding the abuse of vulnerable people, (from the 1969 Ely Hospital scandal – the first big post-war residential abuse scandal) which involved the physical abuse and mental torture of adults with learning disabilities living in a long-stay hospital – to the Pindown Scandal in 1989 (Levy and Kahan, 1991), which exposed the forcible but therapeutically and organisationally sanctioned holding down and secluding of disturbed teenage boys in a secure unit in what were effectively padded cells for long periods of time – to the most recent scandal in April 2012 of a private care facility, graded as excellent by the Quality Care Commission (so much for performance indicators!) where an elderly woman with dementia was repeatedly filmed as part of a Panorama documentary being hit, manhandled and degraded by care staff – would seem to support such a suggestion. With the benefit of the literature contained in this chapter, social welfare workers should now be better able to reflect upon and make responsible, informed and well-justified decisions in relation to touch. Ethical dilemmas, risk, ambiguous situations and misinterpretations will always exist and for the moment most policy directives and managerial dictates appear overwhelmingly concerned about protecting the organisation, even when it is to the detriment of those the organisation is ostensibly there to support and care for.

Further Reading

Gallace, A. and Spence, C. (2010) 'The Science of Interpersonal Touch: An Overview', *Neuroscience and Biobehavioral Reviews*, 34: 249–59: This is a clearly-written, up-to-date and accessible review and summary of the traditional neurological and psychological literature on touch.

Lynch, R. and Garrett, P.M. (2010) '"More Than Words": Touch Practices in Child and Family Social Work', *Child and Family Social Work*, 15: 389–98: This is one of the few articles written that directly links touch to SW. The authors briefly review relevant literature and then contextualise the findings of a small interview study with Irish childcare social workers within such literature, indicating its relevance for social work.

Paterson, M. (2009) 'Haptic Geographies: Ethnography, Haptic Knowledges and Sensusous Dispositions', *Progress in Human Geography*, 33(6): 766–88: This article was written by a social geographer and remains a fascinating and thought-provoking analysis of touch in relation to the social and to time and place.

References

Ashforth, B. and Kreiner, G. (1999) 'How Can You Do It? Dirty Work and the Challenge of Constructing a Positive Identity', *Academy of Management Review*, 24(3): 413–34.

Barnes, H., Green, L. and Hopton, J. (2007) 'Guest Editorial: Social Work Theory, Research, Policy and Practice – Challenges and opportunities in health and social care integration in the UK', *Health and Social Care in the Community*, 15(3): 191–4.

Beck, U. (1992) *Risk Society: Towards a New Modernity*. London: Sage.

Bick, E. (1987) 'The Experience of Skin in Early Object Relations', in M. Harris (ed.), *The Collected Papers of Martha Harris and Esther Bick*. Perthshire: Clinic Press, 114–18.

Blackman, L. and Venn, C. (2010) 'Affect', *Body and Society*, 16(7): 7–28.

Bonitz, V. (2008) 'Practice Review – Use of Physical Touch in the "Talking Cure": A Journey to the Outskirts of Psychotherapy', *Psychotherapy, Theory, Research, Practice, Training*, 45(3): 393–404.

Bourdieu, P. (1984) *Distinction: A Social Critique of the Judgment of Taste*. London: Routledge.

Bourdieu, P. (1990) *The Logic of Practice*. Stanford, CA: Stanford University Press.

Broadhurst, K., Wastell, C., White, S. et al. (2010) 'Performing "Initial Assessment": Identifiying the Latent Conditions of Error at the Front Door of Local Authority Children's Services', *British Journal of Social Work*, 40: 352–60.

Butler, J. (1993) *Bodies That Matter: On the Discursive Limits of Sex*. London: Routledge.

Cameron, C. (2001) 'Promise or Problem? A Review of the Literature on Men working in Early Childhood Services, *Gender, Work and Organization*, 8(4): 430–53.

Cameron, N. and McDermott, F. (2007) *Social Work and the Body*. Basingstoke: Palgrave.

Canvin, K., Jones, C., Marttila, A. et al. (2007) 'Can I Risk Using Public Services? Perceived Consequences of Seeking Help and Health Care Among Households Living in Poverty: Qualitative Study', *Journal of Epidemiology and Community Health*, 61: 984–9.

Carey, M. (2009) '"It's a Bit Like Being a Robot or Working in a Factory": Does Braverman Help Explain the Experiences of State Social Workers in England and Wales since 1971?', *Organisation*, 16(4): 505–27.

Carey, M. and Foster, V.L. (2011) 'Introducing "Deviant Social Work": Contextualising the limits of radical social work whilst understanding fragmented resistance within the social work labour process', *British Journal of Social Work*, 41(3), 576–93.

Chang, S.O. (2001) 'The Conceptual Structure of Physical Touch in Caring', *Nursing Theory and Concept Development or Analysis*, 33(6): 820–27.

Chapman, E. (2000) 'Conceptualisation of the Body for People Living with HIV: Issues of touch and contamination', *Sociology of Health and Illness*, 22(6): 840–53.

Cho, G.M. (2008) *Haunting the Korean Diaspora: Shame, Secrecy and the Forgotten War*. London: University of Minnesota Press.

Clough, P. (2009) 'Reflections on Sessions Early in an Analysis: Trauma, affect and "enactive witnessing"', *Women and Performance: A Journal of Feminist Theory*, 19(12): 149–59.

Connell, R. (1995) *Masculinities*. Cambridge: Polity.

Derlega, V.J., Lewis, R.J., Winstead, B.A. and Constanza, R. (1989) 'Gender Differences in the Initiations and Attribution of Tactile Intimacy', *Journal of Nonverbal Behavior*, 13(2): 83–96.

Dibiase, R. and Gunnoe, J. (2004) 'Gender and Culture Differences in Touching Behavior', *The Journal of Social Psychology*, 144(1): 49–62.

Dolinski, D. (2010) 'Touch, Compliance and Homophobia', *Journal of Nonverbal Behavior*, 34: 179–92.

Douglas, M. (1966) *Purity and Danger*. London: Routledge and Kegan Paul.

Douglas, M. (1992) *Risk and Blame: Essays in Cultural Theory*. London, Routledge.

Dumont, L. (1970) *Homo Hierarchicus*. London: Weidenfeld and Nicolson.

Elias, N. (1978) *The Civilizing Process, Vol 1: The History of Manners*. Oxford: Blackwell.

Erceau, D. and Guegen, N. (2007) 'Tactile Contact and Evaluation of the Toucher', *The Journal of Social Psychology*, 14(7): 441–4.

Ferguson, H. (2011) *Child Protection Practice*. Basingstoke: Palgrave Macmillan.

Field, T. (2001) *Touch*. Cambridge, MA: MIT Press.

Fisher, J., Rytting, M. and Herlin, A. (1976) 'Hands Touching Hands: Affective and Evaluative Effects on Interpersonal Touch', *Sociometry*, 39: 416–21.

Floyd, R. (2000) 'Affectionate Same-Sex Touch: The Influence of Homophobia on Observers' Perceptions', *The Journal of Social Psychology*, 140(6): 774–88.

Ford, J.G. and Graves, J.R. (2007) 'Differences between Mexican American and White Children in Interpersonal Distance and Touching', *Perceptual and Motor Skills*, 45(3): 779–85.

Foucault, M. (1981) *The History of Sexuality, Vol 1: An Introduction*. Harmondsworth: Penguin.

Francis, S., Rolls, E.T., Bowtell, R. et al. (1999) 'The Representation of Pleasant Touch within the Brain and Its Relationship with Touch and Olfactory Areas', *Neuroreport*, 25: 453–9.

Fuller, B., Simmering, M.J., Marling, L.E. et al. (2011) 'Exploring Touch as a Positive Workplace Behavior', *Human Relations*, 64(2): 231–56.

Gallace, A. and Spence, C. (2010) 'The Science of Interpersonal Touch: An Overview', *Neuroscience and Biobehavioral Reviews*, 34: 249–59.

Giddens, A. (1991) *Modernity and Self Identity*. Cambridge: Polity.

Goffman, E. (1963) *Behaviour in Public Places*. New York: Free Press.

Green, L. (1998) *Caged By Force, Entrapped by Discourse: The Construction and Control of Children and Their Sexualities within Residential Children's Homes*, unpublished PhD thesis. University of Huddersfield, UK.

Green, L. (2000) 'Silenced Voice/Zero Choice: Young Women in Residential Care' in P. Cox., S. Kershaw and J. Trotter (eds), *Child Sexual Assault: Feminist Perspectives*. Basingstoke: Palgrave.

Green, L. (2001) 'Analysing the Sexual Abuse of Children by Workers in Residential Care Homes', *The Journal of Sexual Aggression*, 7(2): 3–24.

Green, L. (2005) 'Theorizing Sexuality, Sexual Abuse and Residential Accommodation: Adding Gender to the Equation', *British Journal of Social Work*, 35: 453–81.

Green, L. and Masson, H. (2002) 'Adolescents Who Sexually Abuse and Residential Accommodation: Issues of Risk and Vulnerability', *British Journal of Social Work*, 32: 149–68.

Green, L. and Parkin, W. (1999) 'Sexuality, Sexual Abuse and Children's Homes: Oppression or Protection?' in the Violence Against Children Study Group (ed.), *Children, Child Abuse and Child Protection: Placing Children Centrally*. Chichester: Wiley.

Green, L. Butt, T. and King, N. (2002) 'Taking the Chaste out of Chastisement: An Analysis of the Sexual Implications of the Corporal Punishment of Children', *Childhood – A Global Journal*, 9(2): 205–24.

Guegen, S., Meineri, S. and Charles-Sire, V. (2010) 'Improving Medication Adherence by Using Practitioner Nonverbal Techniques: A Field Experiment on the Effect of Touch', *Journal of Behavioral Medicine*, 33: 466–75.

Halley, J. (2007) *Boundaries of Touch: Parenting and Child Intimacy*. Champaign, IL: University of Illinois Press,.

Heaphy, E.D. (2007) 'Bodily Insights: Three Lenses on Positive Organizational Relationships' in J.E. Dutton and B.R. Raggins (eds), *Exploring Positive Relationships At Work: Building a Theoretical and Research Foundation*. Mahwah, NJ: NJL Lawrence Erlbaum Associates.

Henley, N. (1973) 'The Politics of Touch' in P. Brown (ed.), *Radical Psychology*. London: Tavistock.

Hertenstein, M.J. and Keltner, D. (2010) 'Gender and the Communication of Emotion via Touch', *Sex Roles*, 64: 70–80.

Hertenstein, M.J., Keltner, D., App, B. et al. (2006) 'Touch Communicates Distinct Emotions', *Emotion*, 6: 528–33.

Hochschild, A.R. (1983) *The Managed Heart: Commercialization of Human Feeling*. Berkeley, CA: University of California Press.

Howes, D. (2003) *Sensual Relations: Engaging the Senses in Culture and Social Theory*. Ann Arbor, MI: University of Michigan Press.

Hughes, E.C. (1958) *Men and their Work*. Glencoe, IL: Free Press.

Jones, A. (2004) 'Social Anxiety, Sex, Surveillance and the "Safe" Teacher', *Journal of Sociology of Education*, 25(1): 53–66.

Jourard, S.M. (1966) 'An Exploratory Study of Body Accessibility', *British Journal of Social and Clinical Psychology*, 5: 221–31.

Koprowska J. (2008) *Communication and Interpersonal Skills in Social Work*. Exeter: Learning Matters.

LaFrance, M. (2009) 'Skin and Self: Cultural Theory and Anglo-American Psychoanalysis, *Body and Society*, 15(3): 3–24.

Laming, L. (2009) *The Protection of Children in England: A Progress Report*. London: The Stationary Office.

Lang, M. (2010) 'Surveillance and Conformity in Competitive Youth Swimming', *Sport, Education and Society*, 15(1): 19–37.

Le Breton, D. (2003) 'Touching Another in Suffering', *Revue de Sciences Sociales*, 31: 200–205.

Lee, J.W. and Guerro, L.K. (2001) 'Types of Touch in Cross-Sex Relationships Between Co-workers: Perceptions of Relational and Emotional Messages, Inappropriateness and Sexual Harassment, *Journal of Applied Communication Research*, 29: 197–220.

Lee-Trewick, G. (1997) 'Emotional Work, Order and Emotional Power in Care Assistant Work', in V. James and J. Gabe (eds), *Health and the Sociology of Emotions*. Oxford: Blackwell.

Levy, A. and Kahan, B. (1991) *The Pindown Experience and the Protection of Children: The Report of the Staffordshire Child Care Inquiry*. Stafford: Staffordshire County Council.

Longhurst, R., Ho, E. and Johnston, L. (2008) 'Using "The Body" as an "Instrument" of Research: kim'chi and pavlova', *Area*, 402: 208–17.

Lynch, R. and Garrett, P.M. (2010) '"More Than Words": Touch Practices in Child and Family Social work', *Child and Family Social Work*, 15: 389–98.

Maclean, K. (2003) 'The Impact of Institutionalization on Child Development', *Development and Psychopathology*, 15: 853–84.

McNeil-Haber, F. (2004) 'Ethical Considerations in the Use of Nonerotic Touch in the Psychotherapy of Children', *Ethics and Behaviour*, 14: 123–40.

Mauss, M. (1973) 'Techniques of the Body', *Economy and Society*, 2: 70–88.

McLaughlin, K. (2008) *Social Work, Politics and Society*. Bristol: Policy Press.

Merleau-Ponty, M. (1992) *The Phenomenology of Perception*. London: Routledge.

Montagu, A. (1971) *Touching: The Human Significance of the Skin*. New York: Columbia University Press.

Munro, E. (2011) *The Munro Review of Child Protection Final Report: A Child–Centred System*. London: The Stationary Office.

Neuberger, J. (2008) 'Are We Too Afraid of Touch?' (7 November 2008) *The Sunday Times*.

Owen, P.M. and Gillentine, J. (2011) 'Please Touch the Children: Appropriate Touch in the Primary Classroom', *Early Child Development and Care*, 181(6): 857–68.

Paterson, M. (2009) 'Haptic Geographies: Ethnography, Haptic Knowledges and Sensuous Dispositions', *Progress in Human Geography*, 33(6): 766–88.

Panorama (2011) Undercover Care: The Abuse Exposed, BBC1, 31 May 2011.

Panorama (2012) Undercover Care: Elderly Care, BBC1, 30 April 2012.

Pemberton, C. (2010) 'Should Children's Social Work be a Touch Free Zone?' *Community Care*, 20 August 2010.

Phelan, J.E. (2009) 'Exploring the Use of Touch in the Psychotherapeutic Setting: A Phenomenological Review', *Psychotherapy Theory, Research, Practice, Training*, 46(1): 97–111.

Piper, H. and Sikes, P. (2010) 'Researching Barriers to Change for those in Loco Parentis', *Sociological Research Online*, 15(4): 5.

Piper, H. and Smith, H. (2003) 'Touch in Educational and Child Care Settings: Dilemmas and Reponses', *British Educational Research*, 29(6): 879–94.

Pithouse, A. (1987) *Social Work: The Social Organization of an Invisible Trade*, Aldershot: Avebury.

Reamer, F.G. (2003) 'Boundary Issues in Social Work: Managing Dual relationships', *Journal of Social Work*, 48: 121–33.

Reite, M. (1990) 'Touch, Attachment and Health: Is There a Relationship?' in K.E. Bernard and T.B. Brazelton (eds), *Touch: The Foundation of Experience*. Madison, WI: International Universities Press.

Rees, A. and Pithouse, A. (2008) 'The Intimate World of Strangers – Embodying the Child in Foster Care', *Child and Family Social Work*, 13: 338–47.

Remland, M.S., Jones, T.S. and Brinkman, H. (1995) 'Interpersonal Distance, Body Orientation and Touch: Effects of Culture, Gender and Age', *The Journal of Social Psychology*, 135(3): 281–97.

Rosip, J.C. and Hall, J.A. (2004) 'Knowledge of Nonverbal Cues, Gender and Nonverbal Decoding Accuracy', *Journal of Nonverbal Behavior*, 28(4): 267–85.

Shilling, C. (1993) *The Body and Social Theory*. London: Sage.

Smith, C. (2001) 'Trust and Confidence: Possibilities for Social Work in High Modernity', *British Journal of Social Work*, 31: 287–305.

Steckley, L. (2011) 'Touch, Physical Restraint and Therapeutic Containment in Residential Child Care', *British Journal of Social Work Advance Access*, 1–19.

Strozier, A., Krizek, C. and Sale, K. (2003) 'Touch: Its Use in Psychotherapy', *Journal of Social Work Practice*, 17: 49–62.

Takeuchi, M.S., Miyaoka, H., Tomoda, A. et al. (2010) 'The Effect of Interpersonal Touch During Childhood on Adult Attachment and Depression: A Neglected Area of Family and Developmental Psychology?, *Journal of Child and Family Studies*, 19(1): 109–12.

Tangenberg, K.M. and Kemp, S. (2002) 'Embodied Practice: Claiming the Body's Experience, Agency and Knowledge for Social Work', *Social Work*, 47(1): 9–17.

Thompson, N. (2011) *Effective Communication*. Basingstoke: Palgrave.

Throop, C.J. and Murphy, K.M. (2002) 'Bourdieu and Phenomenology', *Anthropological Theory*, 2(2): 185–207.

Turner, B. (1996) *The Body and Society*, 2nd edn. London: Sage.

Twigg, J. (2000) 'Social Policy and the Body', in G. Lewis, S. Gewirtz and J. Clarke (eds), *Rethinking Social Policy*. London: Sage.

Twigg, J., Wolkowitz, C., Cohen, R.L. and Nettleton, S. (2011) 'Conceptualising Body Work in Health and Social Care', *Sociology of Health and Illness*, 33(2): 171–88.

Ungar, S. (2001) 'Moral Panic versus the Risk Society: The Implications of the Changing Sites of Anxiety, *British Journal of Sociology*, 52(2): 271–91.

Van Dongen, E. and Elema, R. (2010) 'The Art of Touching: The Culture of "Body Work" in Nursing', *Anthropology and Medicine*, 8(2): 149–62.

Wastell, D., White, S., Broadhurst, K. et al. (2010) 'Children's Services in the Iron Cage of Performance Management: Street Level Bureaucracy and the Sphere of Svejkism', *International Journal of Social Welfare*, 19: 310–20.

Whitcher, S.J. and Fischer, J.D. (1979) 'Multidimensional Reaction to Therapeutic Touch in a Hospital Setting', *Journal of Personality and Social Psychology*, 37: 87–96.

Willis, F.N. Jnr and Dodds, R.A. (1998) 'Age, Relationship and Touch Initiation', *The Journal of Social Psychology*, 138(1): 115–23.

Wolkowitz, C. (2002) 'The Social Relations of Body Work', *Work, Employment and Society*, 16: 479–510.

Wrennall, L. (2010) 'Surveillance and Child Protection: De-mystifying the Trojan Horse', *Surveillance and Society*, 7(3/4): 304–24.

Part II
Ethical Tensions? Ambivalent Ethics and Adult Social Work

This second part of the book concentrates upon professional social work with users with mental health needs and older people. Beginning the detailed exploration of the paradoxes and nuances of adult social work, Kenneth McLaughlin and Sean Cordell commence the section by discussing the sites of conflict and ethical dilemmas that can emerge when using Community Treatment Orders (CTOs) within mental health social work. Rather than berating social workers for the adoption of a risk-averse approach to practice, centred upon so called 'revolving door' patients based in the community, the authors skilfully place this development in a historical context in order to highlight the ethical dilemmas that it raises for the social work practitioner. John Hopton continues the theme of mental health related social work in Chapter 6, yet instead questions some of the critiques of and negative assumptions made about the medical model of psychiatry. He asks us to carefully consider the complexity of interaction between heredity, biochemistry, environment and lived experience and shows how a person-centred approach to social work can incorporate a sensitive use of the medical model of mental illness. Perhaps along with safeguarding work with children and families (and increasingly also older people in the community), mental health represents a discursive zone of practices which are traditionally accepted as being at the 'control end' of social work's moral spectrum. Yet each author again highlights the many caveats attached to such implicit assumptions and reveal instead the subtleties often hidden beneath sometimes taken for granted assumptions made about seemingly control- related care work.

In the final chapter of Part II Richard Ward and Sarah Campbell analyse the rise of an extensive system of ethical regulation which now increasingly governs research in health and social care in England and applies across the spectrum from large-scale invasive medical research to smaller-scale qualitative studies involving staff and service users. The chapter charts the progress of a qualitative mixed-method study involving older people with dementia, as it navigates through the highly bureaucratised regulatory system for research ethics. The chapter offers much food for thought and also includes recommendations for making awareness of ethical dilemmas an on-going and integral feature of research.

5 Doing What's Best, but Best for Whom? Ethics and the Mental Health Social Worker

Kenneth McLaughlin and Sean Cordell

Introduction

Of all areas of social work, it is perhaps that of mental health that poses more ethical questions than any other. For the Approved Mental Health Practitioner (AMHP) (a role still held predominantly by social workers although it can also be undertaken by other specified professional groups such as Community Psychiatric Nurses), there is the not inconsiderable issue of the powers given to them by the Mental Health Act (MHA) 1983/2007. The MHA allows the AMHP, subject to having the required medical recommendations, to make an application for the detention in hospital (for assessment or assessment followed by treatment) of someone deemed to have a mental disorder, irrespective of the person's wishes. In other words, the person can be legally detained and medically treated against his will, not necessarily because of what they have done but on the basis of what professionals think they may do in future. And whilst the decision to invoke these powers will be based on an assessment as to the risk that the person (possibly soon to be patient) poses to either themselves or others, it is important to note that detention and treatment under the Mental Health Act can also be solely on the basis that it is, again in the opinion of professionals, deemed to be in the interests of the patient's health.

The ethical issues that arise from this professional role mainly concern issues such as, on one hand, the personal autonomy and rights of mental health clients, and, on the other, the professional, state sanctioned, surveillance and constraint to which they may be subject. Such intrusive measures are justified on the basis that it is necessary for the benefit of the individual and/or wider society; we are, in some way, doing what's best, we are doing 'good'. The most basic ethical question for the reflective and conscientious social worker to consider then, is in which way is such 'good' being achieved. We might say that particular considerations facing a mental health social worker, when making a decision about how to act well or 'best' in her professional role, are 'what or whose good am I trying to promote or protect'; 'why'; and 'who decides?'

These questions are of course illustrative of wider problems in moral and political philosophy. For example, whether or how we can justifiably constrain or coerce people for the sake of some outcome or 'greater good' (such as consequences for carers or relations; wider public security; social capital; law and order; or even economic efficiency); or for 'their own good' (which raises the problem of paternalism). And aside from these particular issues around intervention in individuals' lives and the use of compulsion, a second, and more general way in which the role of mental health social workers can be seen as ethically important concerns their involvement in facilitating the well-being, or 'happiness' of clients. For there is also a more fundamental sense in which 'Ethics', broadly construed, concerns what it means for us to live good human lives (Aristotle, 2009; Williams, 1985). So, insofar as 'mental health' relates in some way to human well-being or happiness, the mental health of individuals or the well-being of society can be said to be the business of Ethics. In this respect there are critical questions for the mental health social worker regarding what 'sound mental health' (or similar) is; and the extent, if any, to which it can or should be promoted in clients' lives.

If mental health social work is fundamentally concerned with these two broad and overlapping areas of ethical concern – the legitimacy of intervention itself and the nature and promotion of 'mental health' (or happiness or well-being), then the social worker working within the field of mental health, which arguably covers each and every social worker to a greater or lesser degree, is embroiled in the business of Ethics. Therefore, both the professional role and the institutions that confer the duties and responsibilities of said role warrant critical ethical justification (Cordell, 2011). This chapter highlights some of these intertwining ethical difficulties in mental health social work primarily using the example of Community Treatment Orders (CTO), which were introduced in England and Wales in the Mental Health Act 2007, but also by considering the government's wider in scope 'happiness agenda' (BBC News, 2010), as it too raises questions over the meaning of mental health, happiness and the role of the state in their pursuit.[1]

---

1   There are several useful critiques of the drive towards empowerment, well-being and therapy. For example, Cruikshank (1999), influenced by Foucault's work

In terms of intervention, one major ethical problem that arises from the introduction of CTOs is that of justifying intervention, constraint or coercion in clients' lives after they have been discharged from hospital; another, in relation to 'happiness', is interpreting the nature and scope of 'mental health' as that which supposedly justifies intervention in the life of both clients and the wider public. A further important issue, which relates to both these aspects of mental health policy, is the need to understand the way in which institutions (through government policy or state legislation) shape the conception of mental health. Through a critical discussion of the arguments supporting the introduction of the CTO and of the ways in which their implementation has been defended, not only do we raise doubts over some of the theoretical and ethical justifications for the use of CTOs, we also raise questions about what we mean when we say we are endeavouring to improve the mental health or happiness of those subject to social work. Our intention is not to provide a blueprint for practice but to create a critical space for social workers to think about how, why and on what basis they are pursuing certain aspects of their professional role.

From Community Care to Community Treatment

Mental health legislation has long provided for the detention and treatment of the 'mentally ill' subject to certain criteria being met. The Mental Health Act (MHA) 1983, enacted prior to the widespread move to care in the community, was held by some to be inadequate for the contemporary period when most mental health care was located within the community rather than in the old long stay psychiatric institutions. High profile tragedies where ex-patients had killed were used to argue that community care had failed and that it had put the public at risk from psychiatric patients, and the patients at risk from themselves due to violence, self harm and/or neglect. Such concerns were hugely influential in the drawing up of the Mental Health Act (MHA) 2007 which amended the 1983 Act (McLaughlin, 2008).

The MHA 2007 provided powers by which patients detained in hospital for treatment, could, upon discharge, be made subject to a Community

---

on governmentality and bio-power, argues that the rise in such measures represents an aspect of neo-liberal welfare policies, and that our 'empowerment' in reality represents our subjection and loss of autonomy. Furedi (2004) similarly sees the management of people's emotions as being representative of a new conformity, although he implicates both the political right and left in the cultivation of such a scenario.

Treatment Order.[2] The CTO can compel the patient[3] to abide by certain specified conditions, most notably, though not exclusively, that they continue to take any prescribed psychiatric medication. Failure to comply could lead to the patient being recalled to hospital, where the drug could be forcibly administered. The introduction of CTOs was controversial in a number of ways, but mainly because it changed the status of psychiatric patients post-discharge from hospital. Whereas previously, under the MHA 1983, patients lost the right to refuse medical treatment whilst subject to hospital detention, once discharged from the section and returned to the community they regained the same rights of citizenship as everyone else,[4] such as the right to refuse medical treatment, even if this went against professional medical opinion and seemed likely to be detrimental to their health.

Given the adverse effects that psychiatric medication can cause,[5] it is perhaps no surprise that many ex-patients exercised this right and stopped taking their medication and/or otherwise disengaged from their clinical team. Such non-compliance was implicated in the so called 'revolving door' patient phenomenon, whereby someone was admitted to hospital, got better with medication, was discharged, stopped taking the medication, relapsed, was readmitted to hospital and so on. Non-compliance with medication was also implicated in several homicide inquiries into cases where ex-patients had killed (Howlett, 1997). Irrespective of this, a history of non-compliance is not necessary for a CTO to be imposed; it can be applied to a patient after his first compulsory admission for treatment, provided the criteria below are met.

A CTO may be made under section 17A(5) of the Mental Health Act 2007 if:

---

2   There has been discussion of the pros and cons of introducing compulsory community treatment orders many times during the latter decades of the twentieth century, although the early years of the new millennium saw a renewed and sustained focus on them which culminated in their incorporation into the MHA 2007.

3   Terminology within the mental health field is an area of contention, with, inter alia, 'patient', 'client', 'service user' and 'survivor' being embraced by some and rejected by others. In this chapter we use the terms patient, client and service user interchangeably merely to avoid repetition. For a discussion of the personal and political meaning behind such identification in relation to mental health see McLaughlin (2012), and in relation to social work more generally see McLaughlin (2009).

4   There were some exceptions, for example those subject to court orders.

5   We deliberately did not use the term 'side-effects' as this can trivialise the symptoms. If they are happening to you they are effects of the drug. They may be unintended consequences but the symptoms are real.

a. the patient is suffering from a mental disorder of a nature or degree that makes it appropriate for him or her to receive medical treatment;
b. it is necessary for his or her health or safety or for the protection of other persons that he or she should receive such treatment;
c. subject to his or her being liable to be recalled, such treatment can be provided without his or her continuing to be detained in a hospital;
d. it is necessary that the responsible clinician should be able to exercise his or her power under section 17E(1) to recall the patient to hospital;
e. appropriate medical treatment is available for him or her.

Given the significant change in status and power dynamics between professionals and patients brought about by the introduction of CTOs, it is worth considering both the basis for their enactment and the evidence as to their effectiveness. In the next section we will first consider the issue of individual autonomy and state intervention in the life of the individual. Second, we look at some ethical arguments for the use of CTOs and whether they are mostly used for the benefit of the patient, society or professionals.

The Autonomous Subject and State Intervention

There are some basic ethical worries about CTOs that are separate from concerns about whether they actually achieve their aims. Perhaps most pertinent are concerns about certain inviolable moral or 'human' rights which recognise the autonomy of the individual subject; rights that one has not by convention or legal decree but simply by virtue of one's status as a human being or a person. Many think that such rights cannot be violated or ignored for the sake of society or for what others see as that individual's good.[6]

The ethical question of intervention in individuals' lives, and whether or not this constitutes a violation of rights or autonomy, is especially pertinent to social work because, in some form or another, intervention in other people's lives is exactly what much of that work is characteristically about. Importantly, intervention is often justified in mental health patients' lives in a way in which it would not be justified in the lives of others, where a widely held anti-paternalist principle is taken to respect the value of personal autonomy, of self governance (literally 'a law unto oneself').The source of this ethical view, on which the autonomy of the rational agent as a

---

6   For further philosophical analysis and discussion of rights see Wenar (2011) and Waldron (1984).

moral being is basic and primary, is most often attributed to the eighteenth-century German philosopher Immanuel Kant. From a Kantian perspective people should be seen as ends in themselves, never merely as a means to some end. This posits persons with an inviolable right to be accorded human dignity which should not be compromised in order to secure some other goal. Much of the language of individual rights and respect for persons is rooted in a broadly Kantian view, and much of the discourse of the ethics and values of social work reflects this approach. According to Bogg:

> the professional needs to ensure that their actions are undertaken in an appropriate, proportionate and informed manner. The ability to exercise coercion should never be downplayed: the aim of a transparent application of power requires the worker to identify the power dynamics and to ensure that the individual's rights are observed at all times. Coercion is neither a threat nor an incentive: it should only be used if it becomes necessary according to the criteria set down in law, and disagreement between worker and user is never sufficient justification. (2010, p. 57)

This view is reflected in many of the explicitly stated aims and ethical guidelines of social work. For example, Banks (2006) examined a selection of codes of ethics for social workers from 31 different countries. She found that most codes start with a list of professional values and/or principles which include variations on such themes as 'respect for the unique value of the individual person; service user self-determination; social justice and professional integrity' (p. 83). In practice then, the mental health social work role entails mediating between different sets of obligations and interests (Yianni, 2009). Of course, respect for service user self-determination may well be a guiding principle, but in the case of statutory powers this is often overridden, with those subject to them, temporarily at least, not accorded the status of autonomous subject. This can be justified in several ways, perhaps most notably with respect to the prevention of harm to others.

The Harm Principle

The eighteenth-century utilitarian philosopher John Stuart Mill famously railed against interference in people's lives for any other reason but the protection of others. In *On Liberty*, Mill stated his famous 'harm principle' thus:

> That principle is, that the sole end for which mankind are warranted, individually or collectively, in interfering with the liberty of action of any of their number, is

self-protection. That the only purpose for which power can be rightfully exercised over any member of a civilised community, against his will, is to prevent harm to others. His own good, either physical or moral, is not a sufficient warrant. He cannot rightfully be compelled to do or forbear because it will be better for him to do so, because it will make him happier, because, in the opinion of others, to do so would be wise, or even right. (2008 [1859], p. 14)

The harm principle does not necessarily preclude preventive detention or treatment of the kind allowed under the Mental Health Act. If there is a 'foreseeable risk' of future harm then Mill concedes that the government (for our purposes in the guise of designated mental health professionals) may be within its rights to intervene before the event in order to prevent its occurrence at some future point. As in other areas of legality and ethics, intervening in someone's life against his will in order to prevent serious harm to them or to others may provide a stronger justification than would (supposedly) intervening to improve his personal welfare. This would appear to be Bogg's (2010) position when she states that 'In circumstances that may result in restrictions being applied, the question must always be asked, is it necessary for the individual's health *and* safety or to protect others?' (p. 79, our emphasis). However, the wording of the MHA is slightly different but this difference has major implications. Detention can be justified if it is deemed necessary for the patient's 'health *or* safety or for the protection of others' (S.3, our emphasis). In other words, compulsory admission and treatment can be justified solely on the basis that professionals deem it to be beneficial to the patient's health; s/he does not have to be a danger to himself or anyone else. Of course, the reality is that with current pressure on psychiatric bed space, only those deemed a risk to self or others are likely to be admitted, nevertheless, legislative powers can be used legitimately whether risk is present or not.

Mill also states that his doctrine 'is meant to apply only to human beings in the maturity of their faculties' (p. 14), which precludes children and others unable to take care of themselves, or more precisely for our purpose, those to whom we have a duty of care. It is recognised that in order to apply the duty of care it is occasionally necessary to restrict someone's freedom and autonomy, to exercise control over him, which can directly impinge on other basic rights. Perhaps it could be argued that in such cases coercion, constraint and intervention in mental health work is no such violation of autonomy when the subject is not autonomous in the relevant sense. That is, following Mill, a line of justification for CTOs can be made which could be quite non-paternalistic and even consistent with anti-paternalism and the value of personal autonomy (Dale, 2011; Munetz et al., 2003). For, it might be said that CTOs are by definition correctly applied only to subjects who, episodically or in the longer term, do not possess the kind or level of autonomy that would include them in the scope of the harm principle; that they are no such 'law unto themselves' is precisely the reason they are subject to constraint, for example by the terms of the Mental Health Act.

However, a problem with this line of defence is that there is a crucial contrast between the initial detention under the Mental Health Act and the imposition of a CTO. At the point of admission to hospital under the MHA it is generally agreed, by professionals if not the patient, that the patient is so 'mentally ill' that they can no longer be left in the community, at which point their individual rights are overridden. However, at the point of discharge the patient, whilst technically still deemed to be 'suffering from a mental disorder of a nature or degree that makes it appropriate for him or her to receive medical treatment', can be otherwise mentally well, have full mental capacity and deemed able to be returned to the community. This is due to the MHA being risk based, not capacity based, and means that, as most patients, at the point of discharge if not admission, will have the capacity to make treatment decisions, 'community treatment orders will commonly be imposed on people who have capacity … [And] we should also not forget that community treatment orders will compel patients to take medication that will be effective to differing degrees and could have seriously debilitating side-effects' (Lawton-Smith, 2008, online).

As mentioned above, prior to the MHA 2007, a discharged patient regained the rights of citizenship that most of us take for granted, in particular with regard to this example, the right to refuse medical treatment, even if to do so would place his health at serious risk. This is no longer the case and marks a major shift in the citizenship status of discharged patients subject to a CTO. The concepts of personal freedom and autonomy entailed the right to make the wrong choices. Here then is a case in which a patient is deemed 'well' enough to be discharged into the community but not enough to enjoy the freedom and autonomous status shared by others within that community. Hence it is not so clear that Millian type exemptions from the 'harm principle' apply in this case. In addition, far from being free to refuse medication that would benefit them, they can be compelled to take medication that can give them adverse medical conditions. The subject of a CTO therefore may be mentally healthy, in relative terms at least, and have full mental capacity but he does not return to full citizenship status but to a reduced social standing, neither full citizen nor patient but a diminished hybrid of the two – the 'community patient'.

For the Good of Society?

In the introduction we referred to one way of justifying intervention in a person's life by reference to the promotion of some 'greater good', a good which benefits society more widely and for the sake of which that individual's interests might be subordinated. This reflects a utilitarian view, on which the right thing to do is always that which will maximise the 'utility', the happiness or welfare, of society overall. Notwithstanding many of the problems with and objections to utilitarianism as a moral or political doctrine (Kymlicka, 2001; Rawls, 1972; Scarre, 1996; Smart and Williams, 1973), there is a clear and plausible line of justification for CTOs which has a distinctly utilitarian form.

According to Maden (2005), a consultant psychiatrist and vociferous proponent of the need for CTOs, the principle at stake 'is not whether we, as a profession or as a society, value dignity, autonomy and choice. The tough choice is whose dignity, autonomy or choice takes precedence? That of the cyclist in Richmond Park, or that of the restricted patient?' (online). Maden is referring to the case of John Barrett, a psychiatric patient, who stabbed a cyclist to death in Richmond Park, London in 2004. The same case was also frequently highlighted by government ministers as they justified the need for CTOs.[7] Maden (2004) argues that mental health professionals 'need to keep in mind the importance of public relations'. This is because 'the people who pay for services have identified safety and public protection from violence as their priorities, and clinicians need to respond to those concerns' (p. 4). Losing this 'public relations battle', will, in his view be to the detriment of psychiatric patients (Maden, 2005). Here, Maden appears to be using a utilitarian argument, in that restrictions on the few will be to the benefit of the many, either in terms of protecting them from possible attack and/or the alleviation of anxiety. Following this logic, Maden also argues that there need be no therapeutic benefit for the patient in order to justify compulsory detention.

In a utilitarian sense then, the decision to place someone on a CTO could be seen as promoting the greater good of society, where in this case the

---

7   The highlighting of this case shows either a careless disregard for the facts or a manipulative use of the media, as linking the John Barrett case to a need for community treatment orders conveniently overlooks the fact that he was actually an in-patient at the time of the killing. He had been given one hour's unescorted leave from the ward but absconded from the hospital grounds. Whilst noting many professional failures in his care, the chair of the inquiry team stated that, 'the remedy for what went wrong in this case lies not in new laws or policy changes' (Barrett Report, 2006, p. 9).

good can be specified in terms of public safety via the prevention of criminal and violent acts. From such a teleological (goal-led) perspective, if the ends justify the means, if a safer society for the majority is achieved then the loss of citizenship rights for an individual or a minority can be justified. Given that a major factor in their introduction was a response to some high profile tragedies in which ex-patients had killed others, and, albeit to a lesser extent, cases where they had killed themselves or otherwise exposed themselves to danger and neglect, issues of public safety and patient quality of life tend to be the areas given most attention in research into the effectiveness of CTOs.

In terms of social and mental health practices, then, it should be borne in mind that utilitarianism *per se* is at odds with the principle of personal autonomy and the inviolability of certain rights. The utilitarian may, in some circumstances, be in favour of upholding some rights or promoting individual autonomy, but only and always when doing so would promote utility (Kymlicka, 2001). Rights or individuals' autonomy could in principle be violated if it could be justified by the actual or expected outcome of greater utility overall.[8] Thus, utilitarian justifications of CTOs should warrant caution from those who see such principles and values as rock solid guides for mental health social work. As well as raising theoretical doubts about the utilitarian rationale in mental health social work, it is also worth considering whether, in fact, the actual use of CTOs achieves the end of public safety; in other words, whether this justification for CTOs succeeds in its own utilitarian terms. As we shall see, this is far from conclusively supported by evidence.

For example, Parker and McCulloch (1999) found that non-compliance with medication is over-emphasised in relation to homicides by ex-patients. A *National Confidential Inquiry into Homicides and Suicides by People with Mental Illness* took place in both 2001 and 2006 (DH, 2001; DH, 2006). The earlier report surmised that compulsory CTOs *may* prevent just two homicides per year, whilst the later one admits that 'We have no reliable way of calculating how many homicides [or suicides] would be prevented by a community treatment order' (DH, 2006, pp. 93 and 139). This raises the question of which two homicides would be prevented.[9] Given the unreliability of risk assessments how many false positives would be needed to ensure the two

---

8   For a stark illustration of the implications of hard utilitarianism from social-science fiction, see Stanley Kubrick's film of Anthony Burgess's novel *A Clockwork Orange* (Warner Bros. 1971). Embroiled in controversy for implementing the 'Ludovico' method of forcibly brainwashing violent offenders to expunge any of their criminal inclinations and make them 'good' (sweet and mechanical, like 'a clockwork orange'), the home secretary declares loudly to Ludovico's opponents in its defence 'the point is that it works!'

9   The problem of assessing the consequences of one's actions or inactions is especially pressing for utilitarians and any kind of 'pure consequentialist' theory

true positives were medicated? Very many according to some reports. The Cochrane review (Kisely et al. 2005) looked at 'compulsory community and involuntary outpatient treatment for people with severe mental disorders'. It found only two relevant trials and concluded that they 'provided little evidence of the efficacy on any outcomes such as health service use, social functioning, mental state, quality of life or satisfaction with care … In terms of numbers needed to treat, it would take 85 outpatient commitment orders to prevent one readmission, 27 to prevent one episode of homelessness and 238 to prevent one arrest' (online). In addition, an international review that considered studies over a 30-year period concluded that there was little evidence that CTOs were effective in such things as reducing hospital readmission rates or compliance with medication (Churchill, 2007). So, the justification for CTOs in utilitarian terms of promoting a greater societal good, such as public safety, is questionable in the very terms favoured by utilitarian reasoning. That is, aside from concerns about patients' rights or autonomy, there is a legitimate scepticism about whether CTOs 'work' in quite the way that some proponents of the measures claim.

For the Good of the Client?

It could be argued that if the CTO effectively promotes the well-being or mental health of the individual subject to it, that this could provide justification for its use separate from whether, or the extent to which, it promotes the wider public good. So, whether or not CTOs make for a safer society, they could be effective in facilitating a better life for the 'community patient'. However, similar doubts may also be raised about the practical efficacy of CTOs as a paternalistic measure, i.e. as a means to promote the 'good' of the client.

First, we need to know to what extent if any does the CTO actually benefit clients themselves. Of those studies that do show benefits they tend to be that some patients found that they gave some structure to their lives, that families found them useful when their relative 'lacked insight' and, perhaps unsurprisingly, that clinicians were the group most consistently positive about the efficacy of CTOs (O'Reilly et al., 2006). The patients' views of CTOs also need to be placed in context. For example, Gibbs et al. (2005) found that many preferred to receive involuntary treatment at home rather than as an in-patient. However, in itself this is just to establish a preference of one option out of the only two available, not that the chosen

which assesses the moral worth of any action or policy on its actual or expected outcomes (see Lenman, 2000).

option is desired or considered beneficial by the patient. To infer the latter would be like saying that because in-patients prefer to be detained for six rather than twelve months that they are in favour of their detention for the lower period.

A second doubt about CTOs in relation to the paternalistic justification is whether their actual use is typically solely directed at the good or well-being of the client in question or, in fact, whether the tendency is towards using them as a means to professional protection, with risk-averse practice being a factor in the imposition of a CTO. It is worth remembering that the use of CTOs was initially said to be necessary for a relatively small number of 'revolving door' patients. Maden argued that they were necessary 'to allow compulsory treatment in the community of patients with a serious mental illness and a history of violence and non-compliance' (quoted in James, 2006, online). In similar vein, Dawson and Burns (2008) argued that the powers 'should give clinicians the confidence to make *selective* use of the new regime' (online, our emphasis). Despite such claims, the early signs are that the use of CTOs far exceeds initial estimates and, rather than being imposed selectively are being used on a wider and less specific group of patients than envisaged by these commentators.

As McLaughlin (2010: 145) points out,

> The government envisaged that between 350–450 CTOs would be issued in England and Wales in the first year. However, the number issued has far exceeded the government's and its advisers' expectations. In the first five months in which professionals were able to issue them, November 2008 to March 2009, there were 2,134 issued in England alone. It may be the case, as some argue, that the initial surge is due to those on a sort of 'waiting list' being put on CTOs as soon as possible once it became an option, and that the rates will stabilise after this initial surge, although you would have thought that the great and the good who worked to bring this legislation through would have accounted for this in their initial estimates.

The numbers subject to a CTO have continued to rise, with 10,071 people being put on one between November 2008 and 31 March 2011 of which only 4,150 (41.2%) had been subsequently revoked (CQC, 2011).

Again, even leaving aside for the moment the debate about ethics, autonomy and citizenship rights, in today's climate there was always the risk that professionals would err on the side of caution and use CTOs as an instrument of managing the risk to themselves of anything going wrong rather than as an option of last resort. There is also the suspicion that due to pressure on psychiatric hospital beds (too few beds, too many patients), many are being discharged early on CTOs rather than having longer hospital treatment. So the paternalistic justification for CTOs can be questioned on grounds of efficiency (are CTOs effective at promoting the good of clients?) and the way in which they are employed (are they used primarily in the interests of professionals rather than those of their patients?).

The Pursuit (or Imposition) of Happiness

If there are many ethical issues for the social worker to consider when it comes to the use, non-use, or indeed misuse of statutory powers in relation to the detention and treatment of mental health service users, the social worker's task may seem far less controversial when it comes to improving the mental health of their clientele. After all, it is often when people are suffering mental distress that they come into contact, voluntarily or not, with mental health services. In working with people who are unhappy, the pursuit of happiness would appear to be a reasonable strategy. Yet consider that the very concept of 'happiness' has exercised the minds of some of the greatest thinkers within Western philosophy, as well as politicians, statesmen, social policy devisors and those professionals, including social workers, responsible for their implementation.[10] For example, Aristotle saw *eudaimonia* (sometimes translated as 'happiness' or perhaps more instructively as 'flourishing') as the condition of living well over the course of a characteristically human life. So being *eudaimon*, living the good human life, is neither reducible to pleasant sensations nor to 'feeling happy' from time to time, and is much more in keeping with what we might think of as good psychic health. In contrast, the 'hedonistic' utilitarian Jeremy Bentham saw happiness purely as the presence of pleasure and the absence of pain, whilst the eighteenth-century economist Adam Smith believed that wealth could produce happiness but also that there was more to well-being than material possessions.

This philosophical controversy over happiness and mental health provides practical problems for social workers at the coal-face of mental health work, for if the concept of happiness itself is unclear and contested, so is its relation to 'mental health'. As we have seen it is important in terms of coercion, constraint and patient autonomy, and it is worth noting that

---

10   Some conception of what it means for humans to live well and the conditions for such – and so to some extent a view of what human well-being or happiness consists of – implicitly underpin many political philosophies. For example, the early Marx, with Engels (1999), argued that the exploitative relationship of the capitalist class over the working class, and the estrangement of the worker from his own productive labour was the root of man's 'alienation': i.e. a disconnection from the capitalist, from his own work, and from other workers in the same situation.

coercion can be of a more subtle variety than the use of statute (Campbell and Davidson, 2009). Also, understanding 'mental health' broadly as a spectrum of human well-being or happiness raises an interpretive problem with justifying a mental health policy or particular act of intervention on the basis of the client's mental health; for example what is measured, who measures it and how is it to be measured? We can even legitimately ask ourselves if it is possible to measure it.

In response, one could insist that 'mental health' is what mental health social work should be concerned with, and that this requires no direct concern with 'happiness'. Perhaps, on this view, mental health is a precondition of happiness; a *capability* one needs for happiness, but that may be all.[11] Indeed, it is possible to argue that implicit in the introduction of CTOs is that for those subject to them, if they cannot achieve happiness they *will* achieve mental health, at least as defined and measured by professionals. However, where delineating 'mental health' and 'happiness' was never conceptually easy, it is also currently practically conflated by policy, where governmental concern with poor mental health goes wider than the measures discussed above in relation to patients subject to mental health legislation. In the contemporary period actual judgements about individual cases are made in a context in which furthering 'mental health' together with 'happiness' are among the stated aims of the government.

The previous New Labour government was so concerned with the rates of unhappiness in the country that it appointed an advisor, Lord Richard Layard, to identify ways to improve the nation's mental health. In 2006 Layard proposed the training of an additional 10,000 Cognitive Behavioural Therapists who were to be based in 250 centres across the country. The current coalition government is also concerned about the mental health of the nation, Prime Minister David Cameron commenting that 'there's more to life than money and it's time we focused not just on GDP [Gross Domestic Product] but on GWB – general well-being' (quoted in Stratton, 2010, online). The mental health and happiness agenda should give the mental health social worker pause for thought. Social work professionals and their organizations are agents and agencies which operate simultaneously under the auspices of public legislation and regulatory frameworks, and also in the private lives of individuals. That is, they work at the interface of the state and its institutions on one hand, and clients – or groups of clients such as families – on the other. In such a position, social work in mental health is perhaps especially susceptible to becoming one of the vehicles through which 'the mental health of the nation' (however that is conceived by

---

11   For the 'capability' approach to welfare see Sen (1985) and also Nussbaum examined in Chapter 3.

governments or their advisors) might be effected, the use of CTO's being a particular case in point.

Importantly, the idea that we can use technical measures to calculate 'happiness' seems to reveal a particularly simplified understanding of the concept which may, arguably, be used to justify practices which are detrimental to 'happiness' proper. For Aristotle, as we have seen, happiness is a way of being and acting over the course of one's life, not merely a state of feeling happy, and it is through our actions in the pursuit of the good and virtuous life that happiness in this sense could be achieved. We need not be Ancient Greeks or confirmed Aristotelians to agree that there is more to human happiness than feeling cheerful; that such things as projects, relationships, achievements, and exercising and developing our intellectual and emotional capacities are a crucial part of what we think of as a worthwhile – 'happy' – life (Nozick, 1974). Similarly, the pursuit of knowledge and awareness of our inability to fully account for the human condition, of facing up to the realities of some of the horrors of the world, can leave us saddened and dissatisfied. From this perspective, it is possible to claim that artificial happiness, or more precisely, drug-induced euphoria or contentment, whether by the voluntary use of illicit drugs or their legal administration under a CTO, is an abdication of the pursuit of happiness and also of responsibility for facing up to both our own and society's problems.

This does not mean, from an individual case-by-case perspective that the use of prescribed medication is never warranted or beneficial, or that psychosocial interventions such as Cognitive Behaviour Therapy cannot help some individuals, it is merely to illustrate that such chemical or technical approaches to the achievement of 'happiness' suggest a view of happiness that is a far cry from the concept's classical philosophical meaning. The practical danger here is that when such approaches also form governmental thinking – CTOs for the few, CBT for the many – it could be argued that to a greater or lesser degree, social policy not only views an ever-increasing number of us as unhappy but also as less than autonomous subjects.

Conclusion

In this chapter we have sought to detail some of the ethical problems that arise in relation to the introduction of Community Treatment Orders for psychiatric patients from teleological (utilitarian) and deontological (Kantian) perspectives and also to highlight the way in which such orders are justified and subsequently used. We also noted that the government's focus on mental health and happiness risks simplifying both concepts and reducing our status as autonomous subjects. Space precludes a detailed discussion of the role of power in shaping the moral and ethical agenda, but we hope that the power differentials between mental health professionals and their patients have been made clear, especially in the power of the former to categorise the latter as mentally ill which can then make them subject to mental health legislation with all that that can entail.

In questioning the evidential base and ethical perspectives in favour of CTOs we have sought to highlight the danger of hiding behind simple ethical assertions such as 'I'm doing what's right'. Unpicking such an assertion necessarily leads to a need to elaborate on what is meant by 'right' and precisely for whose benefit is this 'right' action being implemented. As we have discussed, it is potentially possible to justify the CTO and indeed other aspects within mental health social work by recourse to ethical arguments, so in this respect the CTO or any other measure is not inherently 'unethical' *per se*, so we are not arguing that the conscientious mental health practitioner should categorically refuse to be involved with them. On the contrary, this chapter has to a large extent been motivated precisely by the fact that these practitioners now have a duty to decide upon and justify the use of CTOs in a range of circumstances, and we have sought to show that much greater consideration to the ethical dilemmas of mental health policy in theory and practice is needed at both the level of direct practice and wider political discourse. In this respect, we hope to have suggested that 'doing what is right' in the professional capacity of the mental health social work role cannot simply amount to the correct application of rules or procedures. Most obviously such rules, or measures including CTOs, require interpretation at the ground level of practice, case by case. But ethical professionals may also think about their specified duties and what their role demands of them at a much more fundamental level.

The radical contribution to social work, at its best, endeavoured to make social workers think critically about what they were doing, why they were doing it and on what basis. In short, it endeavoured to stop social workers from being complacent in their role, to make them feel uncomfortable at some or other aspect of their social role and professional practice. This is important not only in and of itself, but also to aid critical evaluation of professional role obligations and the institutions that define those obligations with the aim of improving practice. In questioning the justification for CTOs and the drive for 'mental health' and 'happiness' from utilitarian, Kantian and Aristotelian[12] perspectives, we have sought to carry on that radical tradition.

---

12   For a more detailed defence of a neo-Aristotelian virtue ethical approach to social work see McBeath and Webb (2002).

Further Reading

Campbell, J. and Davidson, G. (2009) 'Coercion in the Community: A situated approach to the examination of ethical challenges for mental health social workers', *Ethics and Social Welfare*, 3, pp. 249–63: This paper discusses the various forms, some formal, others informal, that coercion within mental health services can take, and how the decision can be reached after taking into consideration such issues as legal, organisational, personal or interpersonal circumstances. The paper provides a good discussion of the many complexities involved in the decision to use or not to use coercion and will be of use to practitioners within the mental health field.

Barker, P. (ed.) (2011) *Mental Health Ethics: The Human Context*, Oxford: Routledge: Phil Barker not only edits but substantially contributes to this book that discusses many aspects of ethical importance for those involved in mental health services from a variety of perspectives. There are numerous contributors to sections on ethics and mental health, care and treatment, professional viewpoints, the human context of mental health practices and ideological debates. In each section the ethical dilemmas and debates are discussed providing an invaluable theoretical and practical resource for those engaged in the mental health field.

Mill, J.S. (2008[1859]) *On Liberty*. Oxford: Oxford University Press: Mill defends the value of individual liberty and rejects the legitimacy of paternalistic intervention: coercing someone on the grounds that it would in some way make them better off. Hence this classic work gets to grips with a key philosophical argument, discussed in this chapter, concerning the justification (or otherwise) of social work practices.

References

Aristotle (2009) *The Nicomachean Ethics* (trans. Ross, D.). Oxford: Oxford University Press.

Barrett Report (2006) *The Independent Inquiry into the Care and Treatment of John Barrett*, South West London Strategic Health Authority, http://news.bbc.co.uk/nol/shared/bsp/hi/pdfs/16_11_06_barrett.pdf (accessed 5 December 2006)

BBC News (2010) 'Plan to measure Happiness "not woolly" – Cameron', BBC News Online, 25 November 2010, http://www.bbc.co.uk/news/uk-11833241 (accessed 6 April 2011)

Banks, S. (2006) *Ethics and Values in Social Work* (3rd edn). Hampshire: Palgrave Macmillan.

Bogg, D. (2010) *Values and Ethics in Mental Health Practice*. Exeter: Learning Matters.

Campbell, J. and Davidson, G. (2009) 'Coercion in the Community: A situated approach to the examination of ethical challenges for mental health social workers', *Ethics and Social Welfare*, 3: 249–63.

Churchill, R. (2007) 'International Experiences of Using Community Treatment Orders', *Institute of Psychiatry*, http://www.iop.kcl.ac.uk/news/downloads/final2ctoreport8march07.pdf (accessed 2 November 2011)

Cordell, S. (2011) 'Virtuous Persons and Social Roles', *Journal of Social Philosophy*, 42: 254–72.

CQC (2011) (Care Quality Commission) 'Monitoring the Mental Health Act in 2010/11', Care Quality Commission, http://www.cqc.org.uk/sites/default/files/media/documents/cqc_mha_report_2011_main_final.pdf

Cruikshank, B. (1999) *The Will to Empower: Democratic Citizens and Other Subjects*. New York: Cornell University Press.

Dale, E. (2010) 'Is Supervised Community Treatment Ethically Justifiable?', *Journal of Medical Ethics*, 36: 271–4.

Dawson, J. and Burns, T. (2008) 'Community Treatment Orders are not a good thing' (in debate with Lawton-Smith, S.), *British Journal of Psychiatry*, 193: 96–100, http://bjp.rcpsych.org/content/193/2/96.full.pdf+html (accessed 1 November 2011).

DH (2001) (Department of Health) *Safety First: Report of the National Confidential Inquiry into Suicide and Homicide by People with Mental Illness*. London: Department of Health.

DH (2006) (Department of Health) *Avoidable Deaths: Report of the National Confidential Inquiry into Suicide and Homicide by People with Mental Illness*. London: Department of Health.

Furedi, F. (2004) *Therapy Culture: Cultivating Vulnerability in an Uncertain Age*. London: Routledge.

Gibbs, A., Dawson, J., Ansley, C. and Mullen, R. (2005) 'How Patients in New Zealand View Community Treatment Orders', *Journal of Mental Health*, 14: 357–68.

Howlett, M. (1997) 'Community Care Homicide Inquiries and Risk Assessment', in H. Kemshall and J. Pritchard (1996) *Good Practice in Risk Assessment and Risk Management*. London: Jessica Kingsley.

James, A. (2006) 'CTOS do not work … and that's according to the evidence base', *Psychminded*, http://www.psychminded.co.uk/news/news2006/dec06/ctos.htm

Kisely, S.R., Campbell, L.A. and Preston, N.J. (2005) 'Compulsory Community and Involuntary Outpatient Treatment for People with Severe Mental Disorders', *Cochrane Database of Systematic Reviews*, 3.

Kymlicka, W. (2001) *Contemporary Political Philosophy*. Oxford: Oxford University Press.

Lawton-Smith, S. (2008) 'Community Treatment Orders Are Not a Good Thing' (in debate with Dawson, J. and Burns, T.), *British Journal of Psychiatry*, 193: 96–100, http://bjp.rcpsych.org/content/193/2/96.full.pdf+html (accessed 1 November 2011).

Lenman, J. (2000) 'Consequentialism and Cluelessness', *Philosophy & Public Affairs*, 29: 342–70.

Maden, A. (2004) 'Violence, Mental Disorder and Public Protection', *Psychiatry*, 11: 1–4.

Maden, A. (2005) 'The Point of Principles: Commentary on … The Draft Mental health Bill in England: Without principles', *The Psychiatrist*, 29: 250–51, http://pb.rcpsych.org/content/29/7/250.full (accessed 10 October 2011)

Marx, K. and Engels, F. (1999) *The German Ideology*, (ed.) C.J. Arthur. London: Lawrence and Wishart.

McBeath, G. and Webb, S.A. (2002) 'Virtue Ethics and Social Work: Being Lucky, Realistic and Not Doing One's Duty', *British Journal of Social Work*, 32: 1014–136.

McLaughlin, H. (2009) 'What's in a Name: "Client", "Patient", "Customer", "Consumer", "Expert by Experience", "Service User" – What's next?', *British Journal of Social Work*, 39: 1101–17.

McLaughlin, K. (2008) *Social Work, Politics and Society: From Radicalism to Orthodoxy*. Bristol: The Policy Press.

McLaughlin K. (2010) 'Control and Social Work: A reflection on some twenty-first century developments', *Practice*, 22: 143–54.

McLaughlin, K. (2012) *Surviving Identity: Vulnerability and the Psychology of Recognition*. London: Routledge.

Mill, J.S. (2008) [1859] *On Liberty*. Oxford: Oxford University Press.

Munetz, M.R., Galon, P.A. and Frese, F.J. (2003) 'The Ethics of Mandatory Community Treatment', *Journal of the American Academy of Psychiatry Law*, 31: 173–83.

Nozick, R. (1974) *Anarchy, State, and Utopia*. New York: Basic Books.

O'Reilly, R., Keegan, D.L., Corring, D. et al. (2006) 'A qualitative analysis of the use of community treatment orders in Saskatchewan', *International Journal Law and Psychiatry*, 29: 516–24.

Parker, C. and McCulloch, A. (1999) *Key Issues from Homicide Inquiries*. London: MIND.

Rawls, J. (1972) *A Theory of Justice*. Oxford: Clarendon Press.

Scarre, G. (1996) *Utilitarianism*. London: Routledge.

Sen, A. (1985) *Commodities and Capabilities*. Oxford: Oxford University Press.

Smart, J.C.C. and Williams, B. (eds) (1973) *Utilitarianism: For and Against*. Cambridge: Cambridge University Press.

Stratton, A. (2010) 'David Cameron aims to make happiness the new GDP', http://www.guardian.co.uk/politics/2010/nov/14/david-cameron-wellbeing-inquiry (accessed 20 November 2010).

Waldron, J. (ed.) (1984) *Theories of Rights*. Oxford: Oxford University Press.

Webb, S.A. and McBeath, G.B. (1989) 'A Political Critique of Kantian Ethics in Social Work', *British Journal of Social Work*, 19: 491–506.

Wenar, L. (2011) 'Rights', *Stanford Encylopedia of Philosophy*, http://plato.stanford.edu/entries/rights/

Williams, B. (1985) *Ethics and the Limits of Philosophy*. Cambridge, MA: Harvard University Press.

Yianni, C. (2009) 'Aces High: My control trumps your care', *Ethics and Social Welfare*, 3: 337–43.

6 Ethical Contradictions in Critiques of Psychiatry

John Hopton

Introduction

There are many different ways of conceptualising mental health problems but for convenience most of these competing perspectives can be placed into one of two 'ideal' categories. In simple terms, people who have specific beliefs about the nature and cause of mental health problems and how they could or should be managed can be divided into those who talk in terms of mental illness and those who think of mental health problems as being existential problems or problems in living. The former group believes that mental health problems are abnormalities with similar properties to physical illnesses which can be diagnosed, managed and treated in the same way as physical illnesses can. The most extreme form of this is a strictly bio-chemical model which sees the problem wholly in terms of bio-chemical imbalances and the solution in terms of physical treatments which manipulate bio-chemical and/or neurological processes within the human body and brain.

Most contemporary biological psychiatrists, however, acknowledge that mental illness is the product of complex inter-relationships between biology and environment in which it can be difficult to determine what the exact balance between biological and environmental influences actually is (Hedaya, 1996). The latter group take the view that what are sometimes considered to be mental health problems are simply alternative (albeit less common) ways of being in the world and that, while they may sometimes or in some way be distressing to the individual experiencing them, it is possible for people to learn to manage them without the unsolicited intervention of self-appointed professional experts such as psychiatrists, clinical psychologists, mental health nurses etc. who make decisions about what is normal, what is abnormal and how any presumed abnormalities should be managed. This social model focuses on peer support, self help and addressing political, economic and social factors such as structural inequalities. For convenience, in this chapter these two ideal types will respectively be called the 'medical model of mental illness' and the 'social model of mental distress'.

Many people involved in social work and social care (whether as unqualified workers, student social workers or as fully qualified social workers) have misgivings about the medical model of [so-called] mental illness, and claim to base their practice on a social model of mental distress. Almost invariably, such a preference is linked to endeavours to work in ways which are user-centred and are congruent with what is considered to be good practice in terms of anti-oppressive/anti-discriminatory practice. While the medical model of mental health/illness is far from perfect, such disregard for it can have the unintended consequence of causing people to overlook what positive contributions it can make to the management of mental distress. It may also simultaneously cause advocates of alternative approaches to overlook the limitations of their own favoured approach(es). This risks oversimplifying our understanding of 'real world' activities by compressing complex and nuanced practice-based activities into convenient good/bad binaries. Furthermore, the so-called medical model of mental illness/health is not monolithic as some critics inform us but instead incorporates many eclectic and hybrid approaches to understanding and managing mental distress. For example, since the early and mid twentieth century psychoanalysis and behavioural psychology have been significant influences on medical psychiatry in Western Europe and the USA.

Perhaps the disregard for the medical model of mental illness is an artefact of the way in which the medical model came to dominate Western ideas about mental health. For example, in the British context, political lobbying by asylum doctors during the nineteenth century ultimately led to every asylum (latter to be renamed mental hospitals or psychiatric hospitals) being under the control of a so-called medical superintendent (i.e. a [senior] consultant psychiatrist). In England and Wales, this medical dominance was consolidated via provisions of the 1930 Mental Treatment Act and the 1959 Mental Health Act which replaced it (Jones, 1993; Scull, 1993). Despite the introduction of a new Mental Health Act in 1983 this was not challenged in any way until the introduction of relatively minor reforms to the 1983 Mental Health Act under the 2007 Mental Health Act (such as allowing a mental health professional from any discipline to take overall responsibility for a patient's care). Although the original mission of the medical model was to combat the stigma of madness on the basis that if madness was an illness, no one could be blamed for being mad (Scull, 1993), it is probably true however that the dominance of the medical model slowed down progress in understanding and managing mental health problems. For example, despite the claims by advocates of the medical model, no truly effective physical treatments were discovered until the advent of electro-convulsive therapy

(ECT) in the 1930s and the discovery of anti-depressant and anti-psychotic medications in the 1950s. Furthermore many of these treatments (especially ECT) can have severe and unpleasant side effects and/or are not effective in all cases, while the practice of leucotomy/lobotomy which also began in the 1930s was not only therapeutically ineffective but had unwanted irreversible effects. Nevertheless, the story of medical psychiatry is much more complex than that and it is difficult to see what would be gained by completely eradicating it.

In this chapter it is argued that the distinction between a medical and a social model of mental health problems[1] is not as clear cut as many people would like to believe as many perspectives on mental health incorporate elements of both social and medical approaches. This chapter then continues with a brief history of psychiatry and the critiques of psychiatry, which are then followed by a discussion of anti-oppressive and evidence based practice. A critical examination of initiatives which seek to reduce the stigma of mental health problems and promote greater acceptance of emotional, behavioural and psychological diversity is then presented. Finally, some tentative suggestions are made about how we might be able to develop a new understanding of mental health and mental health problems which takes account of the psychological, behavioural, biological, social and political dimensions of mental health without privileging any one perspective over the others.

Towards a Different Way of Thinking about Mental Health

One way of illustrating the benefits of the medical model is by considering the contributions to our understanding of mental health that have emerged from social psychiatry. Social psychiatry is a movement within medical psychiatry which has its roots in the work of eighteenth century doctors specialising in the treatment of madness. Advocates have included Thomas Withers, William Battie and Nathaniel Cotton; all of whom emphasised

---

1   Throughout this chapter the term 'mental health problems' will be used to avoid the clumsiness of constantly having to refer to mental distress/mental illness all the time or switching between using mental distress and mental illness depending on whether or not the medical model is being discussed. While it could be argued that the use of the work 'health' implies allegiance to the medical model, no true alternative is in common usage at the present time and its use here is intended to imply neutrality.

the importance of relationships, environmental factors and 'purposeful activity' to the development of therapeutic regimes within the 'madhouses' they ran (Nolan, 1993). Although the approaches to mental health care they developed are usually described as moral management, the concerns they had with the environment and social relationships are very similar to the concerns of social psychiatry. The spectrum of social psychiatrists runs from those who concern themselves as much with environmental causes of mental health problems as they do with notions of individual physical or psychological pathology to those who are solely interested in the social, political and economic courses of mental distress. All are interested in how you can structure the environments that people live in to facilitate mental health promotion. The contributions that social psychiatrists have made to our understanding of mental health issues include the development of therapeutic regimes for soldiers who experienced distress as a direct result of involvement in combat during the Second World War; the development of therapeutic communities; the introduction of patients' councils into long stay psychiatric hospitals; as well as recognition of and the development of methods of preventing the damaging effects of institutional living (Barton, 1976; Nolan, 1993; Clark, 1996; Gittins, 1998; Harrison, 2000).

A further illustration of the blurring of the boundaries between the medical and social models of understanding mental health is the case of what is sometimes called anti-psychiatry or critical psychiatry. This movement was spearheaded by the work of Thomas Szasz (who actually prefers the label of libertarian psychiatrist), Ronald David Laing and David Cooper in the late 1950s/early 1960s. Although there were differences of opinion between Szasz and the other 'anti-psychiatrists', they all believed that the mainstream psychiatry of the 1950s and 1960s which relied heavily on psychotropic medication and in-patient care in large Victorian institutions, many of which still had predominantly locked wards, was inherently oppressive. Significantly, all three men were medically trained psychiatrists and although they rejected many of the assumptions of mainstream psychiatry at that time Laing, Cooper and their followers were inspired as much by psychoanalysis, social psychiatry and existentialism as they were by radical political perspectives and influences from the 1960s counterculture (Crossley, 2005). In that sense, while the direct influence of anti-psychiatry on mainstream psychiatry has been marginal, it is nevertheless a movement whose origins are *within* psychiatry while many of the service user perspectives and new psychiatric perspectives that have emerged since the 1960s (such as Pat Bracken and Phil Thomas's concept of post-psychiatry) (Parker, Georgaca, Harper and Mclaughlin 1995; Crossley, 2005; Bracken and Thomas, 2007) may not have existed without it. In contrast, original critiques of psychiatry from writers with a social work background have been conspicuous by their relative absence.

This complex relationship between the social and medical models also raises the following question: If a person with mental health problems is considered to be the person with the most plausible claim to expertise in the understanding and management of his/her own mental health (which is a central concept underpinning the demands of the mental health survivor/ service user movement), how can dogmatic adherence to any model of mental health (whether social or medical) be congruent with principles of anti-oppressive and/or user centred practice? Furthermore, if we operate in a world where it is important that there is a strong evidence base for professional practice don't we have to concede that there is incontrovertible evidence that bio-chemical and genetic factors do have some influence on our mental health; albeit via interaction with environmental and psycho-social factors? (Hopton, 2006).

Additionally, we might ask the following questions:

- How do you impress on the general public the need to give special consideration to people who meet the diagnostic criteria for conditions such as depression, severe anxiety, psychosis, ADHD (attention deficit hyperactivity disorder) without making reference to these diagnoses and the significance of these diagnoses; and how do you get away from the fact that these diagnoses originate in the medical model?

In a social work context, this is an important question because it is difficult to get people the help they need in employment or education contexts unless a person is willing to participate in a process which will give them a diagnosis, as without the diagnosis the relevant authorities are unlikely to recognise the person's 'special needs' and make the reasonable adjustments that are necessary for the person to fulfil a particular job role or achieve educational success. Certainly it is possible for a person to 'go along' with the diagnostic game to get what they need; but this still leaves the question of whether most people in the general population would be quite so accepting of this kind of diversity if we were to completely abandon the medical model and simply take the position that there are different ways of being in the world so we have to make allowances for anyone who appears to see things or react to stimuli differently from the majority. Indeed, it is not uncommon for people outside the caring professions to strongly believe that dyslexia is just a middle class invention to excuse poor standards of literacy or that people who claim that their child has ADHD should just accept that their child wilfully behaves badly.

- If we do not borrow from the medical model – and the idea of normal and abnormal levels of functioning – will this cause as many problems as it solves? For example if, as some thinkers on mental health issues have suggested, we place non lethal self harm on a continuum with socially acceptable practices such as body-piercing and the wearing of high heel shoes (e.g. Pembroke, 1994), does this lead to a weakening of taboos on self harm which could be socially harmful? (For example it might be argued that – inasmuch as there are demonstrable links between suicide and other forms of self harm; a taboo on self harm has a socially protective function.)

For social workers this is not simply an abstract philosophical debate but is rather a real practice dilemma which they may have to address in their day to day role. On the one hand, diminishing the taboo and diminishing the stigma and feelings of shame may go hand in glove but if you 'normalise' self-injurious behaviour too much, are you encouraging a service user to follow a path which may lead eventually to serious injury or even death?

In a social work context, the social model approach has certainly been useful in helping to reduce the sense of shame and guilt people sometimes feel about their own self-injurious behaviours. It has, therefore, made it easier for users to speak about self harm. The social model has also helped to dispel some of the myths about the motivation for self harm and how people might be helped to overcome urges to self harm. In that sense, the contribution to understanding and managing self harm that has come from the social model should not be underestimated. However, it might be argued that at some point in the care of a self-injurious person, there may be some value to exploring with the self harming individual why most people do not engage in that kind of behaviour and, however sensitively and timely that it is done, that would imply that such behaviour was 'abnormal'.

- If all and sundry over-identify with the experiences of those who experience very serious forms of mental distress and very challenging problems in living that result from their intra-psychic experiences (whether we call those experiences mental illness, distress or something else); will that lead to a trivialisation of mental health problems and a backlash where people who require understanding and support will be told to just pull themselves together, toughen up etc.?

Depression is a good example of how such trivialisation could occur as 'depression' means different things to different people. To use a true 'case' example, a person who was on sick leave from work with a diagnosis of depression was regularly and enthusiastically hosting social occasions at his home and setting up a small business throughout the duration of his sick leave. While this kind of behaviour does not mean that he was not experiencing a degree of unhappiness, it is doubtful whether he would have met the formal medical criteria (for example, DSM-IV) for a diagnosis of depression. To contrast this with another example, on being told that a team member was not coming to training anymore because he was depressed and could not find the motivation to get in his car and drive to the gym, the response of one of his team mates was 'Well if he is depressed, that's all the more reason for him to come, because being with your mates is what you need when you're a bit down. He needs to stop feeling sorry for himself and get down here'. Anyone who has experience of working with depressed people would understand the problems of motivation and self doubt that are at the core of depression, but if the team mate in the second example had only had experience of 'depressed' people like the man in the first example, it is easy to see how he might have come to the conclusion that he did. Furthermore, the man in the first example was reacting to changes in his work situation, while there was no obvious immediate cause for the depression of the man in the second example.

Such confusion about what depression is has been the subject of extensive critical discussion by some psychiatrists (Horowitz and Wakefield, 2007). Whether or not we agree with their conclusion that you need to make an absolute clear distinction between 'depression' and 'normal sadness', these examples illustrate how the general public often fail to understand that depression does not always have an identifiable cause, is not always a reaction to disappointment and can affect different people in different ways. It may also lead to unsympathetic reactions to people who are in fact quite severely depressed. Some of the questions posed above are difficult to answer, while the answers to others may in turn lead to more questions than answers. Nevertheless, if we are ever to succeed in developing a truly person-centred approach to working with people with mental health problems, these issues have to be explored.

A Brief History of Critical Perspectives on Mental Health

One of the first organisations to challenge the rise of the newly emerging psychiatric profession in Britain in the mid nineteenth century was the *Alleged Lunatics' Friend Society*. However, although some members of the Alleged Lunatics' Friend Society did take issue with some aspects of claimed medical expertise and treatment, it could be argued that the main thrust of their activism was to critique the existence and growth of asylum-based care and the legal provisions which sustained it (Hervey, 1986). Perhaps, though, the emergence of explicit critiques of the post-nineteenth-century medical model of understanding mental health problems should be considered to date from the middle of the twentieth century with the publication of *The Myth of Mental Illness* by Thomas Szasz (1961) and *The Divided Self* by R.D. Laing (1960).

It would be a mistake nevertheless to suggest that the emergence of psychiatry as a branch of medicine in the mid nineteenth century led to a wholly bio-medical understanding of mental health problems which went completely unchallenged until Szasz and Laing came along. For example, many of the early psychiatrists were as much influenced by the ideology of moral management as they were by medical science. While some writers suggest that moral management was controlling and paternalistic, the significance of this approach which was developed during the eighteenth century was that it emphasised the essential humanity of 'mad' people and the need to have compassion for their suffering. Furthermore, many of the key features of what became known as moral management (which has some overlap with social psychiatry) were pioneered by physicians specialising in the management of mental health problems, such as Philippe Pinel, Nathaniel Cotton and William Battie. Similarly, Sigmund Freud was a neurologist whose interest in psychopathology ultimately led him to develop psychoanalysis (a psychological intervention) rather than pursue the development of effective physical treatments for mental health problems. Social psychiatry (which addresses the relationship between the individual and the social and physical environment and which led to the development of milieu therapy and therapeutic community approaches) was also well established by 1950. Thus, there are a number of traditions both within and on the margins of medical psychiatry which embrace perspectives on mental health which are not wholly defined by biological considerations and physical treatments.

Szasz and Laing's work, however, is significant as each sought to challenge the psychiatric establishment 'head on'. Although they had different concerns about psychiatry, these concerns did overlap. Laing argued that, contrary to received psychiatric wisdom, psychosis was not an illness which led to irrational thought and behaviour but had meaning and significance and that psychiatrists could promote recovery from psychosis if they found a way to interpret the seemingly irrational thought and behaviour and communicate with their patients about their concerns. Szasz's position was even more radical. He argued that as there are no objective markers which prove the existence of a mental health condition, then mental health conditions cannot be defined as illnesses; treatments therefore cannot be applied in exactly the same way as for infections or cancers. He insists that so-called mental illness is socially constructed and that behaviours and patterns of thought are defined as mental health problems when they deviate from widely accepted standards of morality or normality, and that psychiatry (at least when sponsored by the State) is the dishonest use of medical ideology to exercise social control over those whose ideas or behaviours are socially or politically inconvenient.

Neither the ideas of Laing nor those of Szasz have had a major impact on mainstream psychiatry, although many mental health professionals who completed their professional training during the 1960s and 1970s were exposed to their ideas. This in turn has led to the development of further critiques of various aspects of psychiatric, psychological and psychotherapeutic practice and perhaps also to greater open-mindedness to such critiques and to service user perspectives amongst mental health professionals who have completed their professional training since the 1970s. Indeed there is now an established tradition of anti-psychiatry (although the terms critical psychiatry and/or critical psychology are now more usually used). Through the work of writers such as Lucy Johnstone and Peter Breggin coupled with the growth of a mental health service users' movement, it is now widely accepted that ECT (electro-convulsive therapy) and psychiatric drugs can sometimes do more harm than good; people who self harm are no longer universally regarded as undeserving time-wasters; it is recognised that eating distress is far too complex to be effectively managed using crude behaviour modification based interventions; it is now recognised that talking therapies can be used to help people cope with psychotic symptoms; and it has been acknowledged that institutionalised sexism and institutionalised racism exist within mental health services.

Anti-oppressive Practice in Twenty-first Century Mental Health Care

Although its impact on mainstream psychiatry was minimal, the concept of anti-psychiatry and the idea that medical science could offer no worthwhile remedies for mental distress found favour with sections of the intelligentsia. For example, there were strong links between the leftist counterculture of the 1960s and 1970s and the ideas of Laing and his associates, while there is a synergy between the libertarian ideas of Szasz and the libertarian elements of the radical right political movement known as the New Right which emerged during the late 1970s and early 1980s. Anti-psychiatry also emboldened mental health professionals from disciplines other than medical psychiatry to challenge the dominance of bio-medical understandings of mental distress so that many mental health nurses, social workers, psychotherapists and counsellors came to regard the medical model of psychiatry as inherently bad. For example, the 1982 syllabus for the training of Registered Mental Health Nurses produced by the National Boards for

England and Wales was the first such [British] syllabus to be developed without any input from psychiatrists. This placed great emphasis on self awareness and interpersonal skills and only explicitly referred to the theory and practice of medical psychiatry and pharmacology on 2 of its 26 pages.

Perhaps though, medical psychiatry and the psychiatric profession have become something of a convenient scapegoat for mental health professionals who are reluctant to reflect critically on their own ideas and practices. For example, leaving aside powers of criminal courts, between 1959 and 2007 social workers in England and Wales were (along with the 'patient's' nearest relative) the only professionals empowered to make an application to compulsorily detain a person in a psychiatric in-patient facility. Many social workers would argue that as social workers they were/are uniquely positioned to provide an alternative (social and cultural) perspective to the medical model of mental illness during this process, but this claim can not be substantiated. Not only did the majority of the authors of the best known critiques of medical psychiatry and clinical psychiatry come from within those professional disciplines, but (notwithstanding the existence of social work textbooks which do explicitly critique the medical model) authors from social work backgrounds were conspicuous by their relative absence from the roll call of major critics of psychiatry. Thus, whatever merits generic social work ideas around anti-oppressive and anti-discriminatory practice might have in relation to mental health issues, mental health care and mental health services, they were not a direct response to prevailing ideas about mental health *per se*; and neither are they evidence that social workers alone are in a position to critique medical psychiatry, clinical psychology etc. (although they may well be in a position to make useful contributions to the wider debate).

The Mental Health Service Users' Movement

As mentioned previously, there is nothing new about users of mental health services expressing discontent about the quality of those services. However, a truly effective mental health service users' movement did not begin to develop in ways which have led to mainstream acceptance until the 1980s. This was possibly the result of a more general social trend towards consumerism coinciding with the growth of a disability rights movement which was already having some success in challenging the medicalisation of disability. Whatever the reasons though, the emergence of a strong mental health service users movement did make a big difference to the way in which mental health problems were/are understood. For all their radical rhetoric, the likes of Laing and Szasz were still very much playing the role of expert professionals who knew 'the answer' to people's mental health problems and/or what was wrong with psychiatry. With the emergence of a well-organised user movement service users began to offer new explanations of and new ways of coping with problems such as eating distress, self harm, voice hearing, and so on. Although such users' perspectives sometimes refer to people's mental distress being triggered by specific events and series of events and/or (particularly in the case of voice-hearing) family histories which hint at hereditary factors, aetiological factors are not usually a major consideration in these accounts. Instead, the focus of such 'post-modern' approaches tends to be more on how unhelpful it can be when professionals offer rigid dogmatic explanations of what is happening, what its causes might be, how it can or even how it should be managed and what the prognosis is; combined with support for autobiographical accounts of how people have found ways to effectively manage their own distress.

Throughout the 1990s and onwards into the twenty-first century a large body of literature authored by service users has emerged and the involvement of service user representatives in policy reviews, the teaching of mental health professionals in training and, latterly, recruitment to pre-qualifying training programmes for mental health professionals has become the norm. Consequently, the vast majority of people training as mental health professionals since the beginning of the twenty-first century should have been exposed to service user perspectives on mental health problems and mental health care, and should therefore have an understanding of many of the alternative perspectives on mental health problems which have been developed and/or advocated by service user activists. However, although some of the perspectives on mental health problems that are promoted by service user activists are quite radical, the service user movement is no more monolithic than is medical psychiatry. Thus, while there are service users who are highly critical of interventions which are associated with behavioural psychology (such as cognitive behavioural therapy) and medical psychiatry (such as psychotropic drugs and ECT), there are also service users who accept those kinds of interventions because they have found them to be useful. Within any of these sub-groups there may be further divisions. For example, there may be service users who wholeheartedly embrace the bio-medical model of mental health problems and believe that there is a biological base to their problem and that only drugs can resolve the problem, but who dislike the fact that mental health law allows for compulsory admission of 'psychiatric patients'; but there may also be individuals who reject biological explanations for their mental health problems but are content to be treated with drugs or ECT on a pragmatic basis because the treatment makes them feel better or enables them to function better. Thus, although service users may replace the language of traditional psychiatry with more accurate descriptions of their experiences (for example, eating disorders may be referred to as eating distress and vague diagnostic categories such as 'schizophrenia' may be replaced with descriptions of specific phenomena such as voice-hearing or unusual beliefs); their strategy for managing their mental health problems may reflect the same kind of eclecticism that was a feature of twentieth century medical psychiatry.

Textbooks of psychiatry do not usually suggest that you use a particular approach if you believe one particular aetiological theory is stronger than the others and a different approach if you believe another aetiological theory is the strongest. Instead they imply that you should utilise a combination of approaches and – contrary to popular mythology – they rarely suggest that medication is the be-all and end-all (although they may well suggest that medication is usually – or even always – an important, if not essential, part of the care and treatment package). Thus the most significant difference between medical psychiatry and service users' perspectives on mental health problems is the *attitude towards* medication, as service users' perspectives do not ascribe the same pivotal role to medication that medical psychiatry traditionally does. Nevertheless, after over 50 years of anti-psychiatry/critical psychiatry/post-psychiatry there are medically trained psychiatrists who are more open-minded about the role of medication in managing mental health problems, while (as noted previously) there are service users who find that psycho-active medication can be helpful.

Identity Politics and Mental Health

Just as there are arguably as many similarities as there are differences between medical psychiatry and users' perspectives on the management of mental health problems, the question of diagnostic categories is also a complex issue. There is growing acceptance from almost all quarters that certain psychiatric diagnoses are highly stigmatizing. For example, 'schizophrenia' is now considered by many service users and mental health professionals alike to be an unhelpful diagnostic category because of the wide range of behaviours and experiences that can be covered by that umbrella term and the false assumptions that lay people might make about a person given such a diagnosis. Likewise, the diagnosis of 'personality disorder' is problematic because of similar vagueness about what the term actually means coupled with assumptions that some forms of personality disorder are untreatable and that people with such diagnoses are unable to form meaningful and sustainable relationships with others. However, there are other psychiatric diagnoses and similar labels which people seem to be relatively eager to embrace. Thus, in recent years there has been a succession of people in the public eye who have chosen to make public declarations that they are 'bi-polar', 'dyslexic', have a history of depression, have a history of self harm, or have overcome [sometimes multiple] addictions. Although this may help to reduce the stigma sometimes experienced by people who experience mental health problems, when such stories are covered in populist celebrity-focused magazines and other media, readers sometimes over-identify with their idols and may use this kind of language inappropriately so that the profound distress felt by others can inadvertently be trivialised. For example, it is now commonplace for people to refer to quite normal levels of mildly obsessional behaviour as being 'a bit OCD' in ways which suggest that the speaker has no idea exactly how disabling and distressing obsessional compulsive disorder (OCD) can be for some people. Furthermore, as in the earlier discussion of depression, such inappropriate use of the OCD label could paradoxically lead indirectly to a less sympathetic response (rather than a more sympathetic response) to a person with severe OCD. Similarly, people who behave recklessly and/or engage in anti-social behaviour might mistakenly see similarities between their behaviours and the excesses of celebrities who identify themselves as bi-polar and claim the label for themselves in ways that reduce rather than promote understanding of what it really means to be bi-polar.

The question of the pros and cons of 'normalising' thoughts, feelings and behaviours which psychiatry categorises as 'abnormal' raises the question of when a person's mental health problems should be considered to be a mitigating factor when their problems cause them to engage in criminal or anti-social behaviour that they would not otherwise engage in. Although criminal law relating to mental health issues is now more complex than the definition implies, our ways of thinking about this still have their roots in the McNaughton or M'Naghten Rules which date from 1843 and state that

> to establish a defence on the ground of insanity, it must be clearly proved that, at the time of the committing of the act, the party accused was labouring under such a defect of reason, from disease of the mind, as not to know the nature and quality of the act he was doing; or, if he did know it, that he did not know he was doing what was wrong.

However, some radical mental health professionals and service user activists argue that, for example, just because a voice is telling you to kill someone it doesn't mean that you are compelled to do so. They suggest that there are other choices available to you and that allowing people to use such a defence has the unintended consequence of stigmatising all mental health service users by promoting the idea that mentally distressed people may be irrational, unpredictable and could be potentially dangerous. Instead they suggest that if good quality user-friendly mental health services were readily available, most people would usually get help before we arrived at the point where a mentally distressed person committed a crime, and where that did not happen they should be dealt with in the same way as any other offender but given access to user-centred mental health services before, during and after sentencing (Newnes and Holmes, 1989; Beresford and Hopton, 2002). Such arguments have their merits – not least if you use a utilitarian argument about what brings the greatest benefit to the greatest number – but it also raises the question of what the most appropriate response would be to a distressed person who (for whatever reason) did not make use of mental health services until after they had committed a crime. Furthermore, the principle behind the McNaughton Rules would seem to be a good way of assessing whether a person's reckless spending and consequent debts should be re-paid in full in the normal way because a person made a rational choice and should face up to the consequences of his/her actions or should be managed more sensitively because the person had incurred the debts as a consequence of a manic/hypomanic episode or a psychotic break. If you don't accept that a person's mental health problems may sometimes be mitigation for reckless behaviour, might the stress of making them face up to their supposed responsibilities leave them with mental health (and other) problems that spiral further out of control?

Narrowing the Gap between the Medical Model of Mental Illness and Person-centred Social Work

In trying to develop a truly ethical and person-centred approach to social work practice with people who experience mental distress we face two considerable inter-related problems. One is that there are a variety of factors which can combine in many different ways to contribute to a person's mental distress, while different therapeutic interventions work for different people even when their distress seems similar. The other is that it is difficult to find a common language to discuss these issues which is equally acceptable to all concerned. Consequently, even before a social worker begins to explore how a mentally distressed person wishes to manage their distress s/he runs the risk of alienating them by using language which might imply that the social worker has a very different understanding of distress to that of the service user. Furthermore, even if this language barrier can be transcended, there is still the problem of how much confidence service users who believe themselves to be ill can have in a social worker who wholeheartedly rejects the medical model of mental illness – or vice versa.

After nearly 200 years of medical psychiatry and about 50 years of explicit targeted critiques of psychiatry we still do not really know what causes mental distress, how it can be prevented or how we can best facilitate recovery from it. Indeed, it might be argued that all we really know is the following:

- All the thoughts, feelings, perceptions, beliefs behaviours etc. which psychiatry suggests are 'pathological' exist on a continuum with 'normal' thoughts, feelings, perceptions, beliefs, behaviours etc.
- Any human being might experience distress at any time, and there may or may not be an obvious trigger for that distress.
- Some people are more vulnerable to experiencing distress but it is not always possible to predict accurately who the most and least vulnerable individuals are.

We also know that people successfully manage their distress in many different ways and that once someone has found what works best for them they are able to achieve a reasonable state of well-being and live a fulfilling life. Also, many new treatments have been developed, new ideas about well-being and recovery have emerged and despite the persistence of ignorance, stigma and discrimination; many lay people as well as professionals have a better understanding of what it means to experience severe distress and the kind of support that people need to live through it (Pryjmachuk, 2011)

Given the continuing lack of clarity about what causes mental distress, whether or not it can be prevented, whether it is indeed desirable to prevent mental distress or whether it serves some important adaptive purpose, and the impossibility of finding a 'one size fits all' intervention to alleviate mental distress and/or facilitate recovery; there is a need for a radical rethink about how we conceptualise mental distress. Although debates about the aetiology (the study of the origins of problems) of mental health problems can be interesting, they have now largely served their purpose by helping people hypothesise what kind of interventions may help people to manage their mental health problems. We now have a good understanding of what these are. Thus, rather than selecting our favourite theory and sticking doggedly to it or working on the basis of simplistic views of the medical model being inherently bad while social or psycho-social models are inherently more constructive and more person-centred; it might be more ethical to think in terms of what helps a person to cope with their own problems and what the person is comfortable with. Although some service users may be more comfortable trying out approaches which have been shown to be helpful in a statistically significant number of cases, such an approach does not need to be based on hierarchies of what kind of evidence base is the strongest. Instead, what is required is an approach where mental health professionals are able to work their way through a catalogue of interventions which some people have found to be helpful and exploring with service users which they would like to try first and then support them on a journey of discovery during which the service user experiments with different approaches until they find the one(s) that work best for them. Ironically, notwithstanding the prominence sometimes given to biological factors within medical psychiatry, this is not dissimilar to the approach found in many textbooks of psychiatry, where interventions are as likely to be discussed in terms of them being pragmatic ways of managing signs and symptoms as related to specific aetiological theories.

Thus when aspiring to more ethical intervention(s) with a service user who hears voices/experiences auditory hallucinations (for example), a worker might begin by exploring with that person how they themselves conceptualise their voices. Do they consider their voices to be part of themselves, a welcome intrusion from outside themselves or an unwelcome intrusion from outside themselves? Are they supernatural, echoes from the past, one's own thoughts repeated or something else? How powerful and influential are the voices? Does the service user want to engage with them, tolerate but ignore them or eradicate them? If they want to engage with them or find some other way of living with them, how could this be done and where can the techniques be learnt? If the service user wants to eradicate them, do they want to use psychiatric drugs or use some other strategy? If they want to go down the medication route, what kind of information does the service user need and what kind of conversation does he or she need to have with the prescribing doctor or nurse prescriber?

Conclusion

Many new ways of thinking about mental health problems and many new ways of managing mental distress have been developed since the heyday of anti-psychiatry in the late 1960s to the mid 1970s and the approach that is most likely to result in practices which are truly user-centred is what the psychiatrists Phil Thomas and Pat Bracken have termed 'post-psychiatry'. Post-psychiatry is an approach to psychiatry which goes beyond debates about the validity or otherwise of the medical model. It takes account of evidence based interventions, service user and survivor voices and experience, cultural, political and social contexts and the whole spectrum of ideas about mental health and the democratisation of mental health care (Bracken and Thomas, 2009). From a practical point of view, a social worker working with a person with mental health problems might achieve this by putting their personal beliefs about mental health problems and their causes to one side and instead focusing on the following issues:

- What kinds of feelings, thoughts, situations, experiences etc. present problems for you?
- How long have these issues been a problem for you?
- Were there/Are there any triggers for these issues becoming a problem for you? If so is there anything that can be done to avoid or minimise the impact of those triggers?
- Is there anything that makes your problems worse and is there anything that can be done about that?
- How do these problems affect you on a day to day basis?
- What do you find helps you to cope with the problems?
- What aspects of your problems do you feel you need more help with?
- What things have you tried to help you but which haven't worked out, and are there any of those that you would like to try again?
- What other ways of coping have you heard about and would you like to try?
- Where might we go to get further information about alternative approaches to managing the problem?

Such questions could easily be incorporated into a social work assessment and have the advantage of avoiding assumptions about the exact nature of a person's distress (such as that they are 'depressed', 'psychotic', 'obsessional', paranoid or whatever) while leaving the door open to discussing the involvement of a GP or a psychiatrist. At the other end of the spectrum, they allow for a service user to explore with a social worker any negative feelings, anxieties etc. they might have about the possibility of being labelled, 'sectioned', or coerced into taking medication if they seek psychiatric help and for the social worker and the service user to jointly explore possible alternatives.

In conclusion, the early critiques of psychiatry from the 1960s and 1970s played an important role in challenging the ideological supremacy of bio-medical approaches to mental health but are now largely of academic interest. For example, while they have been relatively successful in encouraging more open-minded approaches to mental health problems, other more complex perspectives on mental health have now emerged. However, there is still no definitive answer to what the origins and precipitating causes of mental health problems actually are and there are no therapeutic approaches which are universally acceptable to all people with similar diagnoses. Thus, I would argue that the most ethical way in which social workers can help service users with mental health problems is to help them to navigate their way through the landscape of multiple theories about, and recommended interventions for, whatever mental health problems they may have; and work collaboratively with them to find the approaches ways which will help them to manage such problems effectively in ways which are acceptable to them.

Further reading

David, A.S., Kapur, S., and McGuffin, P. (2011) *Schizophrenia: The Final Frontier*. London: Psychology Press: a comprehensive review of what is known about schizophrenia/psychosis at the beginning of the twenty-first century. Although it focuses only on psychosis, it has been argued by Thomas Szasz (and by others) that psychosis has become the 'core business' of psychiatry and is thus the area where most research has been concentrated. This book provides strong evidence of both environmental and biological factors being important in the development of psychosis.

Hedaya, R.J. (1996) *Understanding Biological Psychiatry*. New York: W.W. Norton: This key book highlights the importance of excluding the possibility that apparently psychiatric illnesses are organic conditions which require medical intervention as well as demonstrating that most contemporary biological psychiatrists are very clear that mental distress is the result of complex interaction between biology and environment

Pilgrim, D. (2009) *Key Concepts in Mental Health*. London: Sage: This book provides a guide to many of the key ideas in psychiatry/mental health care since the mid twentieth century which is both comprehensive and concise.

References

Barton, R. (1976) *Institutional Neurosis*. Bristol: J. Wright and Sons.

Beresford, P. and Hopton, J. (2002) What is Justice? *Openmind*, 114 (March/April), 20–21.

Bracken, P. and Thomas, P. (2007) Postpsychiatry: a new direction for mental health. In Reynolds, J. et al. (eds), *Mental Health Still Matters*. Basingstoke: Palagrave Macmillan.

Clark, D.H. (1996) *The Story of a Mental Hospital*. London: Process Press.

Crossley, N. (2005) *Contesting Psychiatry: Social Movements in Mental Health*. London: Routledge.

Freeman, H.L. (1984) *Mental Health and the Environment*. London: Churchill Livingstone.

Gittins, D. (1998) *Madness In Its Place*. London: Routledge.

Harrison, T. (2000) *Bion, Rickman, Foulkes and the Northfield Experiments*. London: Jessica Kingsley.

Hedaya, R.J. (1996) *Understanding Biological Psychiatry*. New York: W.W. Norton.

Hervey, N. (1986) Advocacy or Folly: The Alleged Lunatics' Friend Society 1845–63, *Medical History*, 30, 245–75.

Hopton, J. (2006) The Future of Critical Psychiatry, *Critical Social Policy*, 26(1): 57–73.

Horowitz, A.V. and Wakefield, J.C. (2007) *The Loss of Sadness: How Psychiatry Transformed Normal Sorrow into Depressive Disorder*. New York: Oxford University Press.

Jones, K. (1993) *Asylums and After*. London: Athlone Press.

Laing, R.D. (1960) *The Divided Self*. Harmondsworth: Penguin.

Newnes, C. and Holmes, G. (1989) The Future of Mental Health Services. In Newnes, C., Holmes, G. and Dunn, C. *This Is Madness*. Ross-on-Wye: PCCS Books, 273–84.

Nolan, P. (1993) *A History of Mental Health Nursing*. London: Chapman and Hall.

Parker, I., Georgaca, E, Harper, D. and McLaughlin, T. (1995) *Deconstructing Psychopathology*. London: Sage.

Pembroke, L. (ed.) (1994) *Self-harm: Perspectives from Personal Experience*. London: Survivors Speak Out.

Pryjmachuk, S. (2011) *Mental Health Nursing: An Evidence-based Introduction*. London: Sage.

Scull, A. (1993) *The Most Solitary of Afflictions*. London: Yale University Press.

Szasz, T. (1961) *The Myth of Mental Illness: Foundations of a Theory of Personal Conduct*. New York: Hoeber-Harper.

7 An Ethics Journey: Ethical Governance of Social Research with Vulnerable Adults and the Implications for Practice

Richard Ward and Sarah Campbell

Introduction

In this chapter we consider the challenges associated with seeking to undertake social research in health and social care settings when vulnerable older adults are involved. Our theme of the *ethics journey* is developed in a number of ways during our discussion but relates particularly to our experience of seeking formal ethical approval for a piece of qualitatively-driven research into the everyday lives of people with dementia. The journey in question, as we describe and discuss below, involved the step-by-step negotiation of a time- and labour-intensive passage from the preparation of an initial application to the final awarding of ethical approval that enabled us to commence our research. In seeking to make sense of this experience, we draw particularly upon the writings of the queer sociologist and critical humanist Ken Plummer (2001) whose own work highlights the long-running tensions between 'ethical absolutists' and 'situational relativists' and who subsequently calls for 'narratives of research ethics and communities of research stories' (p. 227) as a response to the ethical challenges of social research.

Our particular focus is upon the opening stages of The Hair and Care Project. The study, which is on-going, is concerned with issues of appearance, body work and dignity for people with dementia, with particular emphasis upon their use of hairdressing services in care. We outline below the tensions associated with gaining ethical approval for an ethnographic study from a system essentially oriented to positivist scientific medical research. Our commentary contributes to an emerging counter-narrative from within the social sciences in response to what has been described as the 'ethics creep' (Haggerty, 2004) of formal processes for the governance of research in the field of health and social care. We outline both our 'official' ethics journey and dealings with an NHS Research Ethics Committee alongside our own unofficial journey to design and implement a more situated and contextualised response to the ethical dilemmas of research with vulnerable older people. Our experience of the former has led us to conclude that qualitatively-driven research is disadvantaged by the current system for approval; that the process itself serves to alienate researchers from the ethical aspects of their work; and crucially that unhelpful and artificial divisions have been introduced between questions of the ethics of research and the ethics of practice in dementia care.

Our discussion is relevant to practitioner-researchers and practitioners in the field of older people's services as we seek to illustrate the essentially relational nature of ethical dilemmas when working with vulnerable older adults and the overlapping challenges faced by researchers and practitioners in the field. We contend that many of the ethical dilemmas faced by practitioners and other stakeholders are shared by social researchers as we enter into their worlds in order to better understand experiences of dementia and care 'from the inside'. With this in mind we call for a radical rethinking of the current system for ethical governance as it applies to social research in health and social care services and highlight in particular the value and implications of a dialogic approach to ethics that includes opening up a debate in order for researchers, practitioners and people with dementia to share their insights and experiences.

Background

In the UK and abroad, a now well-established system for the ethical governance of research has emerged primarily as a response to a number of medical scandals that revealed the vulnerability of subjects in medical experimentation. The response to these scandals was not however to reconfigure relations between doctors, researchers and patients but instead to introduce regulatory machinery that extended beyond medical science to encompass much social research undertaken in health and social care environments (Boden et al., 2009). This governance 'creep' has met with something of a backlash from within the social sciences with commentators arguing that it represents a form of censorship and a process of deprofessionalisation that has relocated decision-making powers from researchers and their communities to external ethical bodies (Dingwall, 2006; Hammersley, 2010).

An important element to this dispute stems from the tensions between a position of ethical absolutism, i.e. the guidance of research according to firm principles, on the one hand and of situational relativism, on the other, where 'ethics are produced creatively in the concrete situation to hand' (Plummer, 2001, p. 227). While many commentators advocate a blend of the two approaches, the current system for ethical governance in health and social care is clearly weighted to an absolutist or 'principalist' stance, not least because it seeks to pass judgement on the ethical nature of a piece of research before it is allowed to commence. This approach sets at a disadvantage much qualitative research, where the design or detail of the methods may emerge as the research progresses and where researchers themselves are faced with many unpredictable ethical dilemmas that require pragmatic and 'quick-fire' decisions. For instance, Dominelli (2005) stresses the inevitably messy and unpredictable nature of qualitative research that involves disadvantaged groups within community/urban settings. As a result some commentators have questioned whether Research Ethics Committees (REC) can reach a viable judgement on a piece of social research when they have no access to the context in which the research is due to take place (Hammersley, 2009).

Another concern is that RECs are empowered to pass judgement on the methodology employed in a piece of research on the grounds that to subject participants to badly designed research is in itself unethical. One problem here is the implicit assumption that the members of a REC will have the collective expertise to assess the full spectrum of research methodologies. But it is tension over the very nature of research ethics that lies at the heart of the emerging backlash to recent efforts at governance. An absolutist stance leaves little room for pluralism or the possibility that ethical issues may be open to reinterpretation and revision over time. Many of those who are critical of governance measures as they stand argue that we need to recognise the contingent and situated nature of ethics in research and as a result the importance of the autonomous decision-making capacity of the researcher (e.g. Hammersley, 2006). At present, while researchers are held directly responsible for their ethical actions they are deprived of the power to decide what constitutes ethical practice (Boden et al., 2009).

Research with Vulnerable Older Adults

Many of the tensions between absolutist and situational approaches to ethics are amplified in the context of research involving vulnerable adults. A concern to understand and to promote the perspectives of people living with dementia has become an established feature of social research in the last decade or so (Wilkinson, 2002). In order to do so, researchers are required to enter the social world of those affected by the condition and to participate in the 'ethical context' of their lives. When a person with dementia lacks capacity to give informed consent this should not present a barrier to their inclusion. Indeed, to exclude the most vulnerable people from participation in research is in itself unethical. As Boden et al. (2009) point out, the process of being labelled as vulnerable can be 'deeply silencing' (p. 742). But such involvement requires flexibility regarding methods and contingent judgements by the researcher. Commentators on the ethics of research in dementia have placed particular emphasis upon the importance of 'seizing the best moments' to engage with participants, and for researchers to have both the sensitivity and adaptability to tailor their fieldwork to the strengths of individual participants (e.g. McKeown et al., 2010). In this respect the skills required of researchers mirror those of practitioners (Brannelly, 2006).

The Mental Capacity Act (MCA) (2005) was introduced to facilitate and regulate decision-making on behalf of vulnerable individuals and the Act includes provisions concerning their participation in research. With a focus on decision-making, these provisions centre upon the issue of consent and set out a formula for seeking advice from consultees in the event that a person should lack capacity to give informed consent. This emphasis upon consent is mirrored in the literature on research ethics and dementia where an on-going debate has focused upon questions of how best to approach consent and how to sensitively negotiate situations where a person lacks capacity or subsequently loses capacity to give informed consent (e.g. Dewing, 2002, 2007). Useful as this debate has been, we argue that such a focus 'brackets off' certain ethical concerns as research-specific. Many of the more everyday ethical issues that punctuate the lives of people with dementia and those who care for and support them are overlooked, suggesting a failure to consider how researchers are themselves implicated in this broader ethical context. Drawing on the work of Plummer (2001) it is our contention that it is unhelpful, even elitist, to consider ethical issues in research as 'special' and in some way differentiated from the resolution of more everyday moral dilemmas. As such:

> Any attempt to legislate this morality could simply degenerate into mindlessness, rigidity or – as with many professionals – a monopolistic front that perpetuates privileges and elites (those with a higher(!) morality than ordinary mortals). (2001, p. 227)

Connecting Research and Practice

Ethical dilemmas feature regularly in the everyday provision of support and care to people with dementia. While they may arise in the context of 'mundane, ordinary situations' they are nevertheless a challenge and source of stress to carers and carees according to the Nuffield Council on Bioethics (2009). For this reason the Council asserts that 'rules and laws have a particular but limited role to play' (p. 96) and highlight instead the importance of flexibility and compassion to care-based ethical issues. It is clear then that a great deal of commonality exists between research and practice, not least in how we should approach ethical challenges as and when they arise. Rarely is it the case that a simple right or wrong judgement can be made and the resolution of ethical dilemmas routinely requires an awareness of the detail and context of a particular situation. For instance, the Council's report on ethical issues in dementia poses the dilemma faced by a care worker assisting a person with dementia to get dressed. What, they ask, is the most important consideration in this situation? That the person is assisted to dress in a way that is in keeping with how they have always dressed; that their comfort in getting dressed and throughout the day should be the guiding consideration; or that they should be supported to dress as they wish, even when their choices may seem bizarre and likely to lead to stigmatising responses from others?

We argue that such dilemmas are inherently relational, they do not 'belong' either to practice or research but imply a range of direct and indirect participants. Not only should researchers be considering such everyday dilemmas in their research, but it is helpful to understand that, when present during such encounters, they are participants in these 'ethical episodes'. The dilemma for the worker is shared by the researcher in a way that gives both a sense of the challenges that underpin ethical practice. In addition, the person with dementia should not be ruled out of this ethical context, they are also participants and act in ways that demonstrate their own ethical agency. An absolutist approach to research governance is problematic then for a number of reasons. In particular, a system that seeks to decide upon the ethical dimensions of research before it even commences introduces an unhelpful, and we would argue artificial, division between research and practice. Instead of promoting a dialogue between researchers and their stakeholders, the main dialogue on ethics takes place 'behind closed doors' both led and hosted by a Research Ethics Committee.

Seeking Ethical Approval

In this next section we turn to consider our journey through the formal system for ethical approval required of research involving vulnerable adults in health and social care contexts. The account we offer is very much from the standpoint of researchers/applicants and we neither wish nor are we able to comment upon the perspectives of the other 'protagonists' that we encountered along the way.

The Hair and Care Study

The research for which we sought approval is an ethnographic study of issues of appearance and help provided with the presentation of people with dementia residing in different types of care setting (care homes, hospitals and at home). With a focus on hairdressing and support with hair care we sought to include the perspectives of people with dementia alongside care-based hairdressers, care workers, family carers and other stakeholders such as commissioners and managers in health and social care. In order to support the participation of people with more advanced dementia who would likely not have been able to participate in conventional interviews we proposed to include the filming of episodes of care in order to better understand the embodied and non-verbal aspects of these encounters. The study is funded by the Economic and Social Research Council and underwent an extensive process of review and feedback before finally securing funding.

The Ethical Governance of Health and Social Care Research in the UK

While mechanisms to govern ethical research exist in many developed countries comparative research shows that the UK has one of the most 'arduous' systems for doing so (Sherratt et al., 2007). The system itself was set up primarily to regulate medical research but in the absence of a separate system for the social sciences, social research into health and social care is required to follow the same pathway for approval. Following the introduction of the MCA (2005), 30 RECs across England and Wales received training in order to consider research that proposes to involve vulnerable adults. These committees are empowered to prevent research from going ahead if they deem it to be in any way unethical and in this way uphold a requirement for 'pre-emptive accountability' (Boden et al., 2009). While some commentators have suggested that this initial requirement for approval sensitises researchers to ethical issues at an early stage of a study (Teijlingen, 2006) others have suggested that it distances them from the ethical dimensions of their practice as the focus shifts from what is ethically justifiable to what is likely to provide the path of least resistance through the system for approval (Hammersley, 2009).

The Pathway to Approval

Preparations for submission are time- and labour-intensive. Researchers are required to complete an extensive on-line application and are advised not to 'cut and paste' from existing documentation but to answer each question afresh. In our case, the application itself ran to 28 pages and in addition we were required to submit a host of supporting documents that included the research protocol, information sheets to participants, examples of the different forms we would use for consent gathering and draft research tools such as interview schedules. It has been argued that the significance of the administrative burden of this process upon researchers and their work is downplayed (Hammersley, 2009). The burden is intensified if the submission receives only 'provisional' approval where further amendments are required (which happens in roughly two-thirds of submissions [Dixon-Woods and Angell 2009]) or where an 'unfavourable' decision is given (in approximately 8 per cent of cases) in which case the researchers are required to make a fresh application and follow the process through a second time.

In addition to our required preparations we attended a one-day training course offered by the National Research Ethics Service (NRES) on the ethics of qualitative research aimed primarily at REC members. This was a revealing experience as it offered an insight into how committee members are prepared for dealing with qualitative proposals. On the day, the trainer put it to the audience that the nature of many ethical issues associated with qualitative research is much the same as that for quantitative and scientific studies. Asked to share their concerns about qualitative research many trainees cited the low numbers of participants that many submissions propose to involve while others shared their anxieties about research with an emergent design where the detail of what will be done is only decided as the study progresses. These comments revealed that committee members were tending to judge qualitative proposals according to criteria developed for quantitative research but also highlighted their own unease with the requirement for pre-emptive accountability for qualitative research. In effect, members are being asked to second guess possible scenarios for risk. As Haggerty (2004) has argued such 'pronouncements about the risk of research projects are more akin to a subjective imagining of potential scenarios unconstrained by empirical evidence' (2004, p. 402).

Staging of the Committee

Following submission of our application we were required to attend a REC meeting and 'defend' our proposal. This was a highly formalised occasion, despite being furnished with extensive information about ourselves as the applicants, the committee offered scant information on the nine or ten members in attendance, most were not even introduced. We were positioned to take up a subordinate position in this short-lived encounter and it was clear we should not consider this an informal discussion with health and social care colleagues. Of course, these conditions had implications for the committee itself, making it very difficult for individual members to signal the limits to their own knowledge of particular issues or understanding of the ethical implications of a condition such as dementia. The committee is not a discursive forum, our efforts to engage members over their interpretation of our proposal were disallowed and interestingly even in the decision letter that followed we were given no explanation of the reasoning behind the various issues deemed problematic. For this reason, it would be difficult to describe the experience as intentionally educative.

Our proposal received an unfavourable opinion, not for any aspect of the design which was left untouched, but due to our perceived failure to adequately explain the wish to involve people with more advanced dementia and the reasons behind our decision to use filming. The proposed mix of methods was also questioned, despite earlier praise from ESRC reviewers. In the case of our use of visual methods there exist a number of published accounts outlining how or why the use of film can be supportive of the involvement of people with dementia in research (e.g. Cook, 2002; Ward et al., 2008; Hyden and Antelius, 2011) yet it was clear the committee did not have knowledge or recourse to this literature. According to our positioning as subordinate to the committee, this gap in knowledge on their part was reconfigured as our failure to explain and we were required to 'walk through' the reasoning in our resubmission. Hence, despite being embedded in a scientific tradition valuing evidence-based practice, the committee itself did not appear to observe such logic drawing instead purely on its own collective knowledge and experience at the time. In a context where levels of understanding regarding qualitative research appear limited, it is clear that social research is set at a disadvantage in the current system for approval. No researcher can second guess the gaps in knowledge that s/he will encounter with a particular REC and it is likely that a provisional or unfavourable decision will reflect the need to explain based upon such a gap in knowledge as much as account for what is ethically ambiguous according to a principalist stance. The outcome of this particular experience was that the receipt of an 'unfavourable' decision ate into the time available to carry out our research, leading to a requirement that we make time savings later in the project, either abbreviating the fieldwork or time allotted for analysis and writing up.

The 'Unofficial' Journey

Running concurrently with our preparations and application for formal ethical approval were our own efforts to develop and tailor an approach to ethical practice that we considered more sympathetic to the challenges of qualitatively-led research. In our view, a particular challenge was how to take context into consideration in preparing for research. This preparatory work rested upon three key understandings of the conditions we faced:

1. That researchers are participants in a broader ethical context when studying aspects of health and social care.
2. That ethical dilemmas do not 'belong' to the researcher but are shared by everyone in a research setting.
3. That researchers, like practitioners, are not 'fixed'; our ethical practice evolves over time.

The Hair and Care Protocol

Based on this understanding we adapted and updated a 'protocol' for social research in dementia care that one member of the research team (RW) had helped to develop for a study over a decade earlier. The original protocol has been described and discussed in print, see Vass et al. (2003), and comprises three main elements. Firstly, there is a statement of a series of anticipated ethical issues that may possibly occur during the research. Headings include issues such as the well-being of participants, the sharing of information and questions of confidentiality. The second part is a statement of how we intend to respond to these issues and uphold our ethical commitment to the context in which we are working. As with the original use of the protocol, this document has been handed out to the various stakeholders involved in the Hair and Care project and provides a way of sharing ethical issues with practitioners, family carers and people with dementia as well as having a guide to our actions in the field to which we can be held accountable. The third element is a commitment to maintain a log of unpredictable ethical dilemmas alongside some record of how we have responded to them in the field.

By keeping a log of unpredictable ethical dilemmas as and when they arise not only are our actions open to scrutiny, for instance by any auditors, but it means we have a basis for the discussion of ethical issues as a regular feature of supervision sessions involving the team as a whole. This system of reporting back and debating ethical dilemmas reflects our view that such dilemmas are educative opportunities for all concerned and provide a useful opportunity to develop ethical practice and competence as a social researcher. In this respect, our motif of the ethics journey in this chapter also reflects the notion that ethical practice evolves in the course of a research career. Using dilemmas as the basis for ethical debate has a cumulative impact on our capacity to think ethically in the field. We see this as a significant departure from the formal ethics journey we took for the project where researchers are treated as a 'fixed' entity – either they have the knowledge or they do not – and where the application process is not treated as an educative opportunity as a result.

Drawing on the work of Ken Plummer we have also made an addition to the original process of reporting and debate. Plummer, whose work advocates the value of narratives and story-telling to social research, argues in relation to ethics that:

> We need stories and narratives of research ethics to help fashion our own research lives, and to see the kind of broader principle which they can then draw on. (2001, p. 229)

With this in mind, we have involved our wider team and community of research colleagues, many of whom have a background in practice, in order to share and discuss the unpredictable dilemmas that arise in the course of our research. Below, the researcher for the Hair and Care project (SC) outlines how she has put the protocol into action and considers the benefits attached to sharing narratives of research ethics.

Using the Hair and Care Protocol to Put Ethics into Practice

While in the process of gathering data for the project, a number of situations have arisen thus far that have presented ethical dilemmas. To manage, reflect on and improve ethical practice I have drawn on the guidelines of the protocol by noting any such dilemmas within my daily observation notes; for example, recording any situation where I am uncertain of the correct response or action or where I have observed something that I think has implications for practice. Sometimes, however, it is only on reflection that I recognise some kind of ethical tension and will then highlight the event as an ethical dilemma when I read through my observation diary.

Each dilemma is then recorded in a log, which notes the details of what happened, followed by my response to the dilemma at the time and my later reflection on what happened.

The ethical dilemmas that have presented themselves to date have underlined for me that there is a delicate balance regarding my role as researcher and my relationship with staff and participants at the research site. By keeping and maintaining an ethical log I am able to discuss these issues at a later time. For instance, we have begun to share our sometimes differing views during supervision. I have also begun to introduce some dilemmas to discussions in our wider team meetings attended by colleagues from different clinical and professional backgrounds, all working in the field of dementia. This has led to creating a regular slot for different team members to introduce (anonymised) ethical dilemmas from their work in order for the team as a whole to share their opinions and interpretations. Firstly, a dilemma or issue is outlined and then the floor is opened for reactions and views about how the situation might be negotiated or responded to. The proposer will then go on to detail their response at the time and explain their thinking behind this before eliciting further comments where we consider the different perspectives within the group.

Our Research Group Discussions

An interesting aspect to many of the discussions held to date has been hearing the diverse perspectives from different professional or clinical backgrounds. For instance, some of the team with nursing backgrounds have recourse to their professional ethical code as nurses and advocate a course of action in keeping with this. Others of us argue that, as researchers, our role and required response differs from how we might have acted when working as practitioners. According to this line of thinking we are not there to uphold particular professional codes and to do so would lead to intervening in a situation rather than learning what might usually happen when a researcher is not present. What is clear from our discussions to date is that ethical dilemmas can attract multiple responses and interpretations, often they are approached according to the situated knowledge of individual researchers and can be shaped by the professional backgrounds from which we hail.

The opportunity to have such debates with fellow researchers and practitioners at very different stages in their careers thus highlights the complexity of these kinds of issues. By contrast, Research Ethics Committees when asking researchers to consider all the likely ethical scenarios in the field appear to be working with frameworks that are often black and white. Yet, in my experience the life of the social researcher has less clarity. The responsibilities are many: to the funder; to the research project; to the sponsors; the participants in the study; legal obligations; and then we have our responsibilities as individuals with our own set of ethics and values. The need to manage and balance relationships at research sites and with participants is often foremost in the researcher's mind.

Another influence is how long the researcher has been in the field, because in my experience responses can change over time as our understanding of the environment deepens. There is a lot to absorb when first undertaking observations in the field and it can feel overwhelming. If caught off guard, it isn't always easy to speak up. As such, there is much to be gained by researchers honestly discussing the situations that occur in the field and their responses to them. In this way researchers like me can improve our ethical practice and gain a deeper understanding of our role and responsibilities.

Reflections and Conclusions

In this final section we outline what we consider to be a more helpful approach to thinking about ethical practice in the context of qualitatively-driven research. We begin by seeking to put our own research into context, showing why it is that we consider the current system for ethical governance ill-equipped for overseeing such qualitative research.

Clearly, qualitative research differs from much medical experimentation in that the potential to inflict serious or even fatal injury on participants is rare. However, the contrast between quantitative and qualitative approaches is more far-reaching than this. In the field of dementia care, qualitative research has carved out a foothold in the context of a dominant bio-medical model that privileges measurement over meaning and which is characterised by a focus upon the brain and behaviour. The backlash to this line of thinking has questioned the reliance upon the enumeration of fixed, unified categories and variables so beloved of medical science by demonstrating the diversity of experiences and perspectives associated with a condition such as dementia (e.g. Gubrium, 1987; Bond, 1992; Kitwood, 1997). Even more recently, qualitative researchers have begun to question the limits associated with more traditional methods that focus solely upon the reported aspects of social experience, favouring instead methods that better engage with the performative aspects of everyday living. This involves a move away from fixed representations of social life and towards recognition that living is characterised by movement. As the sensory anthropologist Sarah Pink argues:

> When we research what people are doing, while they are in the act of doing it, we are always focusing on how they are moving in and through the world, and how

in doing so they are at the same time uniquely making something of that world and something of themselves. (p. 42, 2012)

Such an approach to qualitative research benefits from methods such as filming that are able to capture life in movement accompanied by an understanding of ethical research practice as situated and evolving. Our own research, which focuses upon the embodied practice of hairdressing and the intra- and inter-personal experiences of service users, is located in this shift towards better understanding such performative aspects of everyday living.

Care Settings as Ethical Events

In this final section we draw on our journeys to date – both official and unofficial – to propose an alternative way of approaching the ethical challenges of social research into health and social care. Drawing on the work of human geographer Doreen Massey and the anthropologist Sarah Pink, we argue that it is helpful to consider each care setting as an *ethical event*. In other words, we see care settings not as fixed spaces but, as Massey (2005) argues, place-events: 'a simultaneity of stories so far' (p. 183). According to this understanding of a care setting, a researcher is not simply 'doing research in place' but is part of what makes that place at any given time. As Pink (2012) contends:

> [P]laces themselves do not exist independently and we cannot go off and find them and do ethnography or interviews in them. Rather, we are part of the constitution of the research-place-event as we do research. (p. 38)

Adding to this conception we would suggest there is an ethical dimension to the place-event and our presence as researchers in them is thereby constitutive of the ethical-research-place-event.

The idea of an event holds appeal for us because it suggests a nexus where many different ethical strands are woven together – these include the combined actions of those inhabiting that environment; the rules and policies that govern it; the routines that structure it and the ad hoc events that alter it. The notion of an event suggests an occasion where many people are participant and influencing of how things unfold at any given time. Thus, when a researcher enters the field, they are taking part in something that extends well beyond them and while they can influence that event they are never fully in control of the ethical conditions under which they are working. Neither should they be made to feel as if they are so entirely in control. The same applies to practitioners in their workplace. The idea of a place-event also suggests something that is fluid and changing over time.

This is applicable to the ethical conditions of a care setting in a number of ways. For instance, conditions may alter at a broader macro level when a piece of new legislation or policy is enacted or it may alter at a much more localised level when a member of staff phones in sick, or a researcher arrives to undertake fieldwork. The value of thinking in terms of an event is that it underlines the interdependent nature of the (direct and indirect) involvement of everyone associated with a given care setting.

In social research, the researcher has to weigh ethical and other considerations against one another and this requires detailed knowledge of the contexts concerned (Hammersley, 2006). And, when the researcher brings these scenarios to supervision it provides an opportunity to consider alternative ethical angles. Hence the idea of an event might also be understood as the wider conditions under which specific *ethical episodes* unfold and are subsequently made sense of. Service users, practitioners and researchers all take part in the event and are all implicated in it. McCormack alludes to this in his critique of the subordination of practice to research: 'there appears to be an assumption that if consent has been achieved from the key participants then we don't have to worry about others who may be less directly involved in the research' (2003, p. 183). In our view it is unhelpful to imagine that particular issues or dilemmas are the property of the researcher or the practitioner, taking part in the ethical-research-place-event means we are unavoidably linked to each other and for this reason any effort to govern and regulate ethical research should promote dialogue between *all* participants in that event. With this in mind we argue for a rethinking of the current system for ethical governance in relation to such movement-oriented social research.

Based on our experiences to date, it seems that one viable way to think about the ethical context of research is as something inherently relational and open to flux and change as well as benefitting from revision and reinterpretation. As Plummer has underlined in his work on narrative, a dialogic approach to ethics through narratives and stories provides the basis to create ethical communities. It is a means to showing that we all seek to lead ethical lives and that no-one is ruled out of such an endeavour. Crucial to this approach is that we understand ethical challenges as educative and practitioners, researchers, service users and other stakeholders as ethical agents who evolve over time. Perhaps one day, even the members of Research Ethics Committees will see themselves as part of the event.

Acknowledgements

The Hair and Care Project is funded by the Economic and Social Research Council. Grant no. RES-061-25-048

Further Reading

Boden, R., Epstein, D. and Latimer, J. (2009) 'Accounting for ethos or programmes for conduct? The brave new world of research ethics committees', *The Sociological Review*, 57, 4, 727–49: this paper tackles the question of how well suited the present system of ethical governance is for overseeing social research. It highlights key aspects of qualitative research that are overlooked or poorly attended to by the current system of governance and outlines the different responses of researchers who engage with it.

Hammersley, M. (2010) 'Creeping ethical regulation and the strangling of research', *Sociological Review Online*, 15, 4, 16: Martin Hammersley has published widely on the issue of ethical governance and social research and is a leading figure behind an emerging backlash within the social sciences against current conditions for ethical governance. This paper captures well the rationale behind his argument and sets out for the reader a compelling case for change.

Plummer, K. (2001) *Documents of Life 2: An Invitation to Critical Humanism*. London: Sage: This book places questions concerning ethical social research in a wider context and theoretical framework based upon Plummer's standpoint as a 'critical humanist'. Plummer offers a useful overview of current tensions over ethics in research and makes a case for a more relational and dialogic approach to ethical practice for researchers in the field.

References

Boden, R., Epstein, D. and Latimer, J. (2009) 'Accounting for ethos or programmes for conduct? The brave new world of research ethics committees', *The Sociological Review*, 57, 4, 727–49.

Bond, J. (1992) 'The medicalization of dementia', *The Journal of Aging Studies*, 6, 4, 397–403.

Brannelly, T. (2006) 'Negotiating ethics in dementia care,' *Dementia*, 5, 2, 197–212.

Cook, A. (2002) 'Using video observation to include the experience of people with dementia in research', in H. Wilkinson (ed.), *The Perspectives of People with Dementia: Research methods and motivations*. London: Jessica Kingsley Publishers.

Dewing, J. (2002) 'From ritual to relationship: A person-centred approach to consent in qualitative research with older people who have a dementia', *Dementia*, 1, 2, 152–71.

Dewing, J. (2007) 'Participatory research: A method for process consent with persons who have dementia', *Dementia*, 6, 1, 11–25.

Dingwall, R. (2006) 'Confronting the anti-democrats: The unethical nature of ethical regulation in social science', *Medical Sociology Online*, 1, 51–8.

Dixon-Woods, M. and Angell, E.L. (2009) 'Research involving adults who lack capacity: How have research ethics committees interpreted the requirements?', *Journal of Medical Ethics*, 35, 377–81.

Dominelli, L. (2005) 'Social work research: Contested knowledge for practice', in Adams, R., Dominelli, L., and Payne, M. (eds), *Social Work Futures*. Basingstoke: Palgrave Macmillan.

Douglas, J.D. (1976) *Investigative Social Research: Individual and Team Field Research*. Beverly Hills, CA: Sage.

Gubrium, J.F. (1987) 'Structuring and destructuring the course of illness: The Alzheimer's disease experience', *Sociology of Health and Illness*, 9, 1, 1–24.

Haggerty, K.D. (2004) 'Ethics creep: Governing social science research in the name of ethics', *Qualitative Sociology*, 27, 4, 391–414.

Hammersley, M. (2006) 'Are ethics committees ethical?', *Qualitative Researcher*, 2, Spring, 4–8.

Hammersley, M. (2009) 'Against the ethicists: On the evils of ethical regulation', *International Journal of Social Research Methodology*, 12, 3, 211–25.

Hammersley, M. (2010) 'Creeping ethical regulation and the strangling of research', *Sociological Review Online*, 15, 4, 16.

Hydén, L.-C. and Antelius, E. (2011) 'Communicative disability and stories: Towards an embodied conception of narratives', *Health*, 15, 6, 588–603.

Kitwood, T. (1997) *Dementia Reconsidered: The Person Comes First*. Buckingham: Open University Press.

Massey, D. (2005) *For Space*. London: Sage.

McCormack, B. (2003) 'Researching Nursing Practice: Does person-centredness matter?', *Nursing Philosophy*, 4, 179–88.

McKeown, J., Clarke, A., Ingleton, C. and Repper, J. (2010) 'Actively involving people with dementia in qualitative research', *Journal of Clinical Nursing*, 419, 1935–43.

Nuffield Council on Bioethics (2009) *Dementia: Ethical Issues*. London: Nuffield Council on Bioethics (accessible at www.nuffieldbioethics.org)

Pink, S. (2012) *Situating Everyday Life*. London: Sage.

Plummer, K. (2001) *Documents of Life 2: An Invitation to Critical Humanism*. London: Sage.

Sherratt, C., Soteriou, T. and Evans, S. (2007) 'Ethical issues in social research involving people with dementia', *Dementia*, 6, 4, 463–79.

Teijlingen, E. van (2006) 'Reply to Robert Dingwall's plenary "confronting the anti-democrats: The unethical nature of ethical regulation in social science"', *Medical Sociology Online*, 1, 59–60.

Vass, A.A., Minardi, H., Ward, R. et al. (2003). 'Research into communication patterns and consequences for effective care of people with Alzheimer's and their carers: Ethical considerations', *Dementia*, 2, 1, 21–4.

Ward, R., Vass, A.A., Aggarwal, N. et al. (2008) 'A different story: Exploring patterns of communication in residential dementia care', *Ageing and Society*, 28, 5, 629–51.

Wilkinson, H. (ed.) (2002) *The Perspectives of People with Dementia: Research Methods and Motivations*. London: Jessica Kingsley Publishers.

Part III
Contesting Modernisation

Part III concentrates upon the tensions that have flourished in the small ethical spaces that can be carved in between the sustained attempts to modernise social work, including initiatives that have encompassed amongst other features: privatisation, participation and managerialism. Each chapter therefore analyses some of the ethical problems generated through the modernisation agenda and related initiatives. Lynne Wrennall begins Chapter 8 with a damning and powerful critique of sectional interests which have, it seems, at times eclipsed the interests of service users in social care. Wrennall skilfully identifies the mechanisms through which the ascendancy of sectional interests (prominently business and power related) over clients' interests is secured and reproduced. Wrennall also broadly assesses the impact of this ascendancy and considers how social workers might ethically engage with the problem. In the penultimate chapter Malcolm Carey then offers a critique of the ethics of service user and carer participation within social work education and practice, questioning whether social work is currently able to fully accommodate meaningful and just participatory methods. In particular he asserts that such seemingly empowering processes are often insensitive to users and carers and can also be used to mask other objectives: such as further privatisation, unethical practices in the field or extend further the power of welfare professionals.

In the final chapter Donna Baines again adds to the assumption made in the chapters by Wrennall and Carey that freer markets invariably generate new obstacles and moral hazards for the increasingly frustrated or perplexed ethical practitioner stood at the coal face. Baines draws upon comparative international data to explore some of the ways that social workers struggle to incorporate their commitment to social justice into increasingly managerialised work in the voluntary or non-profit sector. Though the voluntary sector has long thought of itself as an arena in which workers have opportunities to build close ties with communities, participate strongly in agency decision making, and advocate for socially excluded and exploited peoples, new forms of workplace organisation imposed by government funding have reduced or removed many of the opportunities for these kinds of practices. Nevertheless Baines shows that some practitioners still find ways of resisting such reforms.

8 Where Did We Go Wrong? An Analysis of Conflicts of Interest, Perverse Financial Incentives and NOMBism

Lynne Wrennall

Introduction

This chapter is concerned with the conflicts that arise between sectional economic interests and the interests and needs of service users. It engages with the concern that since the 1980s when marketisation and privatisation within social work began to gather pace, sectional economic interests have gained dominance over the interests of clients in social care (Carey, 2008; Davies and Leonard, 2004; Harris, 2003; Wrennall, 2007, 2010). It aims to identify the mechanisms through which the ascendancy of sectional interests over clients' interests is secured and reproduced, and to consider how social workers might ethically engage with the problem.

In accordance with the tradition set out by Wardhaugh and Wilding (1993), Adams and Balfour (2009) and Preston-Shoot (2011) common themes concerning the 'corruption of care' that affect service provision to a diversity of service users will be addressed. This previous literature addressed the problem in terms of conflicts relating to the role, values and ethics of social workers. This chapter will concentrate upon the economic factors that underpin these conflicts. It is proposed that conflicts about role, values and ethics, predictably reflect conflicts over resources and the abstract theoretical points at issue with practical examples from the lived experience of diverse service users will be outlined. It is because access to scarce resources is at stake that these conflicts are bitterly fought out, often with profound consequences for service users.

171

With varying differences of emphasis, Carey (2008), Garrett (2003), Wrennall (2010) and others have specified the socio-economic and political context within which contemporary social work is practised. Within this context, this chapter's aim is to explicate the precise mechanisms that explain the eclipsing of clients' interests which has occurred over the last few decades. From Orphan Trains to 'Pindown' to Magdalene Laundries to Winterbourne View, centuries of exploitation and institutionalised abuse have created an appropriate and deeply paradoxical caution about regular claims made with regard to helping others. This is most especially when 'help' is imposed through forms of coercion or social control. Arguably, discovering how the interests, needs, wishes and feelings of service users fail to be realised and privileged, and discerning how service users can best be supported, remains the central ethical task facing social work today.

The chapter argues that three of the most significant distorting and corrupting factors in social care are (i) economic conflicts of interest; (ii) perverse financial incentives; and (iii) NOMBism (an acronym for Not On My Budget). It is proposed that these inter-related processes give ascendancy to sectional economic interests above and beyond the interests of clients. They explain how external agendas that are contrary to clients' best interests are imposed on social services. In relation to (i) conflicts of interest, policy and practice are structured by arrangements such as interlocking directorates, horizontal integration and vertical integration, so that decision-making serves sectional interests rather than the interests of clients. Interlocking directorates effectively place decision making by public officials in the hands of directors of companies, because often the same person is performing the two competing roles. Through horizontal integration social or health care companies reduce competition in service provision by taking over competitors, thereby increasing the power of the company at the expense of the Local Authority. Higher prices can then be charged because alternative suppliers have been reduced or eliminated. Vertical integration involves companies becoming self-supplying by taking over an earlier or later stage of the process of service provision, as in, for example, when supposedly independent assessments are undertaken by companies that benefit from recommending services that they themselves provide.

In (ii) perverse financial incentives, unworthy outcomes are rewarded, worthy outcomes are penalised and more worthy outcomes are sacrificed to less worthy outcomes. For example, under current financial arrangements, diverting young people in state care into Higher Education or Further Education is to the short term financial disadvantage of the Local Authority compared to allowing them to enter Young Offender Institutions, because the former are paid for by the Local Authority, whereas the latter are paid for by the Home Office (Sergeant, 2006, 3). The financial incentives do not support the best interests of clients. In (iii) NOMBism, 'false economy' occurs when advantage is achieved on one budget, stimulating costs on other budgets. For example, cuts in child care benefits can increase unemployment, resulting in greater costs for social security and less tax income for the Treasury. More long term, cuts in child care can lead to a range of costly consequences, including the criminalisation of young people, because expenditure on child care correlates with reduced juvenile lawbreaking (Fisher et al., 2000). Failure to invest in appropriate services constitutes NOMBism. For example, failure to invest in reablement, increases the costs of social care. Failure to invest in job creation can stimulate spiralling costs in unemployment, housing, public health and criminal justice. We might also argue that recent austerity measures which have reduced spending within social care will again generate 'false economy', for example through later transferred costs in health care, unemployment, criminal justice through increased crime, and so forth.

In all of these processes, conflicts of interest, perverse financial incentives and NOMBism, as well as acting against the interests of clients, small rationalities work against the larger rationality of the greater good. Service users lose, because their needs are subordinated to corporate interests. Taxpayers lose, because they are manipulated into supporting more expensive options that are less focused on actually solving social problems. Social workers lose, because their ability to practise according to their values, beliefs and ethics is undermined. Given their destructive impacts, there is therefore an urgent need to challenge these processes. The chapter seeks to explore and clarify how social workers can engage with these processes in ways that seek to reorient policy and practice more in the direction of serving the interests of clients.

Prioritising the Needs, Wishes and Feelings of Service Users – The Legislative Basis

Service users can be conceptualised as a varied group, who are often affected by intersecting identities including age, gender, social class, sexual orientation, and a diverse range of abilities and disabilities including giftedness, learning disabilities, physical and mental health problems. In respect of children there is a clear, though oft debated duty, to prioritise the needs of the child, known as the paramountcy principle. The paramountcy principle provides for the welfare of children to override all other factors. This is linked to the principle that the wishes and feelings of the child must be considered. Both of these principles are strongly propounded in the Children Act 1989. In respect of the range of adult service users, the matter of prioritising their needs, wishes and feelings is currently in a state of flux. The *Law Commission* paper on social care states that there is a desperate need for the law on social care to be brought up to date in regard to this issue and argues that there is a compelling case for a statement of statutory principles that maximise the choice and control of service users, support independent living and prioritise home-based living (2010, 24, s 4.3). In respect of people with disabilities, the principles set out in the *UN Convention on the Rights of Persons with Disabilities* (UN, 2006) include respect for 'individual autonomy including the freedom to make one's own choices, and independence of persons'. This is further elaborated by The Council of Europe Commissioner on Human Rights, who states that, 'The bulk of the legal capacity systems in Europe are out-dated and in urgent need of reform. The automatic loss of human rights of those placed under a guardianship regime is a practice which must be changed' (Hammarberg, 2011).

Major problems arise in relation to services provided under compulsion and increasingly, the role of the social worker, at least where social workers are employed by Local Authorities, is one of imposing coercive action on service users (Jordan, 2004). People can be incarcerated and deprived of their other liberties under an increasing range of state powers, including those for Child Protection and Protection of the Person, The Mental Health Act and The Mental Capacity Act. At times these powers have been used unlawfully. For example in *LB of Hillingdon v Neary & Anor [2011] EWHC 1377 (COP)* a young man with autism and a learning disability was forced by the Local Authority to remain in a care home against his wishes and against the wishes of his father. An order for costs was made against the authority in *LB of Hillingdon v Neary [2011] EWHC 3522 (COP)* because the court considered that the authority had acted so improperly. The Mental Health Foundation has expressed concern over the inappropriate detention of 186 people who lack capacity in Out of Home Care settings, during 2010 (Samuel, 2010). It also expressed concern that The Mental Capacity Act was being widely violated in that 52 per cent of professionals were assuming that service users did not have capacity before conducting an assessment and 38 per cent were conducting assessments for unlawful reasons (Pitt, 2010). Official solicitor to the senior courts, Alastair Pitblado, has expressed concerns that people with disabilities were inadequately safeguarded against deprivations of their liberties, particularly in terms of decisions made by the courts (Samuel, 2012). These are especially serious concerns given that, 'More than 100,000 elderly and disabled people are living in care homes that fail to meet basic minimum standards of quality or safety' (Gosden, Ross and Beckford, 2010), and at the time of writing, privately run care homes are still maintaining that they are not covered by the Human Rights Act (Dunning, 2011). Not surprisingly then, in recent months, appeals over Deprivation of Liberty orders, have tripled (Taylor, 2012).

Given this deplorable state of law, policy and practice relating to protecting the liberty of people with disabilities, it is fortunate that the parliamentary Joint Committee on Human Rights (JCHR) has coordinated a case for freestanding legislation to protect the right to independent living of people with disabilities, in UK law. The right to independent living is drawn down from Article 19 of the United Nations Convention on the Rights of Persons with Disabilities (UNCRPD) which states that 'State Parties to this Convention recognise the equal right of persons with disabilities to live in the community with choices equal to others, and shall take effective and appropriate measures to facilitate full enjoyment by persons with disabilities of this right and their full inclusion and participation in the Community'. Arguably the committee has chosen well in focusing upon this particular intervention as the most precise way to protect the liberty of people with disabilities.

Prioritising the Needs, Wishes and Feelings of Service Users – Codes of Practice

At a professional level, the Code of Practice of the British Association of Social Workers (BASW) prioritises 'the safeguarding and promotion of the rights of service users' (2002:1). In accordance with *the International Federation of Social Workers* and *the International Association of Schools of Social Work*, BASW has adopted a definition of social work that focuses on empowerment and liberation (2002, 1). The code gives social workers a duty to place service users' needs and interests before their own beliefs (3.4.2a). Particularly relevant commitments in the Code relate to self determination (4.1.3), informed consent (4.1.4), individual autonomy (3.1.2d), respect for service users' rights to make informed decisions, people's right to have as much control over their own lives as is consistent with the rights of others (3.1.1) and respect for service users' beliefs, values, culture, goals, needs, preferences, relationships and affiliations (3.1.2b). Social workers are asked to give priority to maintaining the best interests of service users, while also showing due regard to the interests of others (4.1.1a).

There are extensive legal obligations/procedures to follow, especially in the UK and stark obstacles of economic and resource related factors which regularly lead to lack of discretion and choice. Banks (2006) discusses this in one of her recent ethics books. Moreover, the code is richly textured by an appreciation of the difficulties that arise in attempting to uphold professional ethics in the murky realities of organisational and social conflict. Significantly, this demonstrates an awareness in the code of the centrality of conflict in the lives of social workers and explicitly that conflicts of interest may bias decision making by social workers (4.1.2). Upholding the ethical principles and responsibilities of the code, is required 'even though employers' policies or instructions may not be compatible with its provisions' (4.3g). Social workers are asked to observe 'the values and principles of this Code when attempting to resolve conflicts between ethical principles and organisational policies and practices' (4.3g).

Conflict surrounds and permeates the role of social workers. In their statement of principles on ethics in social work, *the International Federation of Social Workers* (IFSW) and *the International Association of Schools of Social Work* (IASSW) point out in the first two of the four problem areas that they outline, 'the loyalty of social workers is often in the middle of conflicting interests' and 'social workers function as both helpers and controllers' (IFSW and IASSW, 2004). However, by assuming an individual model of ethical practice, both the code and the statement of principles fall short of helping social workers to confront the forces that undermine their ethical integrity, leaving them isolated and vulnerable. The term 'network' is not even used, nor is 'collective'. Consequentially, individuals are expected to wage a lone battle against powerful economic, legal, organisational and bureaucratic obstacles. When all the fine rhetoric is said, nothing much is to be done. Social workers are not encouraged to question their place in a scheme or order of things that is imposed upon them. However, if the ethical obligations that social workers take on when they subscribe to the code are to be achieved, it is essential that the practical realities that obstruct their achievements are forcefully recognised, analysed and confronted. In the next sections, I shall outline how service users' interests have been undermined and then demonstrate how (i) conflicts of interest, (ii) perverse financial incentives and (iii) NOMBism act as major influences that hamper our ability to fulfil our ethical obligations to service users.

The Loss of Focus on the Needs, Wishes and Feelings of Service Users

There is a well-known disjunction between the services that service users request and those that Local Authorities provide (Farber, 1993; Hill, 1997; Connolly and Seden, 2003; Cortis, 2004; Wrennall et al., 2004). The menu of services from which social workers make their choices concerning referral decisions tends to be limited, if not meagre, and is distorted by sectional interests in the direction of expensive, coercive, Out of Home Services, even though this emphasis is rarely in accord with the interests, wishes and feelings of service users. Arguably, the single most powerful cause of service users' resentment towards social workers concerns the coercive imposition of Out of Home Care services at the expense of In Home service provision. Out of Home service provision involves taking people away from their homes and families and placing them in residential care or in the case of young children, into fostering or adoption placements, rather than assisting them to stay in their homes, with their families and friends. The anecdotal evidence suggests that the impact of this on the relationship between service users and social workers can be devastating. At times, social workers may even, through little fault of their own, be regarded as enemies to be avoided at all costs. The problems that this creates for social workers include lack of cooperation, or at worst, hostility or even violence from service users. The ethical challenge of retaining loyalty to those who are acting with hostility requires a high level of enlightenment on the part of practitioners, as self-care skills in practitioners are needed, alongside empathy and de-escalation skills. Most important though, is the need to address the source of the problem, namely to reduce the imposition of Out of Home services, bringing service provision into closer alignment with the perceived needs experienced by service users.

Alongside limited resources another important problem lies with commissioning. Small disaggregated Local Authorities are unable to commission the appropriate type and range of services because they now lack the scale of public service provisions necessary for diversity which puts them at a disadvantage when negotiating with large corporations. They are swayed by what the market provides and lack the economic resources to promote the necessary initiative and leadership to commission the services that service users regard as necessary. Even more seriously, their decisions can be influenced by corruption, which can consist of many forms but essentially involves the misappropriation of money and other resources. Neild (2002) has argued that corruption in public administration is normal, that the incidence of corruption declined in the mid-twentieth century, only to rise gain towards the end of the century. Bryans (2007, 20) makes the point that health and social care organisations are not immune to fraud and corruption and that these are 'unnecessary burdens on already over-stretched budgets'. Like mistakes and negligence, fraud reduces the resources that are available to assist service users (Bryans, 2007, 2). Research by Gupta, Davoodi and Tiongson (2000) demonstrated that reducing corruption in health and education could produce significant social gains, including the reduction of infant and child mortality. Davis (2009, 311, 321) argues that the risks of corruption in public services are particularly high in the areas of procurement and contracting, that is in the buying of products and services from companies and other external organisations. A report by the Council of Europe (1999) states that few activities offer more opportunities for bribery and extortion than public sector procurement, estimating the costs to taxpayers to be 'astronomical'. Similarly the Organisation for Economic Cooperation and Development (OECD, 2010, 10) has focused on the particular vulnerability of public procurement, to corrupt practices. Transparency International (2006, 14) also emphasises the especial vulnerability to corruption that arises from public procurement, estimating the damage from corruption, 'at normally between 10% and 25%, and in some cases as high as 40 to 50%, of the contract value'. Logically then, Weizsacker, Young and Finger (2005, 357) have demonstrated that corruption flourishes under conditions of privatisation.

Empirically, there is extensive evidence of financial misappropriation in social care (Thoma, 2005a, b). The class bias that resists giving money to the poor to directly ameliorate poverty and its effects has resulted in the diversion of funding to a range of middle-class professionals and private entities. One of the many consequences of this has been that funding has then been spent by the middle classes on themselves, rather than on people in need of help. Numerous auditors' reports collated by Thoma (2005a, b) provide examples of vast amounts of money dedicated for Children's Services, being spent by Foster Care administrators on benefits for themselves in the form of plastic surgery, Country Club membership, limousine services, sports cars, sporting tickets, private swimming pools and cheques made out to cash. To some extent personalisation and personal budgets may be thought to address these problems, but it can only do so inadequately if an appropriate range of services from within the public, private and 'third' or 'voluntary' sectors has not been developed. The challenges for frontline workers are immense. On one level, it is a matter of not taking bribes, but beyond this apparently simple ethical stance lies the complex issue of organisational, or official misconduct and tackling this area is immensely difficult.

The considerable awareness among international organisations of the problem of corruption has led to a series of toolboxes and other preventative mechanisms being developed (Transparency International, 2006; OECD, 2010). Research shows that whistleblower protections are mostly basic, but more sophisticated measures include staff rotation in vulnerable areas, registers of conflicts of interest (discussed elsewhere in this chapter), involving service users in advocacy, democratic protections, i.e. electing public officials, sensitivity to 'red flags', openness to public oversight, Ombudsman and other independent complaints procedures. It would be easier for social workers to confront corruption and advocate for protection if corruption only consisted of individual 'bad apples', but where organisational misconduct is in play, the matter is more serious. Effectively confronting and undermining organisational misconduct requires organised collective action. The three main factors that need to be addressed, conflicts of interest, perverse financial incentives and NOMBism are outlined and further analysed in the next part of the chapter.

NOMBism

Decisions about developing, commissioning and purchasing of social services are distorted by NOMBism. This is the 'Not On My Budget' phenomena, similar to 'NIMBYism', (Not In My Back Yard). Social care or social work services, projects, activities and their associated expenditure are opposed, not because they are unjustifiable, but because they are too close to home. In NOMBism, fund holders make savings that divert costs onto other budgets. Often the net effect of the diversion is the dramatic increase of costs to taxpayers. The manager who makes the savings is applauded at performance review, new items go onto the resumé, but essentially false economy is occurring, the taxpayer is disadvantaged and frequently other forms of social harm result from NOMBism. As well as acting against the interests of clients, small rationalities work against the larger utilitarian rationality of the greater good. Local Authorities have a long history of providing the services that they choose to provide, rather than the services that service users perceive as necessary to meet their requirements (or social workers recognise as necessary following their assessments of need). The assessment functions as an ideological mechanism through which this substitution is given an apparent legitimation. Assessment occurs under a technical rationality that assumes that the judgements about need undertaken by professionals will be objective and seemingly superior to people's own perceptions about their needs. Assessment of service user needs by Local Authorities who broker and fund the meeting of those needs is a conflict of interest in itself. If a service is not commissioned then the LA does not have to provide it, protecting existing services from competition. Assessment also structures the individual consumption of services into consumption that is centralised and to some extent is coercive, so that this consumption may be termed *captive consumption*. Personal budgets, though hampered by several problems such as the lack of independent sources of advice, may at times be justifiable, not only because they can potentially return choice to the service user, but also because they can reduce the opportunities for consumption to be structured around bribery and corruption.

It is not difficult to challenge the veneer of technical rationality that covers captive consumption. For example, very expensive services such as adoption, foster care and children's homes are purchased rather than the far more cost effective services such as *Long Day Care; Watch, Wait and Wonder; Nurture Groups* and *Webster-Stratton* services. Is it because the services that are purchased have better outcomes than those that are not funded, or less funded? Hardly, adoption results in significant difficulties for adopted children. Because previous research studies on adoption had produced discrepant findings, partly due to being based on small clinical samples or on samples biased by self-selection, Miller, Xitao, Grotevant, et al. (2000) analysed the large and reputable archival data set provided by The National Longitudinal Study of Adolescent Health which included a representative sample of adolescents in grades 7 through 12 in the United States, selected through cluster sampling of adolescents, parents and school administrators. The study can be considered to be epidemiological because some '90,000 adolescents completed a self-administered questionnaire at school, and about 20,000 adolescents subsequently were interviewed at home' (Miller, Xitao, Grotevant, et al., 2000, 1460). The results showed that 'adopted adolescents are at higher risk in all of the domains examined, including school achievement and problems, substance use, psychological well-being, physical health, fighting, and lying to parents'. They found 'larger proportions of adopted than non adopted adolescents at the extremes of salient outcome variables' (Miller, Xitao, Grotevant, et al., 2000, 1458). Children who experience Out of Home, have even more deplorable outcomes on a broad series of variables, during and after the experience of 'care', including depression, dental neglect, homelessness, unemployment, substance use problems, imprisonment, breakdown of supportive relationships, medical endangerment and educational underachievement (Polnay and Ward, 2000; Aldgate and Statham, 2001, 33; Richardson and Lelliott, 2003; Sergeant, 2006; Doyle, 2007, 2008). While it is common to explain the disadvantage of children in care, in terms of their experiences before they entered the care system, this explanation does not overcome the problem that care does not appear to be removing their problems. Moreover, active harm is produced by state intervention in the shape of iatrogenic abuse and neglect, educational disruption, spoiled identity, disrupted bonding, damaged relationships, psychological harm, medical neglect, forced maturation, harm to reputation, exposure to adverse influences and criminalisation.

Although Taussig, Clyman and Landsverk (2001) produced findings suggesting that 'youth who reunify with their biological families after placement in foster care have more negative outcomes than youth who do not reunify'. The comparison is biased by the fact that biological re-unified families receive few, if any genuine services, compared to foster families who are generously supported by the Local Authority (Jones, 2001, 558), a point that Taussig, Clyman and Landsverk (2001) acknowledge. Service provision to foster families consists of transport, child care, respite, holidays, gifts and considerable financial support. Ward, Biehal and Farrelly (2011) and Davies and Ward (2011) have discouraged reunification on the basis that two-thirds of children who reunify return into 'care' at some later stage, but the same objection stands – biological families are not given the constructive service provision that is given to foster carers and to children while they are in foster care, nor do these studies identify the causes of further family disruption.

By contrast with the services for children that are routinely and coercively imposed by social services, other services have a much stronger evidence base supporting far more positive outcomes. Reiterating McCain and Mustard's (1999, 37) finding that there are 'well-designed child development studies and longitudinal surveys that show that quality early child development programs that involve parents benefit the children and, in many cases, their families as well', a systematic review of Children's Services conducted by Fisher, McHugh and Thomson (2000, iii) found that 'access to children's services as part of a holistic approach to family support, minimises the risks of abuse and neglect'. Subsidised day care in the form of nursery schools, holiday clubs and before/after school care (that reduces family poverty) is especially effective in reducing child neglect, abuse and juvenile lawbreaking (Fisher, McHugh and Thomson 2000). Attachment-based interventions such as Child Parent Psychotherapy, *Circle of Security*, *Watch, Wait and Wonder* are very well-supported by evidence (Berlin, Zeanah and Lieberman, 2008) and the evidence base for *Webster-Stratton* approaches to develop parental empathy, tackle child behavioural and juvenile lawbreaking problems and build nurturing relationships, is very strong (Webster-Stratton, 2012). Moreover, as Walsh and Douglas (2009, 143) emphasise, 'where parents are provided with material support, the need for more coercive state intervention is reduced'. They conclude that 'Interventions that splinter the family may be inappropriate and more expensive in the longer term, where a focus on capacity building through the provision of material and financial support would have provided better long term outcomes for the child and their family'. Yet social services dealing with children continue to impose approaches for which there is a paucity of supporting evidence. NOMBism, together with the other mechanisms outlined in this chapter, is in the way of rational service provision.

Underfunding, although quite obviously contributing to problems in resourcing, cannot be the entire explanation when more expensive, less effective services are purchased rather than more cost effective evidence based services, as in the examples above involving the purchasing of Out of Home Care, where Day Care, therapeutic services and financial assistance would have achieved better results. Children's care homes frequently cost £80,000 per child, per year (Dispatches, 2004), whereas this funding could have significantly reduced or even eliminated the miserable poverty of an entire family, as well as providing for relationship enhancement, with money to spare. Such interventions are also unlikely to lead to the reduced 'life chances' and unhappiness that so many children in care continue to experience, thus leading to more positive consequences for people who come into the contact of professional social care services.

The perennial conflict between health and social care again provides numerous examples of NOMBism. Delayed discharge occurs when NHS hospitals cannot discharge patients because social care may struggle to make arrangements for the patients' accommodation. On the other hand, social care picks up the cost for patients who have been unlawfully deprived of continuing care by the NHS (White, 2006). In other examples, the NHS deprives patients of medicines, therapies or equipment that results in incapacitation or creates further demands following the side effects of inappropriate or dangerous drugs, or the wrong treatments, that increases the burden on social care, or more insidiously, on the criminal justice system. Cost cutting on one budget creates expense on another. Again the consequential ethical implications of this paradox may remain significant for patients/users or their carers, and it is likely to have economic consequences for taxpayers. The failure of the NHS to provide an appropriate supply of psychotherapeutic services is particularly serious. Chronic, historic underfunding of therapies has been confronted to some extent, but in 2011 it was still the case that of the 6.1 million people in England who suffer from anxiety and depression disorders only 2.0 per cent received therapeutic services (IATP, 2011). Yet figures from the Prison Reform Trust (2011, 10) show the extent to which people with mental health problems end up in prison:

> 72% of male and 70% of female sentenced prisoners suffer from two or more mental health disorders. 20% of prisoners have four of the five major mental health disorders. 10% of men and 30% of women have had a previous psychiatric admission before they come into prison. Neurotic and personality disorders are particularly prevalent - 40% of male and 63% of female sentenced prisoners have a neurotic disorder, over three times the level in the general population. 62% of male and 57% of female sentenced prisoners have a personality disorder.

It is the policy of the Crown Prosecution Service to divert offenders with mental health problems away from the criminal justice system, 'unless the offence is serious or there is a real possibility that it may be repeated' (CPS, 2012), but these figures suggest that the policy is being subverted. The human costs of this are catastrophic and the financial costs to taxpayers are typically immense. The lack of alternative therapeutic disposals compounds the consequences of economic inequality and poverty. There is a clear, inverse correlation between expenditure on welfare and expenditure on criminal justice (Downes and Hansen, 2006) demonstrating yet again, that decisions on expenditure are distorted by class bias. Money is spent on punishing the poor rather than preventing poverty induced crime.

The cuts in services and benefits to people with disabilities also constitute NOMBism. They risk forcing people out of independent living into far more expensive and more oppressive Out of Home 'Care' (JCHR, 2012). In common with other forms of NOMBism, there has been no assessment of the cumulative effects of the piecemeal actions. School exclusions are an example of NOMBism. Despite the enormous social and financial costs of school exclusions, 'It is well documented that some schools permanently exclude pupils on an illegal basis' (Eastman, 2011, 125) and the Office of the Children's Commissioner (2012, 9) has placed this on the official public record. Parsons and Castle (1998, 277) calculated that in England, the costs to other agencies of permanently excluded pupils in 1995/96 were approximately £71 million, and in 1996/97 were over £81 million. More recently Brookes, Goodall and Heady (2007, 1) put the conservative estimated cost of excluding pupils from school at £63,851 per child and since there are over 10,000 new exclusions from school each year, this produces a total annual cost of £650m. The annual social costs including costs to other agencies, such as other parts of the education system, the health service, the criminal justice system and social services were £49,664 per excluded child (Brookes, Goodall and Heady, 2007, 18). Establishing appropriate units within schools to replace exclusions would produce significant financial savings and more constructive social outcomes. More generally, 'underinvestment on education costs £18 billion in underachievement' (The Prince's Trust, 2007, 41). Calculated to age 37, the costs to the taxpayer arising from failure to learn to read at primary school are estimated at between £44,797 and £53,098 for each individual, which is a total of £1.73BN to £2.05BN every year (Reid, 2008, 10). The costs of failing to invest in job creation are also immense. The Prince's Trust (2007, 7) calculated that 'Reducing youth unemployment by one percentage point could save over £2 million in terms of youth crime avoided'. Entirely removing youth unemployment would save about £20 million per week in Jobseeker's Allowance (The Prince's Trust, 2007, 8) and would gain £10 million every day in productivity; and this is without taking into account people who are classified as 'inactive' for other reasons (The Prince's Trust, 2007, 8).

Conflicts of Interest

Conflicts of interest exist when official responsibilities are undermined by conflicting commitments. There have always been conflicts of interest between social work and the state that challenge social workers to consider where their loyalties lie. When misconduct, corruption or institutionalised abuse is detected, a choice must be made about whether to defend and support the victims or to protect the organisation against exposure and possible legal liability. Powerful interests are usually in play, such as insurance companies, whose policies prohibit admissions by organisations of matters that may incur legal liability and hence financial payments of damages to victims. With increased privatisation more numerous and complex financial arrangements develop, intensifying the ethical problems and dilemmas this may create for practicing social workers. The term ethical dilemma is used whenever the application of ethical principles is fraught with difficulty. Where social workers are employed by small and ethically worthy charities, the desire to defend a vulnerable organisation upon which vulnerable clients depend may be in conflict with the need to expose harm by a bullying or exploitative cohort within the staffing of the organisation. In 'for profit' organisations, there will be a strong financial incentive to not reveal mistreatment of clients because such disclosures will discourage future clients from using the service, causing profits to fall and could result in the service being closed. Conflicts of interest pertain to diverse problems and dilemmas where what is at stake at the most serious end of the spectrum can involve matters such as access to life-saving resources and freedom from torture. As Kline (2009) pointed out, 'The failure of staff to whistleblow in the NHS cost dozens of lives at Mid Staffs and Maidstone hospitals in recent years'.

Conflicts of interest frequently arise from a range of business practices such as interlocking directorates and employment (whether concurrent or consecutive). Horizontal integration and vertical integration in which businesses extend their activities into related forms of business, can also create conflicts of interest. By structuring policy and practice, conflicts of interest result in decision making that serves sectional interests rather than the interests of clients. Examples in the field of health and social care would include public servants who are involved in activities such as sitting on the boards of external organisations, external employment, membership of external organisations, receipt of sizable gifts, share ownership, close relationships with people in other organisations and so on, where the other organisations are involved in the day to day business of the Local Authority, government department or other agency. The separation of powers was developed in the Westminster system as an important measure for achieving probity, whereas conflicts of interest subvert that intent.

Registers of interest have been developed because it is recognised that economic interests can bias decision making by public officials, and Local Governments experience particular risks of corruption (Skelcher and Snape, 2001). Under Section 81(1) of the Local Government Act the monitoring officer of each relevant authority must establish and maintain a *register of interests*. Declarations onto the register should be made by councillors and Local Authority employees and they should cover directorships, corporate gifts, shareholdings, other employment and membership of other organisations. Under the Act, the registers must be made publicly available during office hours. Although there is no legal requirement to place registers onto the internet, where they can be easily accessed, some authorities are to be commended for having done so. However, there are some conflicts of interest that are not covered by the registers, for example where an auditor also sells other products and services to the authority that is being audited.

Specific conflicts of interest in health and social care arise when judges, legal services, *guardians ad litem* directors, directors of family law professional associations, social workers and social services managers, members of business councils, regulators, and the boards of relevant charities and companies are interlocking. When law firms represent service users as well as Local Authorities, it can be argued that there is a conflict of interests. There is also a conflict when 'early intervention' or preventative programmes are run by companies that profit from selling the services that the programmes are supposed to prevent (Wexler in Farber, 1993: 48). When regulators and members of regulatory bodies also hold senior positions in the bodies that they are supposed to regulate, this too is a conflict of interest. The problem is compounded when charities are also companies or when charities are set up as 'front units' for companies. Independent Reviewing Officers who are managed by the Local Authority that they are expected to review, are suffering bullying and intimidation as the consequences of being subjected to conflicts of interest (Pemberton, 2012). Vertical integration between family support services and Out of Home services is also conflictual because family support workers can use their position to leverage Out of Home services. This situation helps to explain why surveillance and Out of Home Care, rather than service provision to needy families has been the predominant response to children at risk (Wexler in Farber, 1993: 48). Specific instances of where the conflicts of interest have been manifest involve evidence from the San Diego Grand Jury (1991–92) that social services were deliberately 'setting families up to fail' so that they could retain their children in the highly profitable foster care system. 'Following the money' reveals donations from companies to charities, similarly creating conflicts of interest, incentivising the charity to support business interests at the expense of the interests of clients, where the two are not in alignment.

Conflicts of interest arise between the need to investigate allegations of abuse and neglect in the care system and the agency that organised the placement, because the investigation is conducted by the same agency that chose the placement. This situation that is akin to 'the police investigating the police' undermines the credibility of these investigations and may explain why so many allegations made by children in 'care' do not result in decisive action until the children reach adulthood. If the agency were to find itself responsible for placing the child into an abusive setting, it may be legally liable to pay damages to victims and so the role of the agency as investigator of its own possible negligence is conflicted. The condition of insurance contracts that no admissions of liability will be made, conflicts with statutory duties to investigate allegations of abuse.

As with Children's Services, elderly 'care' companies that provide Home Care as well as owning care homes are similarly conflicted. This is a case of vertical integration that arguably could be unlawful under the 'anti-trust' statutes operating in some states. Difficulties arise for example in that Home Care workers are asked to produce the narrative that will be applied when decisions are made about whether to continue Home Care services and at what level and type, or to coercively remove the elder person into a care home. Clearly there is an incentive for Home Care workers to base their narrative on the financial interests of their employers rather than upon the needs, wishes and feelings of their clients. This narrative then becomes the data upon which social workers will base their decisions.

There is a conflict between clients' needs to not be coercively and unnecessarily drugged and care workers who can benefit from a drugged and therefore presumably compliant client, as well as the pharmaceutical companies who profit from mass coercive drugging. Though 'the chemical cosh' shortens life (Huybrechts, Gerhard, Crystal, et al., 2012) and worsens dementia (Stuart-Hamilton, 2006, 226), there is evidence from covert filming of care workers and managers lying about clients in order to provide an apparent legitimation for forced drugging (BBC, 2010). Indeed forced drugging and other practices of inappropriate prescribing is an issue for all service user populations and given extensive evidence of incentives to prescribe paid by pharmaceutical companies (Kmietowicz, 2004; Steinbrook, 2008), it is at the centre of concerns about conflicts of interest. A related issue is the use of vulnerable populations of service users for involuntary medical research (CBC, 1992; Stolley and Bullough, 2006, 398). Other conflicts arise through information sharing. Data that goes to insurance companies will likely influence the treatment that people receive from a range of companies, particularly insurance companies (Lyons, 2003, 103) and given the close relationship between Local Authorities and insurance companies, the boundaries would likely be permeable (Ericson and Haggerty, 1997; Chandler, 2001, 181). Interstructuring of public services to meet the needs of insurance companies and health and social care companies has been outlined by Ericson and Haggerty (1997). There can be conflicts between clients' needs for privacy and reporting responsibilities established by statute. Privatisation has sharpened the problem of conflicts of interest. Cossman and Fudge (2002) have explained how privatisation has resulted in an individualising of problems, so that punitive carceral approaches have come to bear on difficulties rather than more benevolent collective solutions that would benefit service users. Corruption flourishes under conditions of privatisation because democracy is seriously weakened. Citizens are excluded from decision making and this has a negative impact on the quality of services (Weizsacker, Young and Finger, 2005, 357, xii– xiii).

Conflicts of interest are a matter of serious concern because they express what is arguably the most important mechanism through which corruption occurs. Corruption is raised in an allegation to the *Ryan Inquiry into Child Abuse*, that 'inspectors were taking bribes as an inducement to send children to industrial schools. The report states that inspectors in the early 1950s were accustomed to receiving payment for "expenses", in contravention of the rules' and that this might well explain why. 'The ISPCC faced allegations between the 1940s and 1960s of being too eager to send children into industrial schools, and of not doing enough to work alongside parents' (Nothing about us without us, 2009). (Further detail on the Ryan Inquiry can be found in Garrett's chapter in this book, Chapter 1.) Concerns relating to members of Local Authorities referring clients to agencies or services from which they acquire financial benefit (Wrennall, 2010) are particularly serious when the referrals rely on the coercive power of the state. In one example, Pat More, a whistleblowing social worker in Kentucky was paid $380,000 in compensation for the treatment she received after disclosing a coercive 'babies for order' adoption racket operating in Child Protective Services (Target, 2007, 32). Most ominous, are concerns that coercive powers are used to cover up negligence, malpractice and criminality. Coercive powers are likely to be misused when they are located in settings that have interests to protect that conflict with the interests of service users.

Perverse Financial Incentives

Perverse financial incentives occur when financial incentives produce socially harmful outcomes that are presumably the unintended consequences of financially incentivised public policy. Perhaps one of the most notorious examples involves the iatrogenic abuse of the Duplessis 'orphans' in Canada who were misdiagnosed as having intellectual disabilities so that their institutions could receive extra federal subsidies, allegedly resulting in them being subjected to lobotomies, electroshock, straitjackets and other forms of abuse, including being used as child 'guinea pigs' for unethical medical research (CBC, 1992). This was clearly a result of financial incentives overpowering an ethical commitment to service users.

Lest it be thought that this type of miscategorisation for funding does not occur nowadays, the alarm bells raised by the close relationship between care and imprisonment should be heeded. The majority of inmates in private prisons at the juvenile and adult level have been processed through the care system (Joint Chief Inspectors, 2002, 70; Social Exclusion Unit, 2002; Richardson and Lelliott, 2003). Private prisons have an incentive to increase incarceration (Butts, 2003, 73–4) and this has been expressed in outright bribery (Shover and Hochstetler, 2006, 44; Monbiot, 2009; Shapiro, 2011, 8) and the time-honoured practice of offering lucrative employment contracts to public officials after they leave their existing jobs (Herivel, 2008, 323). Imprisonment operates under a perverse financial incentive in that the more prisons fail to rehabilitate their inmates, the more profitable they are for their owners and controllers. Private prisons at the juvenile and adult level have an interest in setting lawbreakers up to reoffend rather than in rehabilitating them. A rehabilitated offender is a lost customer. Even when they are not ostensibly privatised, they are often built and supplied by the business sector. It is in the interests of prison operators to fail on their avowed objective of reducing crime, because the economic survival of their operators depends on failure to rehabilitate lawbreakers. We might ask how a system that rewards companies financially for housing more criminals can claim to be motivated to also encourage ethical rehabilitation. At times, entire towns are also economically dependent on the prison and hence they are economically dependent on the continuation of crime. There is also the perverse financial incentive that financially benefits Local Authorities if children in care can be sent to prison. As explained by Sergeant (2006, 3):

> The system dictates that the earlier a young person fails, the sooner they cease to be a cost to their local authority. It is better for the local authority's budget to have a young person go to prison, for example, rather than to university. Prison is paid for by the Home Office, university by the local authority. In the topsy-turvy world of care, failure is cheap, success a financial burden.

Perverse financial incentives also exist in Special Educational Needs [SEN] provision. Schools are paid more if they don't teach children to read than if they do. They are paid more if their children have behavioural difficulties, than if the difficulties are resolved, as are foster carers. They are financially rewarded for failure, but not for success. This does not suggest that SEN funding should be removed, but rather that it needs to be tailored to achievement. Education Authorities also benefit financially if SEN children go to prison under the same perverted economic logic that affects children in care.

Perverse financial incentives also operate when offenders are released from prison. Barnardo's (2011) has reported that children as young as 13 are being discharged from custody without so much as basic accommodation being made available to them, quite obviously increasing the likelihood that they will reoffend. Barnardo's 'concluded that supported accommodation could provide savings of more than £67,000 per child over a three year period'. The Youth Justice Board [YJB] is somewhat aware of the problem and is attempting to develop solutions. Frances Done, chair of the YJB said 'We are working on pilots that make local authorities responsible for the failure as well as the success of the options they offer young people leaving custody' (Hill, 2011). Indeed, all public policies that disrupt or underfund rehabilitation are perverse financial incentives in the direction of increased crime, greater profits for prison operators and greater social and financial costs to the public. Further examples would include policies that reduce the ability of lawbreakers to obtain employment such as 'enhanced criminal records checks', public 'naming and shaming', visible markers such as security bracelets and reporting requirements, absence of commitment to job creation and so on. As Cohen (1986) put it, where the penal system is concerned, 'nothing succeeds like failure'. When all these perverse financial incentives are taken into account, it is hardly surprising that as Shapiro (2011) and Monbiot (2009) have pointed out, privatisation of prisons has resulted in mass incarceration

Perverse financial incentives are hotly debated between service users and social services. In the US context, the federal subsidies that reward taking children into state care rather than rehabilitating families are a well-known example of perverse financial incentives (Mundorff, 2003). The consequences have been horrific for children as many of the most extreme examples of child abuse and homicide have occurred in foster care (Wexler, 1995). In the UK, a major contention is the payment of adoption bonuses. Social workers have denied that they had an impact on social work (Holmes, 2008) but service users allege that they have not reduced the number of children in 'care', but rather they have contributed to the commodification of children, incentivising social workers to take the most desirable children who are least in need of intervention, because they are sought after by the financial interests of the adoption industry (Josephs, 2008, 24–5). Other arguably perverse financial incentives that involve the selection by Local Authorities of forced adoption of children, are to do with the costs of alternatives to adoption being borne by Local Authorities, whereas the substantive judicial-legal costs of imposing adoption, particularly those that are bitterly contested by service users, are borne by national government and national taxpayers, rather than by the Local Authority or the service providers who will financially benefit from coerced consumption. This remains the case even though court fees have increased in an attempt by Westminster to return the costs to the Local Authority that is choosing to purchase judicial 'services' rather than the services that clients request and require.

Conclusion

The chapter has argued that the main mechanisms through which the ascendancy of sectional interests over clients' interests is secured and reproduced are the three inter-related phenomena of conflicts of interest, perverse financial incentives and NOMBism. An awareness of conflicts of interest allows us to explain why perverse financial incentives and NOMBism are tolerated even though there is strong evidence that they act against the interests of service users and taxpayers and have other wider destructive impacts. Such powerful forces are likely to significantly undermine social workers capacity to fulfil formal ethical or personal moral principles such as the capacity to protect and support users or challenge forms of social exclusion and oppression. It is unrealistic though, to expect individual social workers, acting through the individual and bureaucratic casework model, to be able to carry the entire ethical responsibility of preventing, confronting and deconstructing such complex forces that compromise the work that they are asked to undertake in the interests of clients. Where then do we go from here? Social workers need to be organised into settings where they can work together to promote the best interests of their clients. If social work ethics are to have an impact, this can only occur in a supportive environment. It has been argued that the current environment undermines social responsibility in favour of sectional economic interests. The challenge perhaps is to create an environment that supports rather than undermines the work that social workers can do to enhance the lives of clients. Individual social workers can still make a difference to individual lives despite the many hurdles that they face in their challenging role. It is my hope, though, that social workers working in networks with service users and other progressive groups, will help to change systems that clearly are often not geared to meeting the complex needs of often vulnerable people, typically living in poverty as well as facing numerous forms of neglect or discrimination. For example, the questioning of overtly bureaucratic cultures of work, inappropriate support services or economic processes that promote vested interests, as well as drawing attention to corruption or neglect wherever possible, remain just a few options which perhaps allows us to practice more ethically in the increasingly dystopian world of enterprise and market-led social care.

Further Reading

Giorgi, A. de (2007) 'Toward a political economy of post-Fordist punishment', *Critical Criminology*, 15 (3): 243–65: This article offers new perspectives on the political economy of punishment and new directions regard critical approaches to contemporary social control strategies.

Preston-Shoot, M. (2011) 'On administrative evil-doing within social work policy and services: Law, ethics and practice', *European Journal of Social Work*, 14 (2): 177–94: This paper explores further the gap between apparent professional ethics and ethics in practice, and between law in statute and law in action. It considers explanations for this tension that include the corruption of care, alongside the concept of 'administrative evil-doing'. The paper also reviews the challenges facing social work practitioners, educators and managers when providing ethics-informed leadership.

Wrennall, L. (2010) 'Surveillance and child protection: De-mystifying the Trojan Horse', *Surveillance and Society*, 7 (3/4): 304–24: This paper alleges the misuse of child protection as discursive policy and practices for ulterior motives. Often concealed behind sanctimonious rhetoric to disarm populations, the extended use of surveillance and new technology promotes sectional economic interests rather than the interests of children. The article collects together extensive empirical and conceptual research to present a groundbreaking thesis that challenges many established assumptions about child abuse, neglect and protection.

References

Adams, G. and Balfour, D. (2009) *Unmasking Administrative Evil*. London: M.E. Sharpe.

Aldgate, J. and Statham, J. (1989) *The Children Act Now: Messages from Research*. Department of Health.

Banks, S. (2006) *Ethics and Values in Social Work* (3rd edn). Palgrave Macmillan Basingstoke.

BBC (2010) 'What have the drugs done to dad?', *Panorama*, last broadcast on Sunday 7 November 2010, 8.30pm on BBC News Channel.

Berlin, L., Zeanah, C.H. and Lieberman, A.F. (2008) 'Prevention and intervention programs for supporting early attachment security', in Cassidy, J. and Shaver, P.R. (eds) (2008) *Handbook of Attachment: Theory, Research and Clinical Applications* (2nd edn). New York, London: Guilford Press.

British Association of Social Workers (BASW) (2002) *Code of Ethics*.

Brookes, M., Goodall, E. and Heady, L. (2007) *Misspent Youth; The Costs of Truancy and Exclusion*. London: New Philanthropy Capital.

Butts, D. (2003) *How Corporations Hurt Us All: Saving our Rights, Democracy, Institutions, and our Future*. Victoria, BC: Trafford Publishing.

Bryans, W. (2007) *Practical Budget Management in Health and Social Care*. Milton Keynes: Radcliffe Publishing.

Carey, M. (2008) 'Everything must go? The privatisation of state social work', *British Journal of Social Work*, 38 (5): 918–35.

Carey, M. (2008) 'What difference does it make? Contrasting organization and converging outcomes regarding the privatization of state social work in England and Canada', *International Journal of Social Work*, 51 (1): 83–94.

Cavadino, M. and Dignan, J. (2002) *The Penal System: An Introduction*. London: Sage.

CBC (1992) *The Duplessis Orphans demand a further investigation into alleged medical experimentation. The Duplessis Orphans 1992–2004*. Canadian Broadcasting Corporation Digital Archives.

Chandler, J.A. (2001) *Local Government Today*. Manchester: Manchester University Press.

Cohen, S. (1986) *Visions of Social Control*. Oxford: Polity.

Connolly, N. and Seden, J. (2003) 'What service users say about services', in J. Henderson and D. Atkinson (eds), *Managing Care In Context*. London: Routledge.

Cortis, N. 2004 '*Evaluating 'performance' in family welfare services: Service users, perspectives'*, Paper presented at the Australasian Evaluation Society International Conference, 13–15 October Adelaide, South Australia.

Cossman, B. and Fudge, J. (2002) *Privatization, Law, and the Challenge to Feminism*. Toronto: University of Toronto Press.

Crown Prosecution Service (2012) *Legal Guidance on Mentally Disordered Offenders*.

Council of Europe (1999) *Corruption in Public Procurement: Proceedings. Programme of Action Against Corruption*, Reports of the 2nd European Conference of Specialised Services in the Fight Against Corruption, Tallinn (Estonia), 27–29 October.

Davies, L. and Leonard, P. (2004) *Social Work in a Corporate Era*. Aldershot: Ashgate.

Davies, C. and Ward, H. (2011) *Safeguarding Children Across Services: Messages from Research*. London: Jessica Kingsley Publishers, 86.

Davis, H. (2009) 'Ethics and standards of behaviour', in E. Löffler and T. Bovair, *Public Management and Governance*. Abingdon: Taylor & Francis.

Department for Education and Skills (2006) *Care Matters: Transforming the Lives of Children and Young People in Care*, Presented to Parliament by the Secretary of State for Education and Skills by Command of Her Majesty, October. London: TSO.

Dispatches (2004) *Profiting From Kids In Care*, Hardcash Productions, last broadcast on Thursday 25 November, 9pm on Channel 4.

Downes, D. and Hansen, K. (2006) *Welfare and Punishment: The relationship between welfare spending and imprisonment*, Crime and Society Foundation, November Briefing 2.

Doyle, J.J. (2007) *Child Protection and Child Outcomes: Measuring the Effects of Foster Care*. MIT Sloan School of Management & NBER.

Doyle, J. (2008) 'Child protection and adult crime: Using investigator assignment to estimate causal effects of foster care', *Journal of Political Economy*, 116 (4): 746–70.

Dunning, J. (2011) 'Human rights should be extended to privately-run homecare users, finds report', *Community Care*, Wednesday 23 November 2011, 00:26.

Eastman, A. (2011) *No excuses: A review of educational exclusion*, A policy report by the Centre for Social Justice, Breakthrough Britain, September.

Ericson, K.V. and Haggerty, K.D. (1997) *Policing the Risk Society*. London: Clarendon Press.

Farber, S. (1993) The Real Abuse, *National Review*, 12 April.

Fisher, K., McHugh, M. and Thomson, C. (2000) *The Link Between Children's Services and Child Protection*, consultancy for the NSW Department of Community Services Office of Childcare, February.

Garrett, P.M. (2003) *Remaking Social Work with Children and Families: A Critical Discussion on the 'Modernisation' of Social Care*. London: Routledge.

Giorgi, A. de (2006) *Re-thinking the Political Economy of Punishment*. Aldershot: Ashgate.

Giorgi, A. de (2007) 'Toward a political economy of post-Fordist punishment', *Critical Criminology*, 15 (3): 243–65.

Glover, J. and Clewett, N. (2011) 'No fixed abode: The housing struggle for young people leaving custody in England'. *Barnardo's*, February.

Gosden, E., Ross, T. and Beckford, M. (2011) '100,000 elderly and disabled people in failing care homes', *The Daily Telegraph*, 18 June.

Gupta, S., Davoodi, H.R. and Tiongson, E. (2000) *Corruption and the Provision of Health Care and Education, Issues 2000–2116*, International Monetary Fund.

Hammarberg, T. (2011) *Persons with intellectual and psycho-social disabilities must not be deprived of their individual rights*, The Council of Europe Commissioner's Human Rights Comment, 20 February.

Harris, J. (2003) *The Social Work Business*. London: Routledge.

Herivel, T. and Wright, P. (2008) *Prison Profiteers: Who Makes Money from Mass Incarceration*. New York: New Press.

Hill, A. (2011) 'Young offenders leaving custody for life of homelessness and reoffending', *The Guardian*, 28 February.

Hill, M. (1997) 'What children and young people say they want from social services, *Research, Policy and Planning*, 15 (3): 17–27.

Holmes, D. (2008) *At What Cost?* BAAF.

Huybrechts, K.F., Gerhard, T. Crystal, S. et al. (2012) 'Differential risk of death in older residents in nursing homes prescribed specific antipsychotic drugs: population based cohort study', *BMJ*, 344:e977, 23 February.

IAPT (Improving Access to Psychological Therapies) programme (2011) *Improving Access to Psychological Therapies (IAPT) Key Performance Indicators (KPIs)* Q1 April–June 2011, A joint Department of Health and Care Services Improvement Partnership (CSIP), The Health and Social Care Information Centre.

International Federation of Social Workers (IFSW) International Association of Schools of Social Work (IASSW) (2004) *Ethics in Social Work, Statement of Principles.*

Joint Committee on Human Rights (JCHR) (2012) *Rights of disabled people may be at risk, says Human Rights Committee*, Twenty-third Report of Session, 2010–12, HL Paper 257, HC 1074, London: TSO, 1 March.

Jones, C. (2001) 'Voices from the front line: State social workers and New Labour, *British Journal of Social Work*, 32, 547–62.

Jones, C. and Novak, T. (1999) *Poverty, Welfare and the Disciplinary State.* London: Routledge.

Jordan, B. (2004) 'Emancipatory social work: Opportunity or oxymoron', *British Journal of Social Work*, 34, 5–19.

Josephs, I. (2008) *Forced Adoption.* North Carolina: Lulu.

Kline, R. (2009) 'We need to protect whistle-blowing social workers', *The Guardian*, 14 September.

Kmietowicz, Z. (2004) 'Consumer organisations criticise influence of drug companies', *BMJ*, 329, 937, 23 October, doi:10.1136/bmj.329.7472.937

Law Commission (2010) *Adult Social Care*, LAW COM No. 326, HC 941. London: The Stationary Office, 10 May.

Lawrence, C.R., Carlson, E.A. and Egeland, B. (2006) 'The impact of foster care on development', *Development and Psychopathology*, 18, 57–76.

Lyons, D. (2003) *Surveillance after September 11.* Cambridge: Polity Press.

McCain, M. and Mustard, J.F. (1999) *Reversing the Real Brain Drain: Early Years Study*, Final Report. Toronto: Ontario Children's Secretariat.

Macarov, D. (2003) *What the Market Does to People.* London: Zed.

Miller, B.C., Xitao, F., Grotevant, H. et al. (2000) 'Comparisons of adopted and nonadopted adolescents in a large, nationally representative sample', *Child Development*, 71 (5): 1458–73.

Monbiot, G. (2009) 'This revolting trade in human lives is an incentive to lock people up', *The Guardian*, 3 March.

Mundorff, K. (2003) 'Children as chattel: Invoking the thirteenth amendment to reform child welfare', *Cardozo Public Law, Policy, and Ethics Journal*, 13(44): 131–87.

Neild, R.R. (2002) *Public Corruption: The Dark Side of Social Evolution*. London: Anthem Press.

Nothing about us without us (2009) *Ryan Inquiry into Child Abuse*, quotes, 23 August.

Organisation for Economic Co-operation and Development (2010) 'Collusion and corruption in public procurement', 15 October, http://www.oecd. org/competition/publicationsdocuments/8/ (Accessed 13 March 2012).

Office of the Children's Commissioner (2012) 'They never give up on you', School Exclusions Inquiry. Children's Commissioner, www. childrenscommissioner.gov.uk/force_download.php? (Accessed 5 April 2012).

Parsons, C. and Castle, F. (1998) 'The cost of school exclusion in England', *International Journal of Inclusive Education*, 2 (4): 277–94.

Parton, N. (1985) *The Politics of Child Abuse*. Basingstoke: Macmillan.

Pemberton, C. (2012) 'Reviewing officers say they are silenced by councils', *Community Care*, 14 May, http://www.communitycare.co.uk/ Articles/14/05/2012/118207/reviewing-officers-face-fear-and-intimidation-at-work.htm

Pitt, V. (2010) 'Professionals fail to comply with Mental Capacity Act', *Community Care*, 17 June.

Polnay, L. and Ward, H. (2000) 'Promoting the health of looked after children', *BMJ*, March 320; 661–2.

Preston-Shoot, M. (2011) 'On administrative evil-doing within social work policy and services: law, ethics and practice', *European Journal of Social Work*, 14 (2): 177–94.

Preston-Shoot, M., Roberts, G. and Vernon, S. (2001) 'Values in social work law: strained relations or sustaining relationships'? *Journal of Social Welfare and Family Law*, 23 (1): 1–22.

Prince's Trust (2007) *The Cost of Exclusion: Counting the cost of youth disadvantage in the UK*, with the Centre for Economic Performance, London School of Economics, London.

Prison Reform Trust and the National Federation of Women's Institutes (NFWI) (2011) *Care Not Custody*, Action Pack, 10 August.

Reid, K. (2008) *National Behaviour and Attendance Review (NBAR) Report*, An independent review conducted on behalf of the Welsh Assembly Government.

Rummery, K. (2011) 'A comparative analysis of personalisation: Balancing an ethic of care with user empowerment, *Ethics and Social Welfare*, 5 (2): 138–52.

Ryan, S. (Mr Justice, Chairperson) (2009) *Commission to Inquire into Child Abuse*. Ireland.

Samuel, M. (2010) 'Concerns raised over wrongful detentions of service users', *Community Care*, 24 June.

Samuel, M. (2012) 'Many deprived of liberty without safeguards, warn experts', *Community Care*, 29 February.

San Diego County Grand Jury (1991–92) *Families In Crisis: A Crisis of Public Confidence in the Juvenile Dependency System*, Report 2.

Sergeant, H. (2006) *Handle With Care: An investigation of the care system.* London: Centre for Young Policy Studies.

Shapiro, D. (2011) *Banking on Bondage: Private Prisons and Mass Incarceration.* New York: American Civil Liberties Union.

Shover, N. and Hochstetler, A. (2006) *Choosing White-collar Crime.* Cambridge: Cambridge University Press.

Skelcher, C. and Snape, S. (2001) 'Ethics and local councillors: Modernising standards of conduct,' *Parliamentary Affairs*, 54 (1): 72–87.

Stolley, K. and Bullough, V. (2006) *The Praeger Handbook of Adoption*, Vol. 1. Westport, CT: Praeger.

Stuart-Hamilton, I. (2006) *The Psychology of Ageing: An introduction.* London: Jessica Kingsley Publishers.

Target 32 (2007) 'Kentucky's child Protection services investigated', The Examiner, http://article.wn.com/view/2012/09/11/Kentucky_launches_new_website_to_report_child_abuse/ (Accessed 3 March 2012).

Taussig, H.N., Clyman, R.B. and Landsverk, J. (2001) 'Children who return home from foster care: A 6-year prospective study of behavioral health outcomes in adolescence', *Pediatrics*, 108 (1).

Taylor, J. (2012) 'Appeals soar after secret courts are opened to public', *The Independent*, 2 January.

Thoma, E. (2005a) *Foster Care and Child Welfare, Studies, Surveys and Audits*, http://www.freeforum101.com/canadacourtwatch (Accessed April 17).

Thoma, E. (2005b) *Close Up: The Petro Foster Care Audits*, http://www.freeforum101.com/canadacourtwatch (Accessed April 8).

Transparency International (2006) *Handbook for Curbing Corruption in Public Procurement*. London: Transparency International.

UN (2006) *Convention of the Rights of Persons with Disabilities.*

Walsh, T. and Douglas, H. (2009) 'Legal responses to child protection, poverty and homelessness', *Journal of Social Welfare and Family Law*, 31 (2): 33–146.

Ward, J., Biehal, N. and Farrelly, N. (2011) *Caring for Abused and Neglected Children: Making the Right Decisions for Reunification or Long-term Care.* London: Jessica Kingsley Publishers.

Wardhaugh, J. and Wilding, P. (1993) 'Towards an explanation of the corruption of care', *Critical Social Policy*, 13 (3): 4–31.

Webster-Stratton, C. (2012) *The Incredible Years*. Library of Articles & Research.

Weizsacker, E.U. von, Young, O.R. and Finger, M. (eds) (2005) *Limits to Privatization: How to Avoid Too Much of a Good Thing*. London: Earthscan.

Wexler, R. (1995) *Wounded Innocents: The Real Victims of the War Against Child Abuse*. London: Prometheus Books.

White, V. (2006) 'NHS care criteria fatally flawed', The NHS National Homes Swindle, *Panorama*, BBC, 5 March.

Wrennall, L. (2004) *Miscarriages of Justice in Child Protection: A brief history and proposals for change*. Paper presented to the parliamentary conference held by the All Party Group on Abuse Investigations, Attlee Suite, Portcullis House, 2 December.

Wrennall, L. (2007) 'The discourse of Munchausen Syndrome by Proxy/ fabricated and induced illness: Does the discourse serve economic vested interests or the interests of children?' *Medical Hypotheses*, 68 (5): 960–66.

Wrennall, L. (2010) 'Surveillance and child protection: De-mystifying the Trojan Horse', *Surveillance and Society*, 7 (3/4): 304–24.

Wrennall, L. Pragnell, C., Blakemore-Brown, L. et al. (2003) *'Taking the Stick Away'* Consultation on the Government's Green Paper on Child Protection, 1 December.

Legal References

London Borough of Hillingdon v Neary & Anor [2011] EWHC 1377 (COP)

LB of Hillingdon v Neary [2011] EWHC 3522 (COP)

9 More Than This?
Some Ethical Doubts (and Possibilities) Regarding Service User and Carer Participation within Social Work

Malcolm Carey

No one talks more passionately about his rights than he who in the depths of his soul doubts whether he has any.

Friedrich Nietzsche

Introduction

The direct involvement or 'participation'[1] of service users, carers, patients and other public sector 'consumers' in spheres of welfare provision (health care, education, social work, etc.) now constitutes part of long-term and widespread policies and practices which look likely to continue or expand into the future (Braye, 2000). Participation can take many forms – including the involvement of users, carers and others in direct training and education, recruitment, research, service regulation, planning or even delivery of welfare services. As a political strategy or even a range of democratic strategies and techniques it may also (to some extent at least) involve users or carers in policy and law formation.

Participation has now become an integral part (to various degrees) of once largely monopolised and self-regulating welfare 'professional' disciplines and activities. In its most common forms it seeks to draw from

---

1 Although many authors distinguish between 'participation' and 'involvement' processes the terms are used as inter-related concepts within this chapter.

service user and carer experience and tacit knowledge in order to improve social care service provision. Despite this, critics now regularly note that most participative practices and concepts tend to be broad ranging, and may also be poorly defined or unclear with regards to their rationale, objectives or desired outcomes (e.g. Hodge, 2005; among many others). Although advocates such as Carr (2004: 6–7) stress that participation 'provides a unique opportunity for organisations to *develop* through user-led critical enquiry … ideas about control, oppression, rights, poverty and citizenship', others such as McLaughlin (2010: 1594) add that as political and cultural process it remains 'open to abuse', and can also be as much about maintaining 'exercises to approve service planning and policy proposals rather than enabling service users to be key players or partners in their formulation'. In other core areas such as research it may also represent a convenient 'whistle' or 'bell' to tag on to a project in order to help secure precious grant income from ever shrinking budgets; or possibly even to fulfill other objectives such as mask a lack of originality, rigor or purpose. In addition, despite initial vigour, often convoluted participative research processes may quickly prove to be detached or tiresome to many users or carers, who may also discover that their hard work and time has had little impact on the final outcomes of any project.

Many of the audacious claims regularly furnished regarding involvement are often either absent from participation processes at closer examination or remain unproven empirically. Also the potential benefits of participation may be exaggerated to, among other things, mask or legitimise very different agendas (Carey, 2010; Carr, 2004; Hodge, 2005). This is not merely by government institutions or academics, but also some professional groups and their various bureaucratic councils, or associations that may seek to secure or extend their legitimacy or power. However advocates have longed stressed that if adequately supported and used to meet needs rather than personal, professional or ideological interests, participation has the *potential* to change welfare services and possibly society for the better (Beresford, 2005; Carr, 2004; Jones, 2000; Whitmore, 2001, and others).

This chapter attempts to look at a fundamental aspect of the participative debate which has largely been overlooked. It asks us to consider whether many central participative or involvement activities within social work (SW) remain unethical. That is it asks if they are unfair and inappropriate or perhaps even manipulative since, beneath a rhetorical and ideological veil, they may actually exploit and oppress vulnerable people whilst maintaining or promoting unequal systems and relations of power? In particular the chapter looks at four areas which include problems (and possibilities) relating to:

- The traditional or continued hostility felt towards some users and/or carers by highly stressed or intolerant SW practitioners.
- That participation may not merely be practically but also ethically inappropriate as part of many core SW practices and responsibilities.
- That participation may be used to extend professional power and control and can therefore be detrimental to users or carers.
- Examples of ethical participation which may have led to positive outcomes for users or carers.

We begin by briefly looking at a not uncommon cultural practice within some elements of social work and more generally welfare; that of suspicion or hostility felt towards service users and their carers.

Attitudes towards and Relationships with Service Users and Carers

Following a survey and interviews with practitioners within recently formed Social Service Departments in England during the early 1970s, Satyamurti discovered common prejudices among SW staff felt towards users:

> The language that social workers use about their clients, often jokingly, seems to be based on an image of them as good or naughty ... It seemed, too, that when social workers referred to a "difficult case" they did not mean that the client presented problems that were difficult to solve, but that she was demanding and time-consuming. (Satyamurti, 1974, cited in Biggs and Powell, 2001, 11)

Similarly Pithouse (1987, 81–5) spent a year with two social work teams specialising in child and family related work in South Wales and again noted practitioners' tendency to codify users into a simple good/difficult binary. For example, he highlights how 'the abstract, formal meaning of the client as worthy participant in the welfare endeavour' was 'matched by practitioner folk-lore of the client as venal and unappreciative and in need of careful management'. Further back in time, Ferguson (2011) notes how in the early twentieth century child protection officers avoided touching children due to a fear of physical contamination from the squalor and 'dirtiness' of the families' houses, clothing and bodies. Anxieties also persisted regarding the possibility of 'moral' pollution which sat alongside a general fear of the feral and/or dehumanised 'other'. Although Ferguson asserts that any such disgust or fear regarding contamination had largely disappeared when social work rapidly expanded (and became a viable middle-class career) throughout the 1970s in Britain, such prejudices still linger and impact on current practices. Indeed in a copy of a once popular English practitioner magazine *Social Work Today* Lamont (1981, 17) is far from ambivalent when he details his contempt for 'clients':

> There is, however, a hardy group of undeserving leeches who take all that is going and put nothing back. As a social worker and a ratepayer, I am beginning to resent the time and money wasted on a section [of clients] that would possibly benefit more from being told: "It's your problem, you deal with it". (Cited in Jones, 1983, 16)

Although the language used by many social workers has softened and become more diplomatic or less discriminatory, tension, hostility and conflict with users, carers and/or their family members or friends still remains a fundamental part of the everyday role for many practitioners (Carey, 2004; Jones, 2001; Wrennall, 2010, and others). Reasons for this are many but they inevitably include that social workers have for some time now remained 'gate keepers' to finite resources utilised for carefully rationed support services, typically put aside for families who more often live in extreme poverty. As well as perform an unenviable and fierce gatekeeper role social workers are also regularly involved in other more social control related or punitive activities that are typically forced onto users rather than being freely chosen as rational welfare 'consumers'. Among others, common enforced interventions or treatments include those that link to 'safeguarding' or adult 'protection' such as the removal of children, the placing of dementia sufferers into residential or nursing homes (including due to financial imperatives) or Controlled Treatment Orders (see Chapter 5) for adults with challenging mental health needs.

Particularly in the more control end of social work when surveys are untaken many practitioners are often perceived by users and significant others as being judgmental, arrogant, impatient, patronising, distant, apathetic or even aggressive. They have also been described or experienced as bullies that lack basic social skills such as patience, empathy, tolerance or the capacity to listen rather than hear. For example, whilst reviewing 47 past studies of user and parent experiences and consulting 35 people involved in child protection work (including users who had previously experienced SW assessments and interventions) Lynne Wrennall and her colleagues (2003) could find few positive responses from users regarding participants' past contacts. The independent researchers later presented their findings to key members of the then New Labour government at the Houses of Parliament. Research participants included mothers (and occasionally fathers) who highlighted how they had been threatened with the removal of their children in the past if they complained following an assessment, or instead would have any remaining children taken away if they grumbled about their first child being removed. In addition some parents had also been threatened with removal proceedings unless they started to look for paid employment, left a current post or unless they ended a relationship with a partner. Although we may not be aware of the perhaps complex mitigating circumstances in some of these cases (for example, involving domestic violence or neglect of a child), what emerges nevertheless is the prevalence of arrogance and hostility on behalf of at least some state officials: very different attitudes to those expressed in much academic or professional literature or local or national policy guidance and legislation. Instead we are repeatedly presented with much more democratic, humanistic or even altruistic claims and processes: from empowerment and anti-oppression to consultation and participation.

In response to Wrennall and her colleagues' findings the government's own *Laming Report* (DOH, 2003, 5) concluded that 'this inquiry saw too many examples of those in senior positions [within social services] attempting to justify their work in terms of bureaucratic activity, rather than in outcomes for people'. Indeed a key finding from the research was that SW agencies spent far too much time and resources on surveillance and assessment rather than the provision of tangible support, such as counselling, positive services such as 'child-minding' and nursery care or help with benefits or other means of financial support and advice. Of equal concern, it was often parents from ethnic minority backgrounds or who had a disability or who cared for a disabled child that encountered some of the most distressing and insensitive contact or interventions from social workers. An earlier White Paper (DOH, 1998, 42) *Modernising Social Services* produced following the then recent election of the first New Labour government again noted that 'many reports and inquiries have highlighted cases where social services have failed vulnerable children'. Examples offered included the high proportion of children previously in the care of local authorities who ended up homeless, unemployed or driven to crime, prostitution or hard drug use. We need to recognise however that social services has always been run on a relative 'shoe-string', and that resources and time for more positive non-bureaucratic or managerially constrained interventions will regularly be in short supply; however this does not necessarily make amends for or justify treating people who typically live in extreme poverty with blatant disrespect or disregard.

Such research or government mandates also help to illustrate the now extensive legal powers that many statutory social workers hold over minority groups such as working-class mothers and their respective children. This is perhaps a fundamental reason why in most economically-deprived and socially-excluded communities distrust and fear of social services (and other associate state welfare staff based in schools, hospitals, GP surgeries, *Sure Start* centres, and so on) now remains part of a long-established and often ingrained tradition among excluded or disenfranchised groups and any subsequent Welfare provisions (Jones and Novak, 1993; Wrennall, 2010). Indeed in Britain at least the tangible legal and political powers held by many social workers over citizens within working class communities are likely to surpass that of the police or the medical profession.

As a consequence many users and carers are less than eager to engage with the still relatively new government and professional panacea known as participation. Of those that do bother many find the formal workings and introspective cultures of welfare bureaucracies impenetrable, intimidating, emotionally distant or simply confusing (Danso et al., 2003; Hodge, 2005; among others). Nevertheless regarding users and carers from the most excluded communities, participation is also often viewed as disempowering or as potentially extending any risks to health or dangers of exposure to control-related practices (Warren, 2007). For example, whilst investigating the participation of black service users within SW, Begum (2006, 20–21) discovered that just as a participative/involvement discourse has grown as political priority over the past 20 years, it has dropped regarding involvement over the same period for ethnic minority service user/carer group members. As well as a lack of direct involvement the researcher also discovered that long held prejudices or scepticism felt towards users on behalf of SW staff were difficult for some practitioners to overcome. Indeed one senior SW manager interviewed as part of Begum's study expressed his fears that extending participation much further would be akin to 'letting sea lions run a zoo'. Begum also discovered a tendency for policy makers and practitioners to approach black professionals or community leaders (also known as 'substitute service users') rather than black families or users about what they need. As the author concludes such surrogate participants 'do not have direct experience of being social care service users and are themselves not immune to holding stereotypical views of service users and what they need'.

Regarding non-paid or informal carers Arksey et al. (2003) found that many professionals' chief focus tends to remain that of the patient or user at the expense of any carer. Indeed not unusually deep suspicion or even hostility may be felt towards (predominately female) carers by many social care professionals (Finch, 1989), or they may play or enforce a dominant role in key decision making such as regards whether or not a user should enter a care home (Davis and Nolan, 2003). The carer may also appear as getting in the way of any serious assessment work undertaken or become a nuisance who asks too many questions or makes too many demands. Worse still the carer might also be viewed, without provocation or evidence, as a liar, potential thief or abuser (Heron, 1998). Such a lack of trust, empathy or tolerance sometimes felt towards 'care givers' by social workers and other professionals is nevertheless often counter-productive, since carers and parents tend to provide an essential yet often invisible low cost support service to the State that also significantly fortifies the wider economy. Buckner and Yeandle (2011), for example, estimate that the economic value of unpaid informal carers (most commonly family, friends, neighbours) in the UK remains around £119 billion per year; which itself is more than it costs to run all components of the National Health Service. Despite this carers are at times recognised as offering little of anything when it comes to participation, other than possibly as associate people to make up the numbers or fulfil quotas set by external bodies. Indeed as part of Wallcraft et al.'s (2012) recent survey of participation activities within 16 Higher Education institutions in England, the general lack of involvement of informal carers in a wide range of activities such as teaching, decision making and course design were again highlighted.

Official guidance and also independent research has continuously stressed the need for dignity and respect for service users or carers during involvement or participation (Crawford et al., 2003). Such recommendations remain sound in principle but they rarely if ever acknowledge the social class and power-based tensions and differences that persist between welfare professionals and most users or carers within SW. Not unusually users or carers also feel that they will not be listened to by professionals or instead that their views will be dismissed (Danso et al., 2003; Warren, 2007). Other studies highlight additional obstacles for users to engage in meaningful participation. These can include a lack of available supporting information or training provided, a lack of legitimate knowledge or power held by participants themselves within alien discursive arenas, or the negative impact of high staff turnover within ever more fragmented or 'outsourced' welfare services.

Severely limited resources and high eligibility criteria for support in social care (in comparison to many health or education sectors) – now further compromised through intense public sector austerity measures imposed by the Conservative/Liberal Coalition government (2010 onwards) (especially as regards adult social care) – also means that the proportion of people with full 'user' eligibility status has fallen further away of any genuine 'needs-led' criterion. In relation to this point, Taylor (2005) notes the exclusion and devaluation of the views of a high number of *potential* users who would otherwise have the option of becoming participants if they received the services that they should be entitled to (if eligibility criteria for social care support reflected genuine needs). This also begs the question that if people with higher dependency needs (for example, regarding later stage dementia or a severe learning disability or children taken into care) are now much more likely to become eligible as 'service users' – adding to ever more established 'risk' management cultures of social work - might such highly dependent 'legitimate' clients struggle to engage meaningfully in participation processes?

Ethically or Practically Inappropriate for Many Social Work Roles?

We have seen that within social work more control-orientated interventions persist within safeguarding or protection work with children and families. Also the 'sectioning' or Community Treatment Orders placed upon people with mental health needs – most commonly women and members of ethnic minority groups for compulsory treatment under the Mental Health Acts of 1983 and 2007 in Britain – remain the other area where punitive or social control practices are more prevalent. Nevertheless although other forms of statutory SW may offer more consistent support – including practical assistance for disabled people or respite care for carers in greatest need – this support tends to be extremely difficult to access and not unusually potential applicants face a raft of bureaucratic hurdles and intense questioning from social workers before being considered for any provisions. Unlike within many health care or education sectors, there is also now likely to be a charge for services whether in receipt of benefits or not.

Alongside numerous allegations of abuse within residential and nursing care homes that nowadays more regularly come to light through the media – such as most recently the exposure in 2011 of the systematic abuse of many older residents by staff within care homes run by the private sector provider *Southern Cross*, or the abuse of older people within NHS hospitals or their homes by 'support workers' – there have also been similar findings within studies of SW support provided for disabled people (Curtis and Mulholland, 2011). Acts of neglect or abuse become even more of a concern for residents and relatives alike when one remembers that the proportion of care home inspectors has steadily declined alongside the increasing proportion of 'for profit' private providers; some of whom such as *BUPA* now dominate the high profit, yet for staff work intensive and low wage, residential and nursing care home sector in countries such as England and Wales. For example, over a 20-year period the number of nursing and residential care homes increased sevenfold since the early 1980s in England, whereas the numbers of care home inspectors employed increased threefold (Kerrison and Pollock, 2001). There have also since materialised original plans set out in 2006 by the Commission for Social Care Inspection to reduce the number and extent of inspections, including of children's homes (CSCI, 2006). In the now distant past, acts of neglect or abuse may have been identified or investigated by social workers in their previous 'generic' role, however under care management and personalisation such roles or responsibilities have diminished in favour of bureaucratic risk assessments, contract and commissioning work, and for some users the setting up of personal budgets.

Despite incidents of neglect or acts of cruelty, a common concern among some adult users is that there may be repercussions, or essential support services might be withdrawn, if complaints against social services are made. For example as part of in-depth interviews with 50 disabled adults receiving local authority support services, Jenny Morris (1993, 117–18) discovered fears of repercussions if users were to upset a social worker:

> A number of people felt they had to behave in a certain way in order to persuade [social] service managers of their need for a particular service. Marcia, for example, said "I feel you have to charm people, you don't get anything otherwise". Michelle explained "I don't want them to think that I've been difficult because I don't think they'll treat me very well then". This was partly why she didn't complain about the home carer who hit her.

Fears of repercussions following criticism or complaints have also been stressed by patients in health care as well as social services, including the possibility that support services may be removed or that individual families may be stigmatised by professionals (Crawford et al., 2003). Such inequitable processes and outcomes strongly suggest that attempts since the 1980s to reconstruct social work on a par with the sub-cultures and practices of business (for example, promoting competition, choice, consumer rights, empowerment, participation, and so on) remain not only unconvincing but also largely unachievable other than in a highly superficial context. Any such doubts are further compounded by reduced budgets and shrinking services across welfare sectors yet disproportionately effecting core adult and family groups such as older or disabled people.

Over the past decade or more new control-related or punitive responses have also developed and continued to grow within social work. For example, in a passionate account Beth Humphries (2004, 95) underlines the complicity of SW to authoritarian policy and law in relation to Immigration. Humphries convincingly highlights how any such draconian measures and practices are 'degrading and inhuman' to already vulnerable and abused people:

> The example of state social work's relationship to immigration controls typifies its relationship to social policy generally, in that on the whole it adopts a role of subservience in implementing policies that have exposed the most vulnerable

UK populations to: "poverty, insecurity, housing and environmental distress and all their social consequences".

As part of her PhD and post-Doctoral research Adele Jones (2000; 2002) looked at the impact of immigration policies in the North of England upon children who had been directly affected. She utilised a participative approach and grounded theory to interview 30 young people and discovered that social service departments, government bodies and voluntary sector organisations involved in child care had a propensity to practice within a narrow cultural and normative framework regarding what constitutes a 'normal' family. Subsequently asylum seeking families were regularly viewed as being outside of any such ideal (and largely mythical) norm and experienced ongoing prejudice and discrimination from numerous welfare professionals. Much as in Lynne Wrennall and her colleagues (2003) findings discussed earlier, surveillance or control techniques utilised tended to be highly disruptive for families and children who were regularly left damaged emotionally and psychologically; especially when, as was common, children had been forcibly removed from their seemingly 'abnormal' or risky families and taken into care.

Within traditional child care social work with families similar themes can persist. For example, Cooper et al. (2003) discovered that many children (alongside their parents or other family members) found assessment processes undertaken by social workers to be traumatising and, from the perspective of children, sometimes more damaging than any previous (or alleged) neglect. Similarly life in care for children may be intrinsically distressing and traumatic, and it's now common knowledge as well as an empirical fact (according to Government statistics) that most 'children in care' experience significantly lower 'life chances' than their peers. For example, despite only 0.5 per cent of children entering the care system (for a short, medium or long term), 27 per cent of the adult population in prison during 2001 were previously in care as children (*Department for Education and Skills*, 2006, 14). It is perhaps therefore of little surprise that so few adults who have previously been in care come forward to engage with participation processes, whether within education, research or practice-related projects or organisations. Such a significant number of the traditional social work client base can also be added to older people and members of minority ethnic groups as three groups who rarely come forward to participate in social work education or practice (Begum, 2006; Wallcraft et al., 2012) which perhaps asks us how such endeavours can ever be truly democratic. My own experience over many years in social work education and practice suggests that it is a relatively small proportion of user groups – such as people with mental health needs or a physical disability – who tend to be well represented as participants. Nevertheless Barnes and Mercer (2006), among others, therefore question whether small groups of disabled people should be relied on to represent the views of many more people.

The prevalence of risk management and control techniques within much modern social work or the limited life chances of children in care beg the question of why subsequent users, family members or their carers would wish to participate in social work education or planning, whether democratic or not. If, for example, you have had your children removed by state officials, or have been subject to a Community Treatment Order under a Mental Health Act and were then forced to take medications or other treatments which subsequently made things worse, why would you wish to educate or advise people to repeat such practices on other 'subjects'? What exactly might you gain from a wider system which may have played a part in severely limiting your life chances or even led to forms of systematic abuse within an institutional care setting? This poses a difficult ethical dilemma: is it ethical to invite or encourage vulnerable people who are the past victims of control-related interventions or poor services to engage in processes that may further promote such outcomes in the future? Alternatively, might the greater and more democratic involvement of such groups lead to more awareness and better practices for some future or current social workers?

There are, nevertheless, other forms of 'social work' which are not necessarily an explicit part of punitive or social control related practices: for example, respite or day care, supported living, residential care, some forms of counselling, advocacy and child support, among others. Such support services are perhaps more suited to some components of participation and involvement, especially those that seek to improve services through quasi-consumerist models of intervention. Nevertheless the implementation and dispersal of care management (in social work with adults and children and families) – and the more recent push for personalisation, direct payments alongside more general forms of 'Big Society' self-governance (including within 'communities') – over the past two decades has rapidly seeped into and colonised every component of what was once 'generic' state social work. In so doing it has in many respects severely hindered the potential options for meaningful involvement with users and carers, and instead supplanted such opportunities or roles with ever more private sector 'service provision', bureaucracy and 'top down' management-led ideological principles. Such political processes have grown in tandem with a culture of intense gate-keeping and economic rationing that have helped to place further strains on relations with users, family members and wider communities (Dustin, 2007; Fenwick and McMillan, 2012; Wrennall, 2010).

The New Labour and Coalition 'modernisation' agenda in the UK has built upon the foundations set by the previous Thatcher and Major governments, and has included a salient role for the private sector in the provision and management of social care and social work. As critics such as Fenwick and McMillan (2012, 368) indicate, participation of not merely users and patients but more generally wider communities has run alongside and supported this process:

> This attempt to move local public services towards a market model envisaged society as a collection of atomized individuals privately "consuming" services, empowered by the existence of competition and by the ostensible growth of choice. Participation was conceived within this framework.

In essence participation has ironically supported the extension of greater market-led inequalities and added to the formation of a more individualistic society, a perhaps dystopian paradox that may be implicitly embedded within wider participation processes and outcomes. Nevertheless as the authors and others such as Orr (2005) and Clarke et al. (2007) point out, participation has developed and grown as a deeply ambiguous, nebulous, even confused concept in practice that engineers a wide range of interpretations and applications. Also, within various rhetorical guises such as 'community involvement' or 'active citizenship', public participation often emerges as a deeply bureaucratic, centrally and/or management/ professionally controlled, prescriptive and disempowering cultural activity for those few citizens who are able or can be bothered to engage. Fenwick and McMillan (2012, 376) question the widespread expansion of public participation on behalf of the New Labour government and add that a core part of the problem remains 'the unitary and relatively centralized state' in the UK, which stands in contrast to 'much of Europe where the tradition of local self-government is long established and where, indeed, the formal decentralisation of federal structures or regional decentralisation would not permit such central direction'.

Whilst offering a summary of the *Joseph Rowntree Foundation's* research projects relating to community participation and involvement, Foot (2009: 18) has concluded that it 'remains difficult to find evidence of the impact of community engagement on service quality' and a 'lack of clarity about the purpose and role of citizens in governance and how they can effect change remains a weakness'. As Fenwick and McMillan (2012) add, participation in most forms has never captured the imagination of communities who have tended to be extremely sceptical if not hostile towards local councils or professional groups and their use of buzzwords, rhetoric or eagerness to wheel out whatever latest project takes their fancy. We might also ask whether the push for participation projects helps neglect or draw attention away from the real issues that impact upon excluded groups, such as poverty, poor housing, domestic violence, cultural disadvantage, and more.

Regards social work practices Davies (2012, 8) also highlights the increased distance between social workers as care managers and user groups:

> Caring has become commodified and subjected to deepening, bureaucratised "instrumentalism" applied within a tightening plethora of contracts and procedures ... On these accounts SW's primary contemporary concern is with superintending neo-liberal regulatory practices ... "At a high emotional cost" (Munro, 2004, 1087) focus is fixated on targets and social work is less orientated towards human relationships than to information management. For Dominelli and Hoogvelt (1996, 46) indeed, "[social work's] concern with ... therapeutic work ... with adaptive responses to life situations have virtually disappeared".

Such institutional and bureaucratic hurdles for practitioners suggest much greater difficulties for practitioners in a challenging role, including in attempts against the odds to meet users' or carers' needs. If SWs are not directly involved in service provision, and also therefore have very limited discretion, (non-negative) power or time available away from their desks and computer screens, this begs the question of what benefits or purpose might involvement offer for users and carers? In particular, are such predominately administrative, technical and information processing roles, tasks and activities likely to be of much interest or validity to people whose needs tend to be so much more personal, emotional, economic, physical, relationship based, family or community orientated?

Of course even long before the advent of care management or personalisation the capacity of SWs to accommodate, never mind meet, complex human needs has always been restricted. This has been partially due a lack of tangible power, owing to factors such as legal, organisational, bureaucratic or economic restraints, or a lack of legitimacy or support from a largely sceptical public and at times hostile working-class communities. In comparison to fully hallmarked traditional male professions such as law or medicine, SW as a mediated, female-dominated, semi-profession simply lacks the resources or legitimacy and tangible (positive) power to deliver the types of supportive or 'emancipatory' practice so readily claimed by its advocates, especially some academics and professional leaders. Its more ambivalent 'community' role has therefore always remained contested and its powers often limited to advice, tea and sympathy, risk-based assessments and minor interventions or more control related negative interventions targeted against disadvantaged groups such as lone parent women, unemployed working-class males, people with mental health needs or asylum seekers. As much as the principles of challenging discrimination, 'fighting oppression' or utilising whichever social model of disability is currently in vogue may appeal, there is little evidence to suggest that such high ideals find their way into 'street level' practices on a *regular* basis. Indeed such paradigms or interventions may actually make things worse by encouraging practitioners to scrutinise and condemn the (perhaps homophobic or racist) beliefs as well as habits of some members of any disenfranchised client base. Some commentators point out that such emancipatory principles have never really received much tangible support beneath the surface and that individualism, private practice and moral conservatism are much more in keeping with the professions raison d'être or yearning for survival, legitimacy and power (Hardcastle et al., 1997; Spect and Courtney, 1994). It seems more likely however that as an occupational force social work is more likely to draw from a wide demographic with diverse values, viewpoints and approaches to practice.

The extensive movement of decision making and provider-related powers away from once reasonably stable local authorities or statutory agencies, and towards a deeply fragmented kaleidoscope of private, state and voluntary sector service providers, nevertheless brings into question how participation within social work organisations can, to use a cliché, make a difference. Exactly where do loyalties lie, how and where are decisions made or is power located among so many different providers of social care services? The empirical research has also noted extensive obstacles to meaningful participation due to such and other many changes imposed through care management (Braye, 2000). Among many other examples these have included the detrimental effects of staff shortages and high turnover within social work (and other state welfare) organisations, a subsequent lack of continuity regarding local authority support and not uncommon problems encountered contacting remaining or more transient staff, whether they be long-term or as likely private recruitment agency employed (Carey, 2009; Danso et al., 2003; Janson and Law, 2003; Roulstone et al., 2006; Warren, 2007, 54).

Extending Professional Legitimacy and Power?

If we assume a positive and democratic role for social work and participation then another danger that prevails with greater participation remains the possibility that professional powers may increase further following more involvement with users and/or carers. That is power differences such as articled through decision-making processes or capacities to stigmatise or exclude may extend rather than narrow or disappear. John Swain and his colleagues (2003: 133) highlight the not uncommon perception of professionals felt by users:

Professionals have been perceived, by their clients and sociologists alike, as controlling, distant, privileged, self-interested, domineering and the gatekeepers of scarce resources. Furthermore feminists have spoken about the patriarchal nature of the professions where high-ranking doctors and lawyers tend to be white, male and with "social connections".

Foucault (1975) especially has stressed the centrality of power, dominance, control and normalizing surveillance techniques inherent within welfare professional labour processes. Here it seems essential capabilities such as the collection and processing of information, regulation or the monitoring of potentially deviant populations persist. As with so much else within politics and culture, however, power is rarely sovereign but instead has to be earned and gained through forms of consent, trust and public sanction. Participation and involvement therefore offers the potential of playing a crucial role in helping professions to *legitimise* their role and grip on power by promoting partisan interests as democratic, open, altruistic and serving the interests of customers.

In contrast, however, numerous empirical studies have revealed that when applied in practice participation can subtly or more explicitly become quickly regulated and carefully controlled by professional groups (Barnes and Mercer, 2006; Carr, 2004; and many more). Institutional settings such as a social work department, hospital or university can also intimidate participants and quickly influence or even mould their behaviour, dispositions and attitudes. In contrast however, expectations regarding appropriate behaviour can sometimes be contested by users which may subsequently lead to sanctions. For example, Barnes (2008, 462–3) highlights the centrality of emotions such as enthusiasm, passion and anger for many users who participate in official public welfare meetings, ceremonies or focus groups. Such responses often surprise or are resented by professionals who may then attempt to impose more controlled and rational norms of behaviour on participants. Indeed Barnes uses the example of Church's (1996) study of the involvement of psychiatric survivors within a participative legislative subcommittee in Canada to stress her point:

> Many of the officials involved in this process found the angry and emotional input from service users very hard to handle. One young woman started to cry as she told her story and challenged officials to act quickly because if they didn't it would be too late for her – she would be dead. Officials thought the approach adopted by service users was too confrontational and tried to rule personal stories as outside the remit of the committee. Questioning of officials was described as "grilling" and overall the behaviour of service users was constructed as "bad manners" ... [in this case example] we see the absence of emotion among the jurors being cited as grounds for questioning the authenticity of *their interest* in

the issues they are deliberating. There is a sense that they are "going through the motions", that they do "not really care" about the issues "in any significant sense".

Problems with professionals vary yet prevail throughout empirical studies with different service user groups from older people to disabled children and people with mental health needs, among others (Carr, 2004). These include professionals appearing to be fixated upon what users are unable to do (Beresford, 2000), who may also paternalistically stigmatise clients as dependent and passive or incompetent or view them as largely invisible or as a nuisance (Davies, 2003; Jones, 1983; Watson, 2007). There can also remain a significant gap between rhetoric and what finite social care 'budgets' are able to offer (Barnes and Mercer, 2006) or even that socially constructed terminology such as 'service users' implicitly assume that people who use social work services are dependent and inferior (McLaughlin, 2010). Of course individual attitudes and practices will again vary yet institutional and cultural group pressures – from the discursive to the ideological - may instil a set of binary outlooks (good/bad, dependent/independent user or carer, and so on) and inculcated professional dispositions and narrative-based responses which the hard-pressed social worker may find difficult to resist.

Hodge (2005, 164) adds that many forms of participative governance continue to involve users 'in an ad-hoc way'. Also professionally controlled processes of involvement regularly normalise, regulate and/or dismiss user views whilst maintaining the interests of elites. In particular, professional discourses and paradigms (theories, practices, traditions, normative beliefs and procedures, etc.) may surreptitiously and/or openly distort, regulate and control the views and behaviour of users whilst also circumscribing their finite powers. As Hodge illustrates with empirical evidence, such often tacit cultural processes developed within the knowledge-centred domains of the professional are sophisticated, flexible, subtle yet also potent in carefully filtering or excluding the views or stances of clients or patients. Hodge drew on critical discourse analysis, ethnographic and interview data collected within and among members of a semi-independent mental health advocacy forum, comprising users and health care officials. From this rich data Hodge was able to illustrate the subtle yet elaborate ways in which service users' views or experiences are marginalised or dismissed within some health care environments. This was especially in formal meetings between officials and users and any related discussions. For example, topics of discussion during formal meetings with users tended to be limited and controlled by health care professionals. This was often done by stopping or limiting participant references to structural forms of disadvantage (poverty, poor housing, etc.) as being a common cause of mental health needs for users. Such topics were kept off minutes and agendas or subsequent 'difficult' conversations were averted by chairs or non-participant attendees during meetings. As Hodge notes participant discussions of personal experience were deemed 'relevant only in so far as they [could] be incorporated instrumentally into [dominant] discourse', which helped to establish 'discursive inequality between service users and officials which mirrors and thus reinforces wider institutional power inequalities'.

In a similar vein Hodgson and Canvin (2005, 54) again question the sincerity and ethics of using participants within health-based research projects. The authors present involvement as a political process that ultimately supports established institutions and professional practices. A fundamental problem remains that 'Lay' experts and participant knowledge bases lack the cultural and linguistic competency or agility, principle scientific knowledge or technical detail gained through long-term formal training or practical experience within institutional domains; all of which remains crucial for survival in the stressful and fiercely competitive arenas of health care research and practice. In such discursive arenas that rely so heavily upon cultural capital the user or carer may quickly lose confidence or effectively become perplexed and excluded within complex projects that nevertheless claim inclusion and participation as part of any initiative, project or service.: In addition participation may also be used to attract research funding, promote brilliant careers or improve professional capabilities and practices, and again further legitimacy and power. There is then a structurally induced paradox held within the system that may ironically extend professional powers the more patients become involved!

Similarly within social work, examples of empowerment-led or democratic participation projects which are not tokenistic or actively controlled by professionals are difficult to find. Brian Corby and his colleagues (1996, 488–9) utilised a questionnaire and interviews with 35 parents attending social work case conferences regarding allegations of neglect or abuse towards their child. They also distributed questionnaires to professionals present at 110 case conferences the researchers attended in the North of England. The researchers discovered that parental participation in this inevitably sensitive, stressful yet also long winded and bureaucratic process was extremely limited:

> Most of [the parents] we interviewed had little opportunity to disagree with assessments either before or during conferences. They felt unable to challenge professionals views or put forward their own concerns and had no say whatsoever in the final decision making. [Case] conferences seemed to be carefully stage-managed to avoid conflict in the presence of parents. Great pains were taken both before and during conferences to ensure that parents were carefully groomed and moulded into the process.

The authors do however argue that in some other countries such as New Zealand engagement and involvement by parents in child protection processes tend to be more sincere and embedded into the organisational and professional cultures of statutory social work. Nevertheless as among other case examples there remains a tendency for participation to be regularly circumscribed or subtly controlled by professionals. Again such inequitable processes and traditions are often held together by intricate rods of power which are generated through the knowledge and ideological practices or procedures developed by professionals themselves and which may push away or sanction people and their 'deviant' behaviours, attitudes, beliefs and dispositions, etc., that do not fit within a remit built upon rational and clinical (patriarchal) processes and cultural norms. With regards to statutory social work in countries such as Britain the influence of legal and policy lead sanctions – fortified and codified by often imposing financial or bureaucratic parameters – may also help to enforce further externally driven constraints upon attempts to achieve less superficial forms of active participation.

Discussion: Creating Ethical Spaces for Meaningful Participation?

We have seen that participation as political and cultural process has generated as many practical and ethical problems as it has offered solutions: especially regarding factors such as how best to accommodate a representative number of users or carers to engage meaningfully in decision-making processes, especially those that are then able to change practices, beliefs and working cultures for the better. It has been proposed that there are also inevitably complex moral questions and dilemmas regarding whether it is ethical to encourage often disenfranchised social groups, such as asylum seekers, members of ethnic minority communities or parents who have had safeguarding measures enforced – and who regularly receive the brunt of imposed social work assessments or control-related interventions – to become involved in, say, the education and training of future state employees. After all such employees are likely to then go on to breathe further life into dystopian policies that may counter the needs or basic human rights of already disadvantaged people. Simply involving a few people through a physical presence is unlikely to make much if any difference to outcomes or policies at a "street level" and although levels of participation tend to vary they are generally much more limited the closer we move upwards towards key decision making processes, policy making and other forms of traditionally centralized or hierarchal "top down" power.

Many such thorny questions in relation to meaningful or ethical participation have sometimes been avoided, often in favour of simpler interpretations which may conceal complex debates and political processes within a dualism that proposes either 'bad' managerial or 'good' democratic models of involvement, or worst still assumes implicitly that any form of participation is inevitably a good thing for us all. Crucial mitigating details such as that many social work interventions in core areas such as child protection or community mental health are often forced onto users; lead to poor outcomes for children in later life following long-term care (as well as being dehumanizing for some parents) and are typically caused by underlying and powerful structural factors such as poverty, cultural disadvantage, exclusion and discrimination, have often also been bypassed within some debates and assumptions. Braye (2000) however notes that many feminists in particular have stressed that so much seemingly 'good' participation appears largely intent on at best improving the quality of *current* welfare service provision. In contrast it is claimed that such processes should also seek to challenge and reform normative traditions and structural outcomes, including professional practices and the often unregulated negative powers that self-appointed 'experts' may hold over users, patients, carers, and others.

Krysia Canvin and her colleagues (2007, 984) drew from case study research and interviewed 25 adults living on welfare benefits in deprived parts of London, Wales and North West England. This research highlighted the distrust and scepticism typically felt towards welfare professionals – including social workers, teachers, GPs, social security clerks, and others – as well as the entrenched power differences that continue to persist despite more than two decades of participation and other 'democratic' reforms or initiatives. Users or carers interviewed articulated their embedded distrust and fear of the welfare professional, especially regarding their capacity and not uncommon tendency to judge them unfairly, misunderstand their points of view and potentially take away benefits or children:

> Approaching services was perceived as akin to taking a gamble that might or might not result in their needs being met. Faced with this "choice", participants employed strategies to minimise the risks that on the surface may appear risky to health. If public services are to succeed in providing support to disadvantaged families, greater efforts are needed to build trust and demonstrate understanding for the strategies these families use to maintain their well-being against formidable odds.

We must remember, however, that practitioners remain a diverse breed and some if not more will be fair and reasonable with users and carers. Such findings also imply that there is a *potential* positive role for future participation and involvement, especially if they lead to greater understanding of needs, and more particularly perhaps empathy on behalf of any distant or otherwise unsympathetic professionals. Indeed among the numerous costly research projects and barrage of subsequent professional, government and university reports dedicated to what has become a 'participation industry' of sorts, there are examples of projects which are built upon at least some of the egalitarian principles from which welfare participation first emerged. For example, Littlechild and Glasby (2001) offer a less rhetorical yet practically beneficial social care model of involvement within health care. The researchers drew support from older people as 'participating patients' to challenge many of the findings and recommendations held within previous health and medical research that explored appropriate patient care responses as part of Emergency Hospital Admissions. As they show within their participatory qualitative approach that involved 52 patients admitted to a hospital in Birmingham, England over a 4-month period, previous studies within health care had neglected the views of patients as well as drawn conclusions which contrasted with their own. Among other points, this research highlighted the divisions between health and social care services, the marginalisation of social services within health care and, in particular, the corrosive impact of ever more fragmented service provision upon older people. The authors conclude that participation research should do more than merely seek to understand participants and improve established services, it should where possible lead to other outcomes such as the 'personal development' of participants and encourage moves towards creating fairer systems of support.

In another example briefly discussed earlier Adele Jones (1998; 2000; 2002) drew upon feminist and participative action research to undertake interviews with 30 young people directly affected by draconian immigration controls in England. As well as again draw attention to often poor treatment from welfare professionals experienced by vulnerable children, alongside relatively commonplace examples of institutional racism, Jones was able to elicit from a methodology which it seems allowed otherwise passive participants significant control and power over how any data was collected and used. As Jones (2000: 31) notes, representing children as users in research can only be considered ethical if it helps to 'dislodge adult certainties and address inequalities'. Also confronting cultural processes that disempower users and carers such as those stressed in this chapter should be central to participation:

The focus of participative research should be as much as about *disempowerment* as empowerment, meaning that there must be a personal and political understanding and commitment to identifying and dismantling disempowering processes both at the level of personal dynamics and also in achieving change within a wider social context. (Jones, 2000, 37)

Fenway and McMillan (2012, 372) again highlight the possibilities for more meaningful and ethical participation when they note the importance of *relations* held *within* participative processes alongside a chance to *tinker* with policies, mechanisms or processes generated externally by other bodies. In relation, Clarke and Newman (2007) have elsewhere 'focused on the multiple identifications available to users of health services – including patient, citizen, and consumer – as a means of exploring active and passive forms of participation and "dissent"'. Clearly participation can be used for very different purposes by user or carer collectives than those envisaged or constructed by managers, professionals and various committees or wider government. As Barnes and Prior (2009) also suggest, 'closer cooption of the "responsible citizen" in the delivery of public services can give the citizen (and public services staff) the opportunity to transform or "subvert" the relationship that is offered to them by the state, changing – inverting – the meaning of the relationship'. Such approaches, what we might loosely term deviant or ethical participation, may offer a challenge to what Forbes and Sashidharan (1997) depict as the all too commonplace use of participation in its various guises to give legitimacy to inequitable state professional practices and policies, as well as fail to acknowledge or address structural inequality or the further exclusion of dissenting voices.

Although the capacity of individual practitioners to influence wider structural dynamics such as government policy or legislation will tend to be limited, much of the empirical research cited in this chapter suggests that it is also the attitudes held and micro-practices applied by practitioners at street level that regularly imposes so much damage to service users, carers or family members. In this regard relations and personal prejudice may be, as, if not more, important than wider structural factors from a user perspective. We might therefore seek to creatively encourage proactive participations to move from a now long running tradition in some quarters of viewing the largely powerless and passive client or carer with a despairing or cynical eye; and to instead encourage practitioners to look up and question the often corrosive impact of negative policies, procedures and organisational practices and norms which disempower or disenfranchise those people within and around the ideological domains of social care. Here ethical participation does not exist alone or in isolation to other events or practice cultures, as is often the case if built around a purely consumer led or pseudo-democratic model that may seek to extend efficiency, save resources or implicitly promote normative self-governance or adherence to reductive professional norms disseminated among objectified clients. Instead ethical participation may entwine with other dynamics or trends that link involvement with an understanding of structural disadvantage, hidden ideological objectives or recognising and revealing the potential powers of surveillance that professionals may hold over users, as well as calling for and moving towards greater equality.

Further Reading

Canvin, K., Jones, C., Marttila, A., Burström, B. and Whitehead, M. (2007) 'Can I risk using public services? Perceived consequences of seeking help and health care among households living in poverty: qualitative study', *Journal of Epidemiology and Community Health* 61: 984–9: a succinct yet incisive account that draws upon a small qualitative study to reveal the tensions and class conflict held between many users and welfare professionals. The paper suggests that contact with welfare services represents a risk or gamble for most users that may lead to service provision but may as likely make things much worse for families living in poverty.

Hodge, S. (2005) 'Participation, discourse and power: A case study', *Critical Social Policy* 25(2): 164–79: an excellent piece of case study research which reveals in great detail the largely unwritten rules attached to participation within health care services and mental health. In this example users are carefully regulated implicitly by professionals through discursive processes such as the meeting at which they are able to prioritise their own agendas and largely evade or silence the more critical views of users.

Fenwick, J. and McMillan, J. (2012) 'Public participation and public service modernisation: Learning from New Labour?' *International Journal of Public Administration* 35(6): 367–78: an up to date critical overview of the policy initiatives and implicit objectives that lie behind public participation and involvement as a seemingly democratic political process. A detailed and extremely well written account.

References

Althusser, L. (2003) *The Humanist Controversy and Other Writings*. London: Verso.

Arksey, H., Jackson, K., Wallace, A. et al. (2003) Access to Health Care for Carers: Barriers and Interventions Report for National Co-ordinating

Centre for NHS Service Delivery and Organisation Research and Development (NCCSDO), www.sdo.Ishtm.ac.uk/files/project/24-final-report.pdf

Barnes, C. and Mercer, G. (2006) *Independent Futures: Creating User-Led Disability Services in a Disabling Society.* Bristol: Policy Press.

Barnes, M. (2008) 'Passionate participation: Emotional experiences and expressions in deliberate forums', *Critical Social Policy* 28(4): 461–81.

Barnes, M. and Prior, D. (eds) (2009) *Subversive Citizens: Power, Agency and Resistance in Public Services.* Bristol: Policy Press.

Begum, N. (2006) Doing It for Themselves: Participation and Black and Ethnic Minority Service Users: Participation Report 14. London: Social Care Institute for Excellence.

Beresford, P. (2000) 'Service users knowledge and social work theory: Conflict or collaboration', *British Journal of Social Work* 30(4): 495–503.

Beresford, P. (2005) 'Theory and practice of user involvement in research: Making the connection with public policy and practice', in Lowes, L. and Hulatt, I. (eds), *Involving Service Users in Health and Social Care Research.* London: Routledge.

Biggs, S. and Powell, J. (2001) 'A Foucauldian analysis of old age and the power of social welfare', *Journal of Aging and Social Policy* 12(2): 93–112.

Braye, S. (2000) 'Participation and involvement in social care', in Kemshall, H. and Littlechild, R. (eds), *User Involvement and Participation in Social Care: Research Informing Practice.* London: Jessica Kingsley Publishers.

Buckner, L. and Yeandle, S. (2011) Valuing Carers: Calculating the Value of Carers Support Leeds, Carers UK; CIRCLE; University of Leeds.

Canvin, K., Jones, C., Marttila, A. et al. (2007) 'Can I risk using public services? Perceived consequences of seeking help and health care among households living in poverty: qualitative study', *Journal of Epidemiology and Community Health* 61: 984–9.

Carey, M. (2003) 'Anatomy of a care manager', *Work, Employment and Society* 17(1): 121–35.

Carey, M. (2004) *The Care Managers: Life on the Front-line After Social Work.* Unpublished PhD thesis: University of Liverpool.

Carey, M. (2009) 'The order of chaos: Exploring agency care manager's construction of social order within fragmented worlds of state social work', *British Journal of Social Work* 39(3): 556–73.

Carey, M. (2010) 'Should I stay or should I go? Practical, ethical and political challenges to 'service user' participation within social work research', *Qualitative Social Work* 10(2): 224–43.

Carr, S. (2004) Has Service User Participation Made a Difference to Social Care Services? Position Paper 3. London: Social Care Institute for Excellence.

Clarke, J. and Newman, J. (2007) 'What's in a name?', *Cultural Studies* 21(4): 738–57.

Clarke, J., Cochrane, A. and Smart, C. (1987) *Ideologies of Welfare: From Dreams to Disillusion*. London: Hutchinson Education.

Clarke, J., Newman, J., Smith, N. et al. (2007) *Creating Citizen Consumers*. London, Sage.

Cooper, A., Katz, I. and Hetherington, R. (2003) 'The Risk Factor' Demos, http://www.demos.co.uk/publications/riskfactor

Corby, B., Millar, M. and Young, L. (1996) 'Parental participation in child protection work: Rethinking the rhetoric', *British Journal of Social Work* 26(4): 475–92.

Commission for Social Care Inspection (2006) 'Changes to the frequency of inspection', http://www.csci.org.uk.

Crawford, M., Rutter, D. and Thelwall, S. (2003) User Involvement in Change Management: A review of the Literature Report to the National Co-ordinating Centre for NHS Service Delivery and Organisation Research and Development (NCCSDO), www.sdo.Ishtm.ac.uk/files/project/18-final-report.pdf

Croft, S. and Beresford, P. (1995) 'Whose empowerment? Equalizing the competing discourses in community care', in R. Jack (ed.), *Empowerment in Community Care*. London: Chapman and Hall.

Curtis, P. and Mulholland, H. (2011) 'Panorama Care Home Abuse Investigation Prompts Government Review'. *Guardian*, 1 June.

Danso, C., Greaves, H., Howell, S. et al. (2003) The Involvement of Children and Young People in Promoting Change and Enhancing the Quality of Services: A Research Report for SCIE from the from the National Children's Bureau. London: National Children's Bureau.

Davies, C. (2003), 'Workers, professions and identity', in Henderson, J. and Atkinson, D. (eds) *Managing Care in Context*. London: Routledge.

Davies, H. (2012) 'Contextual challenges for crisis support in the immediate aftermath of major incidents in the UK', *British Journal of Social Work*. Advanced access 27 January, 1–18.

Davies, L. and Leonard, P. (2004) 'Introduction', in Davies, L. and Leonard, P. (eds) *Social Work in a Corporate Era*. Aldershot: Ashgate.

Davies, S. and Nolan, M. (2003) 'Making the best of things: Relatives experiences of decisions about care home entry', *Ageing and Society*, 23: 429–50.

Department for Education and Skills (2006) Children looked after in England (including adoption and care leavers) 2005–2006, http://www.education.gov.uk/rsgateway/DB/SFR/s000691/index.shtml

Department of Health (1998) *Modernising Social Services*. London: HMSO.

Department of Health (2003) *The Victoria Climbié Inquiry report of an inquiry by Lord Laming*. London: HMSO.

Dustin, D. (2007) *The McDonaldization of Social Work*. Aldershot: Ashgate.

Eagleton, T. (1991) *Ideology: An Introduction*. London: Verso.

Fenwick, J. and McMillan, J. (2012) 'Public participation and public service modernisation: Learning from New Labour?', *International Journal of Public Administration* 35(6): 367–78.

Ferguson, H. (2011) *Child Protection Practice*. Basingstoke: Palgrave Macmillan.

Foot, J. (2009) *Citizen Involvement in Local Governance*. York: Joseph Rowntree Foundation.

Finch, J. (1989) *Family Obligations and Social Change*. Oxford: Polity Press.

Forbes, J. and Sashidharan, S.P. (1997) 'User involvement in services – Incorporation or challenge?', *British Journal of Social Work* 27: 481–98.

Foucault, M. (1975) *Discipline and Punish – The Birth of the Prison*. London: Penguin.

Hardcastle, D., Wenocur, S. and Powers, P. (1997) *Community Practice: Theories and Skills for Social Workers*. New York: Oxford University Press.

Heron, C. (1998) *Working with Carers*. London: Jessica Kingsley.

Hodge, S. (2005) 'Participation, discourse and power: A case study', *Critical Social Policy* 25(2): 164–79.

Hodgeson, P. and Canvin, K. (2005) 'Translating health policy into research practice', in Lowes, L. and Hulatt, I. (eds), *Involving Service Users in Health and Social Care Research*. London: Routledge.

Janson, K. and Law, S. (2003) *Older People Influencing Social Care: Aspirations and Realities Research Review on User Involvement in Promoting Change and Enhancing the Quality of Social Care Services*. Care Equation Limited.

Jones, A. (1998) *The Child Welfare Implications of UK Immigration and Asylum Policy*. Manchester: Manchester Metropolitan University, Department of Applied Community Studies.

Jones, A. (2000) 'Exploring young people's experience of immigration controls: The search for an appropriate methodology', in Humphries, B. (ed.), *Research in Social Care and Social Welfare: Issues and Debates for Practice*. London: Jessica Kingsley Publishers.

Jones, A. (2002) 'Family life and the pursuit of immigration controls', in Cohen, S., Humphries, B. and Mynott, E. (eds), *From Immigration Controls to Welfare Controls*. London: Routledge.

Jones, C. (1983) *State Social Work and the Working Class*. London: Macmillan Jones.

Jones, C. (2001) 'Voices from the front-line: State social workers and New Labour', *British Journal of Social Work* 31: 547–62.

Jones, C. and Novak, T. (1993) 'Social work today', *British Journal of Social Work* 23(3): 195–212.

Kerrison, S. and Pollock, A.M. (2001) 'Caring for older people in the private sector in England', *British Medical Journal* 323: 566–9.

Humphries, B. (2004) 'An unacceptable role for social work: Implementing immigration policy', *British Journal of Social Work* 34(1): 93–107.

Lamont, A. (1981) 'Social workers: A soft touch for spongers?' *Social Work Today*, 3 March.

Littlechild, R. and Glasby, J. (2001) 'Older people as participating patients', in Kemshall, H. and Littlechild, R. (eds), *User Involvement and Participation in Social Care: Research Informing Practice*. London: Jessica Kingsley Publishers.

Lymbery, M. (2012) 'Social work and personalisation', *British Journal of Social Work*. Advanced access 2 April.

McLaughlin, H. (2006) 'Involving young service users as co-researchers: Possibilities, benefits and costs', *British Journal of Social Work* 36(8): 1395–410.

McLaughlin, H. (2010) 'Keeping service user involvement in research honest', *British Journal of Social Work* 40: 1591–608.

Morris, J. (1993) *Independent Lives: Community Care and Disabled People*. Basingstoke: Macmillan.

Orr, K. (2005) 'Interpreting narratives of local government change under the Conservatives and New Labour', *British Journal of Politics and International Relations* 7: 371–85.

Pithouse, A. (1987) *Social Work: The Social Organisation of an Invisible Trade*. Aldershot: Avebury.

Roulstone, A., Hudson, V., Kearney, J. and Martin, A., with Warren, J. (2006) Working Together: Carer Participation in England, Wales and Northern Ireland Position Paper 5, www.scie.org.org.uk/publications/positionpapers/pp05.pdf

Spect, H. and Courtney, M. (1994) *Unfaithful Angels: How Social Work Has Abandoned Its Mission*. Free Press: New York.

Swain, J, French, S. and Cameron, C. (eds) (2003) *Controversial Issues in a Disabling Society*. Maidenhead: Oxford University Press.

Taylor, D. (2005) Governing through evidence: Participation and power in policy evaluation, *Journal of Social Policy* 34(4): 601–18.

Wallcraft, J., Fleishmann, P. and Beresford, P. (2012) The involvement of users and carers in social work education: A practice benchmarking study, *Work Force Development Report* 54, London: Social Care Institute for Excellence.

Warren, J. (2007) *Service User and Carer Participation in Social Work*. Exeter: Learning Matters.

Whitmore, E. (2001) '"People listened to what we had to say": Reflections on an emancipatory qualitative evaluation', in Shaw, I. and Gould, N. (eds), *Qualitative Research in Social Work*. London: Sage.

Wittgenstein, L. (1967) *Philosophical Investigations*. Oxford: Blackwell.

Wrennall, L. (2010) 'Surveillance and child protection: De-mystifying the Trojan Horse, *Surveillance and Society* 7(3/4): 304–24.

Wrennall, L., Pragnell, C., Blakemore-Brown, L., et al. (2003) Taking the Stick Away, Consultation on the Government's Green Paper on Child Protection, 1 December,.http://john.hemming.name/national/familylaw/takingthestickaway.html

10 Resistance In and Outside the Workplace: Ethical Practice and Managerialism in the Voluntary Sector

Donna Baines

Drawing on comparative international data from Canada and Australia, this chapter looks at a number of practice examples to explore some of the ways that social workers struggle to incorporate their commitment to social justice into increasingly managerialised work in the voluntary sector. Though the voluntary sector has long thought of itself as an arena in which workers have opportunities to build close ties with communities, participate strongly in agency decision making, and advocate for socially excluded and exploited peoples, new forms of workplace organisation imposed by government funding have reduced or removed many of the opportunities for these kinds of practices. Instead, social workers are increasingly required to follow tight scripted practices and meet performance targets rather than building the capacity of service users and communities to defend and expand their rights. The vignettes show that practitioners maintain their sense of integrity and ethics through ongoing resistance within and outside the workplace. The chapter concludes with a discussion of ways to foster critical thought and resistance as central components of social justice practice and ethics.

Introduction

Social work codes of ethics and practice guidelines face the near impossible task of attempting to reflect and build consensus between and among workers holding very different sets of values and deeply rooted disagreements about the underlying causes of social problems and their solutions. Though generally presented as a single field with a singular, helpful ideology, the boundaries of social work are porous, extending into many areas of practice, reproducing and extending a diverse amalgam of ideologies running the gamut from very radical to ultra conservative (Baines, 2011; Carniol, 2010). Most social work codes of ethics erase and undermine the credibility of more collective, activist and policy-based solutions by a) giving them short shrift within the multiple clauses aimed at confidentiality, appropriate boundaries and conflict of interest (Weinberg, 2010, 40) and b) simultaneously centralising individualised practice through their preoccupation with practice with families, individuals and couples.[1] These processes marginalise more politicised forms of intervention and, in the minds of many social workers, place them beyond the boundaries of good, professional practice. As Rossiter et al. (1996, 315) note 'the individualism of mainstream ethics is disciplinary: it renders the professional an individual subject of correction and at the same time it creates the totalising category of professional'.

Though many assert that codes of ethics were developed to provide accountability to the 'public' and set acceptable standards for 'professional' social work practice (Reamer, 1999), Weinberg (2010) argues that ethics are always political and though putatively neutral, benign positions, in actuality, ethics reproduce moral and normative positions on issues such as distribution of power, privilege, resources, and what kind of social order we want to construct (Weinberg, 2008, 2).

In the social work literature, moral and normative questions are often expressed as values. Similar to codes of ethics, social work values attempt to assemble a pluralist consensus among opposing ideological and practice models, and to stake out values common to all social workers. Postmodernists argue that this kind of universalist approach ignores important differences among and between social groups and encourages solutions that are best suited for the privileged majority, often causing increased exclusion for those in less powerful subject and identity positions (Leonard, 1997).

Though sympathetic to the postmodernist claims above, this chapter adopts a more structuralist approach (Corrigan and Leonard, 1978; Lundy, 2004; Mullaly, 2007) or that which Healy (2000) calls a moderately universalist position by arguing that the notion of common values generally falls to the lowest common denominator creating a false and conservative cohesion. In addition to erasing important differences between and among people, the pluralist model places limits on how we can think about social

---

1   Hardina (2004) notes that the NASW Code of Ethics does not cover most of the practices typical of community organizing, leaving ethical dilemmas to be resolved on a case-to-case basis (p. 595).

problems, their origins, what fuels them, and how to address them in ways that provide relief to those in need as well as provide deeper solutions aimed at removing the reasons for their prevalence and persistence. The position adopted by this chapter also explores some of the ways that social workers are constituted and constitute the practices they undertake within and beyond their workplaces. In short, there is no place of innocence (Rossiter, 2001) or 'politics free zone' (London Edinburgh Weekend Return Group, 1980) within social work. Even workers who are sceptical of the kinds of things they are asked to do at work are part of the larger processes of a highly gendered, racially stratified and increasingly polarised global capitalism, and find that while a perfect approach to ethics does not exist, a consistently ethic approach to social work practice and personal integrity involves collectively and individually resisting inequity and unfairness *within* and *beyond* their workplaces (Baines, 2011; Carniol, 2010; Smith, 2011).

The aforementioned themes are intensely political and social workers are often uncomfortable with the notion that their practice is political (Baines, 2011). As Rossiter et al. (2000) argue, many practitioners regard the larger context of their practice such as policy and hierarchical management structures as outside their decision making capacity. They therefore consequently see this as having little or nothing to do with the ethical dimensions of practice (see also Gray, 2010). Likewise, many social workers are uncomfortable with the notion that the field is strongly divided between those who consciously or inadvertently support inequity and those working to resist and change them (Baines, 2011). Though the source of this discomfort can be a personal aversion for conflict, it is also part of a larger liberal philosophy of pluralism[2] and a way of diverting attention away from how difficult it is to introduce robust discussions of, let alone practices fostering social justice and far reaching, equity-based social change within the social work context. This chapter will argue that in order to maintain personal and social integrity (Banks, 2010), good social work practice and ethics must be based on the central value of social justice and that this pivotal value is missing from most framings of professional ethics and values (see the International Federation of Social Workers Ethic's Statement of Principles, 2004, for an example of an exceptions to this norm, though note it is a statement of principles, not a code of ethics, and hence serves more as a set of guidelines than a prescription for proper practice). This

---

2   Pluralism refers to the notion that society consists of various ethnic, political and religious groups with equal access to power, resources and affirming identities. The role of government is to adjudicate their competing claims. This framework ignores differences that are woven into our social, economic, cultural and political systems and that are shaped by and reproduced by race, gender, class, disability, and so forth.

chapter will also argue that as long as social justice is sublimated within professional ethics or recast as liberal pluralism it is very difficult to practice social work in ways that remain within the mainstream boundaries of the workplace and professional codes.

Using social work practice in the voluntary sector as an exemplar of practice in a challenging and intensely political environment, this chapter starts with a short discussion of ethics, social work values and the managerial context of most contemporary social work practice. Drawing on two vignettes from my international research projects and other practice examples drawn from larger studies of restructuring in the nonprofit social services, this chapter argues that ethical practice requires that one works for change both within the workplace as well as within the larger society.

Ethics, Values and Managerialism

Gray (2010, 1974) argues that the dominant approaches to ethics within social work have had i) a deontological focus on duties and rules or ii) a consequentialist-utilitarian focus on managing and reducing risk/harms. Noting further that 'in the harsh, risk-aversive, managerial environments of contemporary practice, it becomes increasingly difficult to maintain an ethical perspective', Gray asserts that codes of ethics have a tendency to 'force practitioners into a narrowly prescriptive approach with little space for professional autonomy' (Gray, 2010, 1796). Webster (2010) concurs, observing that the re-emergence of a Taylorist scientific model has contributed to questionable ethics and a general deskilling of social work practice under the guise of new managerial effectiveness, efficiency and economy (p. 29). Weinberg (2010, 40) likewise argues against rules-based and risk-minimising frameworks typical of managerial approaches, noting that social work ethics must move away from technical functions and towards redressing the causes of social problems.

Service users and practitioners often remind us that even before the era of neoliberal reform, social work processes were not always helpful. Reflecting the mixed frameworks and politics from which social work draws its theory, many practices reinforced oppressive norms and extended unequal and harmful relations of power (Baines, 2011). Unfortunately, over the last couple of decades, neoliberalist management models, such as New Public Management (NPM) have reduced or removed the capacity of even the most well-intentioned social workers to respond holistically to social and individual problems. Claiming to improve practice and reduce costs, these performance-based models 'lean out' social work practices (Carey, 2009, 2007; McDonald, 2006) removing social justice-oriented practice such as community action and organising advocacy, policy critique and staff participation in developing agency policies and priorities (Baines, 2004a, 2010a; Ross, 2011; Smith, 2007). The loss of these interventions narrows practice and limits the space in which workers can think about their work and its broader social values and ethical impacts. Social justice values have difficulty finding purchase in the arid soil of technical and routinised practices, prompting some social work scholars and practitioners to seek alternative ethical models.

Though absent from most social work codes, some models of ethics emphasise social relationships as the core of ethical being and rather than hard and fast rules to fit every situation, these models assert the need to develop the capacity to think critically about problematic situations and pursue appropriate actions based on our virtue- or care-based web of interconnections to each other (Gray, 2010). The feminist ethics of care, for example, asserts that our sense of moral conduct is founded in and reproduced through interpersonal relationships in which we are constantly giving and receiving care (Noddings, 1984; Tronto, 1993). Similarly relationship-based, virtue ethics assert that in any social context it is 'good to be good' and that practitioners and wider society need to foster conditions under which good ethical decisions are easy to make. As Gray (2010, 1807) notes neither 'compassion or care or any other virtuous attitude happens automatically. It is not a natural human response, but a learned and increasingly inculcated moral attitude gained through socialisation'. Rather than depending on individuals to behave in ethical situations regardless of working conditions and the larger society, these models[3] recognise the ways that the social relations and larger ideology shape interactions, limiting ethical practices or in more social justice-oriented circumstances, promoting diversity-embracing equity and social care.

Other critiques of the deontological or utilitarian-consequentialist models include postmodernist/poststructuralist approaches (Rossiter et al., 2000; Webster, 2010; Wilks, 2005). These approaches discourage totalising, all-embracing theories of ethics (Banks, 2004) and encourage narrative, diverse, pluralist approaches. The common critique of these models is that they tend towards relativism, making it nearly impossible to judge better courses of

---

3   The notion of an ethics of care has been critiqued as overly rooted in women's current roles in society rather than in social justice. As Gray (2010, also see Orme, 2002) argues,

'There must be an agreed standard of care for those in need to avoid paternalism, subjectivism and unfairness. Care must be connected to justice or it would become a random practice. It is crucial, then, to acknowledge the inextricable links between the political "rights and justice" agenda and the moral "care" agenda and to recognize the impact of each on the other' (1805).

Social Justice

For the purposes of this chapter, social justice will be understood as based in critical theories that analyse all aspects of social life from an explicitly political perspective intertwining theory and practice.

Social justice approaches need to:

- expose bases of subordination and domination in society;
- demystify rival approaches that obfuscate or rationalise oppressive and exploitive relations;
- promote equitable and fair access to resources, power and affirming identities;
- view social movements and struggles for social change as the subjects of their critiques and political practice as the ultimate test of the validity of their claims (Fraser, 1989, 113).

---

action from worse (Baines, 2011; Fook, 2002; Mullaly, 2007).[4] Though not theoretically consistent with postmodernist/poststructuralist tenets many of these ethical models embrace modernist, normative social justice values redistribution, equity, fairness and full participation. Webster (2010), for example, provides a three-part prescriptive (modernist), but simultaneously, narrative (postmodernist) model to redress the historical exclusion of Maori knowledge and ways of being and to counter standardisation and deskilling in social service work. Noting that 'the future of social work codes in the light

---

4   Moral or normative theories and ethics contain a ballast or central tenet which assists in determining better from worse or right from wrong. A core aspect of structural theories, such as feminist, anti-racist, Marxist and anti-oppressive, is the identification of oppressed groups (e.g. women, racialised groups, working class and poor people) who require liberation through the fundamental reorganisation of social relations (including structures). This dynamic provides a moral-political project within the epistemological centre of these theories and a moral compass for their supporters.

In contrast, postmodernism is an epistemological theory about ways of knowing and how language and discourse exercise power not a moral theory for political action (Fook, 2002). In order to avoid constructing oppressive discourses, postmodernism avoids moral projects preferring to deconstruct and reveal the operation of oppressive uses of language and knowledge. Mullaly (2007) argues that despite this epistemological dissonance, critical postmodernism, Marxist, feminist and other social justice-oriented approaches can be jointly mobilised to develop social theory and address social problems.

of the postmodern project is uncertain and fraught', Briskman (2001, n.p.) observes that 'by not specifying the nature of justice, a social worker cannot be expected to understand the form of their responsibility'.

Although a consensus exists among the critical social work literature that NPM has harmed social work and threatens its capacity to be an ethical endeavour, beyond philosophical debates, there is little in the ethics literature about how practitioners can infuse social justice into their everyday managerialised work lives. Ross (2011) argues that social justice practices need not always be on a massive scale; smaller everyday acts of resistance within the workplace can carve out spaces for creative and critical reflection and energise those depleted by under-funding and managerialism. In the same vein, though under-theorised in the literature and often incremental in their impact, collective and individual acts of resistance within *and* outside the social services workplace can provide dignity and respite for clients and workers, and provide a context for the emergence of an ethics of social justice.

Examples from the Field

Non-profit social services (NPSS) provide a particularly rich research node epitomising some of the central themes and tensions criss-crossing the restructured welfare state. In particular, NPSS are an arena in which paid and unpaid staff are involved in projects explicitly aimed at unmet and emerging needs, using interventions that have the potential to empower others, knit social solidarity, and expand democracy – or contribute to their unravelling. Unfortunately, like social services provided in other sectors, NPSS can be stripped of their collectivist content and delivered in bureaucratic, standardised ways that demobilise and disempower those who provide services, as well as those who receive them (Baines, 2004b; Cunningham, 2008, 2001; McDonald and Marston, 2002).

The next sections of this chapter discuss examples drawn from a number of studies undertaken in the NPSS or voluntary services in Canada and Australia. Though these countries have much in common, non-profit workers in Australia are connected through the agencies that employ them to central advocacy organisations known as peak bodies. Most of the Australian workers interviewed for my studies felt that though under duress, these peak bodies continued to provide a venue through which their concerns could be voiced to government and the larger community. The example below and my other research shows that even with the advocacy opportunities provided by peak bodies many non-profit social service workers still resist changes within their workplaces through individual and shared actions and ethics. My research also shows that in addition many workers joined/join causes and social movements outside the workplace to pursue larger social change and challenge the conditions that compel clients to seek services (Baines, 2010a, 2010b).

Taylorised Care – Australia

In 2007, as part of a larger, multi-country study of restructuring in the NPSS, we conducted an intensive case study in a fairly typical, mid-sized, multi-service, multi-site non-profit agency in a small city in Australia (Baines et al., 2010). The agency was widely regarded as 'best practice' and had developed a 'unique' approach to fostering the full community inclusion of marginalised clients. This approach involved the introduction of an explicitly Taylorised model known as 'technologies of supports' in which workers were coached and tightly scripted to avoid building relationships with service users and co-workers. They were therefore directed to restricting themselves to providing the physical tending required by service users, facilitating opportunities for the service users to participate in the community and to build relationships with 'average' people in the wider community, eschewing any sort of relationship with workers beyond 'positive regard'. In particular, female-associated sentiments such as care and emotional ties were to be avoided. Commitment to social justice was also not seen as desirable within this highly structured and technical model of support.

The Director of Human Resources claimed he had moved staff people to new units and jobs when they seemed to be getting 'emotionally attached' to service users, underscoring his commitment to ensuring that workers did not become 'caring'. Though the literature underscores the contribution supportive relationships make to productivity and stress reduction (Garfield, 1980; McCalister et al., 2006), this same director was also sceptical of the need for friendships or affinity between and among staff members. Pointing out that opportunities for staff friendships were limited because most staff worked alone or with only one or two others, he argued that employees should get their workplace satisfaction from providing the 'right

---

Taylorism

A way of organising work in order to optimise profits or cost savings in which work practices are broken down into their smallest component pieces in order to standardise them and make them easy for anyone to undertake.

amount and kinds of support' to clients rather than building workplace connections with fellow employees.

The workers we interviewed were highly sceptical of this narrow and leaned-out model of service delivery and found various ways to maintain their sense of integrity and ethics by covertly and overtly resisting management's neoliberalising agenda. Acknowledging that the model was more restrictive than earlier models of practice used in the agency, one senior worker noted:

> We used to call it individualised intervention plans or something. Now it has a new name and we have to write it out and get it approved and it's just the same old thing. But, mostly you need to use the knowledge you get from working with these guys (service users) every day. You have to have a real connection with people and through trial and error work out what works for them and for you. It's pretty straightforward.

Another long-time worker agreed, noting that the rigidity of Taylorised plans could prove harmful for clients and workers:

> I don't like these rigid plans and strategies – when we have a problem we need to draw on our experience and the immediate situation and think on our feet. Every situation is slightly different or completely new and one size does not fit all.

> These plans just hamstring you, make you less effective, and harm the clients. They (the service users) need us to know them and know what works and make changes as we go along. You can't write all that stuff down. By the time you've developed a strategy, the situation has changed.

A mid-level worker also wondered if providing 'technologies of support' rather than older models based on 'care' were partially motivated by cost savings inherent in managerialism. Noting that providing tightly scripted intervention plans purportedly removed emotion and connection, as well as 'dependence', waste and error while simultaneously rationing services to service users, a mid-level worker argued,

> I think if you do (the work) properly you're not going to create dependence anyway. I'm sometimes cynical ... I think it's the powers that be worrying about money. I think that's my gut instinct. It's not so much about building independence at all.

> For most workers resisting the technologies of a support model focused on practices they felt were more ethical, such as self-determination and care,

You gotta care about these guys or you wouldn't do the work. I provide care for these guys (the service users) and some of the care is supports and some is doing it for them when they need it, and most of it is about really connecting with them and knowing them. (SNORTS) Caring, support – whatever, I just do the job.

Even workers and supervisors who claimed a strong affinity with the new model deviated from it when discussing front-line practice dilemmas and individual clients. For example, the supervisor in charge of training staff in the new approach noted the following in reference to a client with very challenging behaviours:

God love him. He's such a lovely man. I know we're supposed to support people and not care for them but you gotta love him. All the staff love him, we all just love him.

The technologies of support model attempted to intervene at the level of professional practice, by remaking relationships both among staff and between staff and clients, as well as reshaping the kinds of work people undertook, how they did it, and the interpretive screens they were encouraged to embrace. However, the evidence from our case study suggested that the technologies of support model was largely unsuccessful at changing practice or people's sense of how to maintain integrity and ethics on the job. Instead, social service workers continued to draw on other bases for their practice, and to resist a model that seemed unethical and inhumane. It is worth noting that as contradictory and technocratic as many of the social work codes of ethics are around the globe (Mullaly, 2007) some of the new models of lean and standardised care directly and indirectly contradict central tenets of these codes such as social justice and service user self-determination. This leaves social service workers in a position where they need to advocate with

---

Neoliberalism

An approach to social, political and economic life that discourages collective or government services, instead encouraging reliance on the private market and individual skill to meet social needs. In the social welfare arena, this approach has resulted in reduced funding for social programmes, new service user groups, and workplaces with fewer resources and increased surveillance, management control and caseload size. Worldwide it has resulted in the growth of poverty, decrease in democracy, and increased social and environmental devastation.

and for service users in order to maintain a minimal standard of care that does not stand in contravention of professional ethical codes.

Social Unionism – Canada

In Canada non-profit workers do not have access to the kind of advocacy provided by peak bodies in Australia and report that, under neo-liberal restructuring, most of the avenues within their agencies for advocacy and activism had been shut down. Frustrated with this situation, some workers have sought out new venues through which to have a voice on issues within and outside the agency. Indeed, many workers reported the equivalent of 'being unable to sleep at night' if they failed to respond to the ravages of neo-liberalism. The short quote above came from a worker who was dealing with a 300 per cent increase in her caseload at the same time as service users tried to make ends meet after a 22 per cent across the board cut to social assistance payments (Baines, 2000). Other workers added their commitment to buffer the worst effects of welfare state downsizing by taking on unpaid overtime, working through lunch hours and coffee breaks and taking work home with them on weekends and holidays in order to try to meet soaring service user needs. One worker argued that though she knew putting in many hours of unpaid and unrecognised overtime on behalf of her clients did not really change the larger oppressive system, she felt that at least her long hours made society less cruel, which these days could be constructed as an act of resistance itself. Moreover, it constituted a strategy that permitted her to maintain her sense of integrity within her job (Baines, 2004).

As discussed later in this section, my research shows that another popular strategy for maintaining a sense of personal integrity while simultaneously contributing to larger strategies for social change was the pursuit of social unionism, a type of activist, participatory unionism that is highly compatible with social work values and the best of the non-profit ethos (Baines, 2010a). I became interested in the way that social service workers involved in social unionism responded to the crises of neo-liberalism and undertook a study of the experience of unionised non-profit social service workers in the context of restructuring. Some of the findings are discussed below. Findings from earlier studies regarding resistance, and by extension ways of grappling with social justice and ethical practice, are also discussed at the beginning of this section.

In all my studies of workplaces and social service workers, the research participants have provided numerous examples of everyday resistance against parsimony and narrow work practices. These practices helped workers feel a sense of personal integrity and ethics and included: making an agency's resources and space available to client actions and social change groups; co-facilitating client-led social change and social service initiatives; bending and breaking 'unethical' policy for clients; encouraging clients to 'go over my head' or complain to the worker's supervisor in order to get access to greater resources, advocating for clients, sometimes with the full participation and support of the client and sometimes without the client's explicit knowledge in order to protect them from possible reprisals.

Reflecting on the increasingly narrow, standardised interventions permitted in her NPSS workplace, one child and family worker argued that although she still wants to do advocacy and community mobilisation:

> We don't have time like we used to. I can't work with a family to build their skills, and link them up with what they need and stand up for them when they need it. It's just in the door, quick assessment, promise to call next week with a case plan and back out the door to file the paperwork. I find it soulless and they (the clients) just look at me like "what is the point of all this?"

Some workers were very clear that they wanted to work in ways that were consistent with social justice values rather than with 'professionalism' and managerialism. As one mid-level mental health counsellor put it:

> Most of us are here because we want to work with people in not just in a way that makes a difference, but in a different way – we don't want to just fill in reports and push paper ... We want to work in a way that empowers people and challenges systems that harm people. We want to organise with the community to take control back, not just put band aids on a few of the more obvious victims.

The official model of unionism in Canada is social unionism – representing members at the bargaining table while simultaneously campaigning for social justice 'in every aspect of the economic, social and political life of Canadians' (Canadian Labour Congress, 2010). This model is popular with many non-profit social service workers as it is consistent with their social justice values. When pathways for expression of social justice values, and therefore ethics, were blocked by NPM restructuring, some non-profit workers used their union locals as vehicles through which to pursue social justice content no longer possible on the job.

Through participation in public events, lobbying, building coalitions and joining other organisations, research participants, explicitly used their unions as a way to extend care for clients and communities, linking agency level and larger issues. For example, concerned about deaths among homeless people during the winter, two of the NPSS locals became involved in mass organisations such as the Toronto Disaster Relief Committee and the 'Ontario Coalition Against Poverty'. Reflecting the interests of their members and the clients they served, some of the locals were involved in community actions aimed at stopping deportations and organising around immigrant policy and service issues. After a number of assaults occurred against gay, lesbian and trans people, some of the NPSS locals also became involved in a mass campaign against homophobia in the downtown core. This broad-based campaign was eventually extended to challenge all forms of discrimination in the inner city. Echoing the linkage of issues expressed by many interviewees, a settlement worker with 22 years experience in the non-profit sector noted,

> Our work doesn't stop at the end of the day or at the door of the agency. We bring the world in with us to work and the world walks through those doors everyday looking for help and assistance. It's only natural that we would get involved in activist work *in this city*. Heck, activist work *in this world*, 'cause it sure never needed it more. (emphasis in original)

In the same vein, while acknowledging that 'only one in a hundred' clients follow through on political action, workers regularly made referrals to social action groups, often ones in which they themselves were active, in order to link clients with collective solutions (Baines, 2010b, 2011). As one worker asserted

> it means putting our energies alongside those who are most pushed to the margins in our society. Showing them that we are outraged at the ways things are and that we think there is a better way to do things.

In some cases, employers applauded social unionist activism and even joined in coalition work and protests (Baines, 2010a). In other cases, employers were hostile and punitive. Front-line workers I interviewed for my studies tended to feel that regardless of their employer's response, social unionism provided an outlet and organisation through which to maintain their sense of social justice, ethics and morality.

Concluding Thoughts

The examples discussed in this chapter show that social workers are constituted both by resistance to and compliance with workplace managerial and practice modes. Compliance can be a reflexive and strategic decision adopted consciously while one explores other options, seeks like-minded allies in and outside the workplace, and learns more about how new managerial models exert power and the many ways that social workers are implicated in reproducing oppressive relations. Strategic compliance is a form of resistance itself, though not a sufficient one. Like the social unionist social workers in the second example, other forms of resistance and organising in- and outside the workplace are necessary and can restore a sense of dignity and integrity, provide hope that things can change and involve social workers, their employers and community members in efforts to build a more equitable future for all. In short, if as Rossiter (2001) notes, there is no place of innocence within social work then it is necessary to consciously choose sides and take action in order to protect and extend ethics of social justice, fairness and equity.

There is little in the literature on the ethics of social work resistance. Ross (2011) reminds us that social work resistance is a 'big tent' and takes many forms, not just those associated with political rallies and protest. Smaller everyday efforts to sustain and extend human rights and dignity are also important to building a culture and ethics of resistance, incrementally shifting an ethos of professional compliance to an integrated and ongoing struggle for social justice. Further research is required to explore an ethics of resistance and ways to push professional organisations, agencies and other organisations to adopt more social justice-based concepts of ethics, and to promote the kinds of critical thinking necessary to overcome the individualism and pluralism of mainstream practice, instead placing social work energies and ethics alongside those marginalised and exploited within our current mode of social organisation. On a practical level this can start with a recognition that social work is not neutral and benign but a wholly political endeavor as well as by: centralising resistance within codes of ethics; educating practitioners and their employers in critical thinking, strategic compliance and other practices of social change and resistance; and joining social workers' efforts with those of others aimed at building the kind of society in which equitable, ethical and fair decisions are easy to make.

Further Reading

Baines, D. (ed.) (2011) *Doing Anti-Oppressive Practice: Social Justice, Social Work*. Halifax/Winnipeg: Fernwood Publishing: this extensive edited collection covers the historical and theoretical roots and the specific contexts of anti-oppressive social work practice. It uses practice vignettes, personal experience and case work examples to discuss a variety of issues including child protection, poverty and welfare rights, disability rights, working with unions and standardised assessment procedures.

Gray, M. (2010) Moral sources and emergent ethical theories in social work. *British Journal of Social Work*, 40: 1794–811: this well written and focused paper examines the ethics of care and other approaches to promote the use of a diverse range of theories to enhance care centred practices.

Weinberg, M. (2010) The social construction of social work ethics: Politicizing and broadening the lens. *Journal of Progressive Human Services*, 21: 32–44: within this article the author suggests that structural barriers and paradoxes of practice lead to ethical tensions for practitioners. The article then offers an explanation of how the construction of ethics has evolved before suggesting ways to broaden the lens of focus.

References

Baines, D. (2004) Caring for nothing. Work organization and unwaged labour in social services. *Work, Employment and Society*, 18(2): 267–95.

Baines, D. (2010a) Neoliberal restructuring/activism, participation and social unionism in the nonprofit social services. *Nonprofit and Voluntary Sector Quarterly*, 39(1): 10–28.

Baines, D. (2010b) 'If we don't get back to where we were before': Working in the restructured nonprofit social services. *British Journal of Social Work*, April, 40(3): 928–45.

Baines, D. (2011) An overview of anti-oppressive social work practice: Neoliberalism, inequality, and change. In Baines, D. (ed.), *Doing Anti-Oppressive Practice: Social Justice Social Work*. Halifax/Winnipeg: Fernwood Publishing, pp. 25–48.

Baines, D., Cunningham, I. and Fraser, H. (2010) Constrained by managerialism: Caring as participation in the voluntary social services. *Economic and Industrial Democracy*. Published online.

Banks, S. (2004) *Ethics, Accountability and the Social Professions*. Basingstoke: Palgrave Macmillan.

Banks, S. (2008) Critical commentary. Social work ethics. *British Journal of Social Work*, 38: 1238–49.

Banks, S. (2009) Integrity in professional life: Issues of conduct, commitment and capacity. *British Journal of Social Work*, Bcp152.

Briskman, L. (2001) A moral crisis for social work. Critical practice and codes of ethics. *Critical Social Work*, 2(1): n.p.

Canadian Labour Congress (2010) 'Canadian Labour History'. Ottawa: Canadian Labour Congress.

Carey, M. (2009) It's a bit like being a robot or working in a factory: Does Braverman help explain the differences in state social work in Britain since 1971? *Organization*, 16(4).

Carey, M. (2007) Some ethical dilemmas for agency social workers, *Ethics and Social Welfare*, 1(3): 342–7.

Carniol, B. (2010) *Case Critical: The Dilemma of Social Work in Canada*. Sixth edition. Toronto: Between the Lines.

Corrigan, P. and Leonard, P. (1978) *Social Work Practice Under Capitalism. A Marxist Approach*. London: Macmillan Press.

Cunningham, I. (2001) Sweet charity! Managing employee commitment in the UK voluntary sector. *Employee Relations*, 23(3): 192–206.

Cunningham, I (2008) *Employment Relations in the Voluntary Sector*. London: Routledge.

Fook, J. (2002) *Social Work, Critical Theory and Practice*. London: Sage Publications.

Fraser, N. (1989) *Unruly Practices: Power, Discourse and Gender in Contemporary Social Theory*. Minnesota: University of Minnesota Press.

Garfield, J. (1980) Alienated labor, stress, and coronary heart disease. *International Journal of Health Services*, 10(4): 551–61.

Gray, M. (2010) Moral sources and ermergent ethical theories in social work. *British Journal of Social Work*, 40: 1794–811.

Hardina, D. (2004) Guidelines for ethical practice in community organization. *Social Work*. 49(4): 595–604.

Healy, K. (2000) *Social Work Practices: Contemporary Perspectives on Change*. London: Sage Publications.

International Federation of Social Workers (2004) Ethics in Social Work. Statement of Principles, http://www.ifsw.org/f38000027.html. Accessed April 15, 2011.

Leonard, P. (1997) *Postmodern Welfare: Reconstructing an Emancipatory Project*. London: Sage.

London Edinburgh Weekend Return Group (1980) *In and Against the State*. London: Pluto Press.

Lundy, C. (2004) *Social Work and Social Justice: A Structural Approach to Practice*. Peterborough, ON: Broadview Press.

McCalister, K., Dolbier, C., Webster, J. et al. (2006) Hardiness and support at work as predictors of work stress and job satisfaction. *The Science of Health Promotion*, 20(3): 183–73.

McDonald, C. (2006). *Challenging Social Work: The institutional context of practice*. Basingstoke: Palgrave Macmillan.

McDonald, C. and Marston, G. (2002) Fixing the niche: Rhetorics of the community sector in the neo-liberal welfare regime. *Just Policy*, 26.

Mullaly, B. (2007) *The New Structural Social Work*. Third edition. Toronto: Oxford Press.

Noddings, N. (1984) *Caring: A Feminine Approach to Ethics and Moral Education*. Berkeley: University of California Press.

Orme, J. (2002) Social work: Gender, care and justice. *British Journal of Social Work*, 32: 799–814.

Reamer, F. (1999) *The Philosophical Foundations of Social Work*. New York: Columbia University Press.

Ross, M. (2011) Social work activism amidst neoliberalism: A big, broad tent of activism. In D. Baines (ed.), *Doing Anti-Oppressive Practice: Social Justice Social Work*. Halifax/Winnipeg: Fernwood Publishing, pp. 251–64.

Rossiter, A. (2001) Innocence lost and suspicion found: Do we educate for or against social work? *Critical Social Work*, 2(1): n.p.

Rossiter, A., Prilleltensky, I. and Walsh-Bowers, R. (2000) 'A postmodern perspective on professional ethics'. In Fawcett, B., Featherstone, B. and Rossiter, A. (eds), *Postmodern Feminist Perspectives: Practice and Research in Social Work*. London: Routledge, pp. 83–103.

Smith, K. (2007) Social work, restructuring and resistance: 'Best practices' gone underground. In D. Baines (ed.), *Doing Anti-Oppressive Practice: Building Transformative, Politicized Social Work*. Halifax/Winnipeg: Fernwood Publishing.

Smith, K. (2011) Occupied spaces: Unmapping standardized assessments in health and social service organizations. In D. Baines (ed.), *Doing Anti-Oppressive Practice: Social Justice Social Work*. Halifax/Winnipeg: Fernwood Publishing, pp. 251–64.

Tronto, J. (1993) *Moral Boundaries: A Political Argument for an Ethic of Care*. London: Routledge and Kegan Paul.

Webster, M. (2010) Complexity approach to frontline social work management: Constructing an emergent team leadership design for a managerialist world. *Social Work and Social Sciences*, 14(1): 27–46.

Weinberg, M. (2008) Structural social work: A moral compass for ethics in practice. *Critical Social Work*, 9(1), pp. 1–10.

Weinberg, M. (2010) The social construction of social work ethics: Politicizing and broadening the lens. *Journal of Progressive Human Services*, 21: 32–44.

Wilks, T. (2005) Social work and narrative ethics. *British Journal of Social Work*, 35: 1249–64.

Index